Biblical Counseling

by
WIM MALGO

©Copyright 1979 by
Midnight Call, Inc.

Published by
The Midnight Call, Inc.
Columbia, S.C. 29202

Preface

The pages of this book are filled with a selection of original letters written by people from all walks of life who have turned to the counseling ministry of Dr. Wim Malgo in a search for a Bible-based answer to their questions.

The questions as well as the answers are unique in two ways; 1) the questions have come from a cross-section of Christianity, from many different countries of the world. 2) Dr. Malgo has answered each individual according to his or her need, and has not followed a pattern or dogma established by any theological direction but rather has based it on his understanding of the Scriptures.

The deepest motive in publishing this selection of letters is to help those in need of counseling and at the same time, to be a guide to the layman and minister alike in their counseling ministry to others.

The author confesses with the Apostle Paul that "we know in part only," and points out that the day will come when all our questions will be answered, for the Lord Jesus Christ Himself stated "In that day ye shall ask me nothing" (John 16:23).

Prayerfully we dedicate this book to all who have set their hearts on following Jesus unconditionally; who uphold the unfailing truth of the Scriptures at any cost, and who in preparing themselves, help others to prepare for the soon coming of our Lord Jesus Christ.

The Staff, Midnight Call Ministries.

CONTENTS

THE BIBLE IS TRUE!

The Authority of God's Word

P.K. in K.: From (comparatively) early youth, I have followed different streams in the Christian religion. After I discovered "anti-Semitic" writings of Luther, against which no official church authority has taken a stand up until now, I left the Evangelical Lutheran Church (at seventeen years old). I must confess however, as you probably assume, that I see things quite differently from you. It would be a great pity however, if you were to classify me for this reason as a "servant of the devil" or "helper of the wicked one." I think you would only be avoiding the problem in doing this. I have one elementary principle in trying to understand those of a different opinion, and that is the belief that everyone who sincerely represents a social idea, an ideology, a religion, etc., seeks good, I believe this of Jesus, Marx, Mao, Adenauer, deGaulle, and not least, of yourself. Where do we find a measure whereby we can tell to what extent, or whether at all, something is good? In its benefit to health, the production of food, culture, freedom, love or faith?

Answer: Don't worry, we do not give people the ultimatum — either you're my brother or my enemy! We do not claim either that the knowledge that we have is the absolute and ultimate. Only on one point do we differ: our (that is, my) source is in actual fact the Word of the Living God. And this Word says something quite different from what you say, namely that not everyone is seeking good, not everyone is good, but that none is righteous, no not one. It also says that we can only obtain the righteousness that counts with God through faith in the atoning blood of Jesus. Please compare Romans 3:25. You will probably reply, with your tolerant attitude which believes that everyone is right, "Why should the Bible be the only source, and why should it be the only measure and standard, and the only truth?" Here, my dear Mr. K., is where we separate. This is a free-will decision of faith. I have decided to bring my reason (which is darkened by sin) into subjection to the Bible because I have realized that the Eternal, Almighty and Only Wise God's way is not "into our hearts via our understanding," but vice versa. "Via the heart into the understanding." Read carefully 1 Corinthians, chapter 1. And whoever **does not want** to believe that the Bible is God's Word, may leave it and indulge in the worship of Communism, Buddhism, Islam or even some kind of Maoism. You will find however, if you are unbiassed and objective, that all ideologies and religions outside of Jesus Christ have not brought man what he seeks in the depths of his soul, and that is peace with God, eternal life. Here is my personal foundation: I believe that the Bible is God's Word, not only because I was told so, or because I was brought up in Christian surroundings, but also because I experience daily that Jesus Christ lives and dwells in me, as it is written in Ephesians 3:17. But he who does not want God, and does not want Jesus, says "no" to Him. He should consider however that death is not followed by a full stop, but a comma, as it is written, "It is appointed unto men once to die, but after this the judgment." (Hebrews 9:27). You, with your broad-minded tolerance, also have this assurance in your heart that God exists, even if you were never to read the Bible. This assertion can be proved with a statement in the Bible, which you would perhaps like to read, in Romans 1:18-20. You have this revelation of God in your conscience so that you will have no excuse when you stand before Him one day. What you are doing here is extremely dangerous, because you are generalizing and putting Jesus Christ, the Son of God, on a par with deGaulle, Mao, Adenauer, etc. In doing this, you are ultimately suppressing what in your heart you know about the Living God. You know, you are not alone in your views, nor even modern, but very, very old-fashioned. Pilate, the Roman governor, said, according to Matthew 27:11 as Jesus stood before him, (although in actual fact it should be the other way round, because Pilate was standing before Jesus) "What is truth?" because he did not want to believe the ultimate truth of the presence of the Son of God of whose reality he was convinced. Consider for one moment the hour of your death. Your elastic view of life will not be of any use to you then. Only the precious blood of Jesus, the Son of God, which cleanses from all sin, can help you then, or else you will discover there, on the threshold of eternity, that it is too late. There have been greater men than you in this world who have cried this on their deathbeds, for instance, Voltaire, who cried out as he lay dying, that he was going to hell. You probably know what Goethe wanted written on his tombstone. He said, "When I am dead, let it be written on my tombstone: All his life he was lucky, but he was never happy."

To sum up, I would like to say to you: Your elementary principle is not good, because — according to your letter — you believe in man. We believe in the Living God and His Son, Jesus Christ. This is the only principle which will endure in eternity! I have the impression from your letter that, basically, you are a person who does want to know the truth. Or am I wrong? If I am right, I have hope for you, because the Lord Jesus said, "Everyone that is of the truth heareth my voice." You see, there are doubters who doubt for the sake of doubting, because they say regarding Jesus Christ: **It isn't true.** And when they are convicted in their conscience of sin, through the Word of God which is made alive through the Holy Spirit, they say: **It can't be true.** And when they are absolutely cornered, through the powerful working of the Holy Spirit in their hearts, they cry: **It mustn't be true.** I take it that you do not belong to this category of people, that is, those who doubt for the sake of doubting, but that you doubt for the sake of truth. The truth however, is indivisible. This is not in a deGaulle, nor in a Mao Tse-tung, but only in Him who said, "I am the Way, the Truth and the Life: no man cometh to the Father, but by me." (John 14:6).

Inspired by the Holy Spirit!

E.E. in D.: If the Bible is really the WORD OF God why then is it written by people? These men were not without fault, either.

Answer: The Bible is the unerring word of God, "for the prophecy came not in old time by the will of man: but holy men of God spake as they were moved by the Holy Ghost." (2 Peter 1:21) 2 Timothy 3:16 says: **"All** scripture is given by inspiration of God, and is profitable for doctrine, for reproof, for correction, for instruction in righteousness."

Modern theological teaching does not say: "the Bible **is** the Word of God" but, "The Bible **contains** the Word of God." How terrible! So when I read my Bible and am moved by one portion of the Bible and receive a blessing by reading it in my quiet time then soon doubts arise, is this really the Word of God? To be very sure, I would have to call professor "A" or "B", after each reading of the Bible, to ask: Was this, which I just read, the Word of God, or was it just human reports? — No, the Bible **is** God's Word! So-called Theological views come and go, but the Bible outlasts them all.

Verbal Inspiration

E.W. in C.: While studying the Bible I came across a sentence which troubles me considerably in Psalm 137:9.Can we still speak of verbal inspiration here? I do not doubt that God speaks to us through the Bible, but is all Scripture really given by inspiration of God, that is, given by God directly to His servants. In Mark 10:4 onwards it is clear that there is a difference between God's original commandments for His people and the commandments as Moses delivered them (cf. Num. 23:19). In Leviticus 24:13 it says, "And the Lord spake unto Moses, saying . . . ," and in verse 20 it continues, "Breach for breach, eye for eye, tooth for tooth . . . " In Leviticus 19:18 God says, "Thou shalt not avenge, . . . love thy neighbor as thyself." This is all very contradictory! Or do I fail to see the connection? Please give me an answer to these burning and tormenting questions.

Answer: The whole Bible, word for word, is in its original text the infallible Word of God, inspired by the Holy Spirit. In the Old Testament the holy and righteous God reveals Himself and attempts to show His love to those who are willing to keep His commandments. We often see how God's holiness and righteousness conflict with His love: because of the first two attributes He has to condemn and destroy man, but His love longs to save and have mercy on him. This conflict is very clearly expressed in Hosea 11:8 for instance, where He says, "How shall I give thee up, Ephraim? how shall I deliver thee, Israel? how shall I make thee as Admah? how shall I set thee as Zeboim? mine heart is turned within me, my repentings are kindled together." Your trouble is your lack of recognition of the perfect nature of God. Let us continue, however. On Calvary's cross God accomplished the great and inconceivable in that He gave His Son, Jesus Christ, laid the sins of the world upon Him and judged and condemned Him in our place. Here God's conflict was solved. His perfect holiness and righteousness as well as His immeasurable love were revealed in the sacrificial Lamb, Jesus Christ. Nothing has been taken away from God's law — Jesus has fulfilled it all! God does not take back anything from the curse of the law in that He was cursed for us, as it is written, "Cursed is every one that hangeth on a tree." Death as the wages of sin, has never been abolished, but Jesus died on Calvary's cross that we might live. All that which seems to your intellect to be contradictory is answered in Jesus Christ, the Crucified One, in whom divine wisdom and divine power are united.

Every Jot and Tittle

H.J.S. in A.: In your May 1969 issue you discuss the verbal inspiration of the Bible in the Correspondence Column. As I wrote you last year, Dr. Ivan Panin's discovery spells death for modern theology, and even more: every modern theologian is silenced when confronted with Panin's discovery. I sent you the enclosed leaflet last year and you promised to publish the suggestion at an opportune time. I take it that the matter has been forgotten. (Dr. I. Panin discovered that the original text of the Holy Bible, from the first letter of the first chapter to the last letter of the Revelation of St. John is based on a secret, hidden, numerical system, so that the whole Bible is like a precious carpet of numerical figures and patterns and it is therewith proved beyond any doubt that every word, every jot and tittle, is spoken and given by God: everything which over the years has been left out is restored and everything controversial made plain):

Answer: No, the matter concerning Dr. Panin is not forgotten. On the contrary, I possess his book and believe it. The most important thing, however, is overlooked. Proof of the truth of the Bible does not help anyone to believe, because what has been **proven** can no longer be **believed.** We believe with our hearts, without having proof. Panin, by the way, is not the only one to have made this discovery. The Jews also know exactly the numerical value of the Hebrew language. A few months ago I spoke with a well-known Jewish author who is also aware of this. And if the Bible is of divine inspiration — which we believe it to be — it is also perfect in its numerical combination. But, I repeat, all this will not convince any unbelieving people. The Bible has to be **believed** by bringing one's intelligence into captivity to the obedience of Christ (2 Cor. 10:5), and not on the grounds of rational proof. This is not faith and does not lead to revival. Take the biblical example of Elijah. When he was on Mount Carmel and sacrificed the burnt offering in the presence of many, many thousands, God answered with visible proof of His existence. Fire fell from heaven and they cried, "The Lord is God. The Lord is God." Were they converted? No! That is why the Lord always reveals Himself **through His Word.** He did this after His resurrection. He could have said to His depressed disciples, "Look, it is I, Jesus." But He did not do this. He opened the Word to them (Luke 24:25-27). Then He revealed His work of redemption through the breaking of bread (Luke 24:30), and it was only then that they saw Him. But then He disappeared again from their eyes, so that they could believe.

GOD IS GOD!

Proof of God's Existence!

G.K. in U.. Recently someone asserted that there is no way to prove God's existence. I did put forth the argument that it can be proved by nature, such as the seasons of the years, etc. I would appreciate your help in letting me know what else one could bring as proof.

Answer: How foolish are such people! The proof of God's existence is first of all placed into the conscience of each human being. We have come forth from the hands of God (Romans 1:19). Second, if one still wants to deny the existence of God and refuses to believe, of such Romans 1:20 says, "For the invisible things of him from the creation of the world are clearly seen, being understood by the things that are made, even his eternal power and Godhead; so that they are without excuse." To extreme people, who deny the existence of God, the Scripture says, "The fool hath said in his heart there is no God" (Psalm 14:1). There is no difference, if a man says "maybe there is no God." Basically, these two assertions are the same. Both put the existence of the Eternal into question. That means, they deny Him.

Why then does the Bible call such a person a fool? This not only because such a person closes his eyes to the creation; in order to kill his conscience, but more so because by his denial of the existence of God he actually brings a proof that God exists. For nobody can deny something which does not exist! Would not such a person be a fool if he sits on a chair on his table and asserts continuously there is no such thing as a table and a chair?!

He who denies God is in actual fact fleeing from the inescapable fact — of which he knows deep down in his conscience — that he ultimately will be confronted by God, whom he is denying. In this great and terrible hour, in this last judgment, heaven and earth will be permitted to *flee* from the face of Him who is sitting on the throne (Revelation 20:11), but sin will not be able to flee. Then happy is the man who has not fled from God, but has fled to Him through the Lord Jesus Christ, and therewith his life is protected with Christ in God for eternity (Colossians 3:3).

Is God Unchangeable?

K.H. in R.: Is God really unchangeable? The Bible continually says, "God repented" and He then decided to act differently. Surely God could therefore change His plan for us personally or for our nation merely through our prayers.

Answer: Yes, the eternal God is unchangeable. The Bible teaches this very clearly. In James 1:17 He is called "the Father of lights with whom there is no variableness, neither shadow of turning." When we read that God repented, it is always only in view of man's sin and not in view of His own deeds. God does not change His plans, for His intentions are perfect and immaculate from the beginning until all eternity. Through our prayers we are unable to bring about any change in His plans and ways, but instead, the opposite is true: through intensive prayer, **we** are changed so that God at last, because of who He is, can do what He has wanted to do all along, i.e. to bless, save and set apart. Man will never be able to change God; to believe such a thing is incomparable arrogance and shows that we have in no way recognized His holy Majesty. He is always the One who blesses. When, for instance, a person is unconverted are his sins actually upon him? Is he really guilty before God? Certainly! Does God not want to forgive these sinners of their sins then? Of course He does! Why are they not forgiven then? It is because an inner state of mind and heart is lacking, namely that of repentance and conversion. When a person fulfills this condition, however, he immediately receives what God has long wanted to give him in Christ Jesus, i.e. forgiveness of sin. Has God changed in regard of such a person? Not at all! The person changed! It is the same in the case of a believer too; does God not want to send a revival into his soul? Yes, He does. **He wants to!** But the necessary condition of mind and heart is lacking, i.e. earnest prayer ... He that hath ears to hear let him hear!

The Holy Trinity

R.S. in B.: Lately I have become so unsure about the doctrine of the Holy Trinity I would hesitate to call B. Branham a false teacher or prophet, but in his book *The Age of the Church* the Trinity of God is rejected. Please help me so that I do not go astray.

Answer: I can well understand that you are having a fight with this question as to whether there is a triune God or not; and yet the Bible teaches this. Even if the word "trinity" is not used, the Bible still teaches and reveals the Trinity of God. The Trinity is one divine Being which comprises three different persons, namely, Father, Son and Holy Spirit. In their existence, majesty, will and attributes, these **three** persons are **one.** God is one divine Being, but in the one divine Being there are three different persons, each person being truly God i.e. not three gods. From the very beginning when the Lord said, "Let **us** make man" and many other Bible verses which I will not enumerate here, we are taught of the Trinity. Here is one example. In Ephesians 4:4-6 it speaks of one Spirit, one Lord, one God and Father. If the Holy Spirit is not God how can He then "speak," "separate" and "convict"? I know about these false doctrines which have emanated from the B. Branham movement. But we must resist them because we believe on God the Father, God the Son and God the Holy Spirit — One God, according to the Bible. This biblical doctrine is denied by most of the cults which is also the case with the Jehovah's Witnesses. They even start to mock and to blaspheme and talk of three Gods, only because in their limited receptivity, resulting from the presence of indwelling sin, they cannot understand rationally that God the eternal Father is the **initiator** of our salvation, and that Jesus Christ, in the fullness of time on the cross of Calvary, is the **executor** of God's plan of salvation, and that The Holy Spirit, according to Ephesians 1:13 is the One who **seals our salvation.** Do not listen to all the devilish and misleading false teachings, but instead hold fast onto the sound truth of the Bible.

Is God Cruel?

D.S. in H.: People often say that the God of the Old Testament is so cruel and cannot be compared with the God of the New Testament, for instance 1 Samuel 15:3 and 1 Kings 18:40b. What is the proper answer to this?

Answer: These ignorant people who even dare to call God, the Lord, cruel do not know God at all and themselves even less. They do not know that horror and destruction and inevitable judgment of sin did not originate in the heart of God but in the heart of the devil. They also do not know of God's perfect holiness and righteousness which compels Him to destroy the sinner and even less do they know that in a totally inconceivable way God solved His conflict through Jesus Christ on the cross of Calvary. Which conflict? The conflict between His **holiness** and **righteousness** on the one side and His burning love for us on the other side. This unsolved conflict becomes very obvious for instance in Hosea 11:8, "How shall I give thee up, Ephraim? how shall I deliver thee, Israel? how shall I make thee as Admah? how shall I set thee as Zeboim? mine heart is turned within me, my repentings are kindled together."
Nobody realizes this, otherwise they would be amazed and worship God seeing what actually happened on Calvary's cross where God's holiness and righteousness and love met together **in and through Him** who was given for us so that righteousness and peace — which are otherwise mutually exclusive — kiss one another (Psalm 85:10b).

Understanding God's Plan For Man

S.G. in M. According to my understanding, man was not created when Lucifer fell. Evil had come into being, but how could this happen before the eyes of the Almighty? Why was man created and given a free will to choose, if it was known from eternity that Adam and Eve would fall? Oceans of tears and misery, and also the painful sacrifice of Jesus later on, must have been known of by the omniscient God before man was created. This looks as though — however heretical it may sound — at some time God was not the almighty and omniscient God; it looks as though there was a mistake in the cosmos of which man must bear the consequences to the bitter end. Why must future generations suffer because of the sin of the first men? Why is a baby born a sinner although he could at no time decide whether he wanted to be conceived or not?

Answer: The Bible gives no answer to the question of how sin occurred in Lucifer. But we do know that it came into being, and this was through pride (Isaiah 14:12-15).
God created man in His own image and equipped him with a free will to choose. Man had the ability to choose between good and evil, between God and Satan. Why? Because God is love and He expects reciprocation of His love. Love can only be given on a free-wil basis. Did God know everything beforehand? Yes, He did! Why did He allow it then? We are treading on very dangerous ground when we attempt to explain God. I decline to do this, but I would like to say this to you, that I have come to see that the deepest motive for the Eternal One's allowing all this — the fall of man through sin and his redemption later on — is His great, inconceivable and glorious love. God could have exterminated Satan with one breath of His mouth. With this, evil would not have been conquered, however, but only put out of the way. But behold, the almighty and eternally wise God manifested that light is stronger than darkness, that love is stronger than death, and that the holy and righteous God is the only God to whom glory, laud and honor belong from eternity to eternity.
I would like to confront your other question as to why the baby is born a sinner etc., with Romans 9:19-20, "Thou wilt say then unto me, Why doth he yet find fault? For who hath resisted his will? Nay but, O man, who art thou that repliest against God? Shall the thing formed say to him that formed it, Why hast thou made me thus?" In other words, do not be so vain as to think that your feeble, sin-darkened understanding could understand God and judge His actions, and also, do not be so presumptuous

as to require God to give account of Himself. Let us rather wonder at God's inconceivable mercy, expressed in the words of the Psalmist, "What is man that thou art mindful of him?" and cry with Paul in Romans 11:33 & 34, "O the depths of the riches both of the wisdom and knowledge of God! how unsearchable are his judgments, and his ways past finding out! For who hath known the mind of the Lord? or who hath been his counseller?" You know, this age-old "why" that you put to God, is ultimately rebellion against His holy will. I have often said it, and I will say it again at this point, there is only one "why" that is justified in the whole of history. It is the "why" of the Son of God as He cried on the cross at Calvary, "My God, my God, why hast thou forsaken me?" God was silent at this question. The reason for His silence we find in Zephaniah 3:17, "He will rest in his love" (K.J.V. Margin says "be silent"). God was silent then as His Child carried away the sins of the world — including your sins — because He so loved us.

God's Love — Holiness & Justice

O.E. in D.: I have to ask several questions about your sermon, yesterday. I was deeply touched so was my friend — she even cried. You spoke harshly with the entire congregation. Although, I am learning, that God does not permit to be fooled with, but John writes: "God is Love." The human race needs love. Preach on the love of God! Why do you do this so little?

Answer: I have to refuse your invitation to preach only on the love of God, especially since people of today have only an emotional understanding of God's love. Where the love of God is preached without His holiness and justice, it is misunderstood. We cannot even understand God's love before we are touched by His holiness and justice. These three characteristics of God cannot be separated. Look at Jesus on the cross: The revelation of the love, the holiness and the justice of God! Whoever wants to hear only of the love of God remains in his character a rebel and starts using the dangerous expression: "the loving God." His wonderful love is being misused as a cover-up for continuing in sin. That's why I have to heed the Word of Isaiah 58:1: "Cry aloud, spare not, lift up thy voice like a trumpet, and shew my people their transgression, and the house of Jacob their sins." When under the power of the Word of God the believer breaks through in a spirit of repentance, and frightened by the earnestness of their sin in the light of God's holiness, then, and only then, they begin to recognize the love of God in its unending breadth and length, and depth and height. (Ephesians 3:18-20).

JESUS IS LORD!

The Precious Blood of Jesus!

M.R. in B.: A friend of mine went to a meeting some time ago, where the minister said that Jesus Christ had Godly blood. In Hebrews 2:14, it says "Forasmuch then as the children are partakers of flesh and blood, he also himself likewise took part of the same." Jesus was true man and true God. He was equipped with the Holy Spirit. If He had Godly blood, then how could He with only Godly substance be tempted as a man? Could He be true man if He had Godly blood? Also, it is written, flesh and blood cannot inherit the kingdom of God.

Answer: Jesus Christ is true God and true man. As the Son of man, He poured out His eternal life in His blood. When you ask if Jesus Christ had Godly blood you should rephrase this statement: God became man in Jesus Christ (1 Timothy 3:16). However, since He did not know sin in His life as man (2 Corinthians 5:21), His blood was eternal and did not carry the seed of death in it. As such, the Lord Jesus was able to redeem us with His blood from our sin and death. He was **as man** just like Adam before the fall, that's why He is called the last Adam in I Corinthians 15:45. There is a cunning, almost unnoticable misleading in the statement that Jesus Christ had Godly blood. With this, Satan tries to put a question mark after the fact that we are redeemed by a man who was God at the same time.
In a different place we read the undeniable fact which we can never grasp with our mind: the Eternal God really became in every way man, even in our temptations except for sin, wherefore Paul calls it a great mystery of godliness in I Timothy 3:16.

Immanuel

A.R. in Z.: I have often wondered why in Matthew 1:21 the angel told Joseph to call the child Jesus and not Immanuel according to Isaiah 7:14. Is there an explanation?

A second question: It is striking how often the name of Jesus is misused even by refined and educated people and even by believers. One only has to be surprised or shocked or to have forgotten something and out comes the word "God!" although sometimes in changed forms like "Gee," "Golly," "Gosh" etc. But it still refers to the name of our Lord. What should one do? Warn when possible or just quietly pray "Lord forgive"?

Answer: The precious name of Jesus was not allowed to be revealed in the Old Testament because the name "Jesus" means "Saviour." This was only revealed in the fullness of times. It is a fact that in the Bible people's names always represented their character, work titles of our blessed Lord are mentioned in the Old Testament except the name "Jesus." But the name "Immanuel" — God with us — points to Jesus and He Himself said, "He that seeth me seeth the Father."

Because Satan trembles at the power in the name of Jesus, he used millions of people as his mediums in order to dishonor this holy and exalted name. For the child of God, it cuts to the heart to hear thoughtless, degenerated people abuse the name of God at the slightest provocation. Such people are not aware how they are sinning against the commandment "Thou shalt not take the name of the Lord in vain," and how they are tools in the enemy's hand. You should warn them when you can. The best is usually to have a suitable tract on hand to give to the one concerned.

Jesus Believed the Scriptures

C.S. in S.: You write in a back issue of the *Midnight Call* that Jesus believed in the historical reports of the Old Testament. Are you not one of the greatest of the false teachers yourself? Please answer this question. In Jesus, God became the Word which was spoken to the prophets, thus a Holy Spirit of truth was in Jesus who **knew** everything. Therefore it is not true, as you write, that Jesus **believed** the Scriptures. You make Jesus a liar with your statement, in the same way as every other false teacher.

Answer: And how our blessed Saviour **believed!** He, the Son of God, became in every respect the Son of man, but **without** sin. He was no superman. In all things He was made like us, "For," says Paul in 2 Corinthians 8:9, "ye know the grace of our Lord Jesus Christ, that though he was rich, yet for your sakes he became poor, that ye through his poverty might be rich." Again the Scriptures say, "Wherefore in all things it behoved him to be made like unto his brethren" (Heb. 2:17a). He was tempted, just as we are, so that we could overcome temptation (Heb. 2:18). He was hungry, so that He could give us the Bread of Life (Matt. 4:2). On the cross He cried "I thirst" so that He could give us the Water of Life. It is written of Him that He was weary (John 4:6). Thus He was able to give us rest for our souls. He believed to the end, even then when the priests stood before His cross and cried mockingly, "He trusted in God; let him deliver him now . . . " (Matt. 27:43). In Hebrews 12, Jesus is even called the Author and Finisher of our faith. Paul had only one boast, "The life which I now live in the flesh I live **by the faith of the Son of God"** (Gal. 2:20). If Jesus had not believed, how could we then believe. You are way off mark, my dear Mr. S. Appropriately the Post Office stamped the envelope containing your letter as follows, "Wrong zip code led to misdirection of letter." It would be a good thing if you were to see your spiritual misdirection.

Friendly Yet Strict

H.M. in R.: In one of your Radio Messages (not in English Ed.) you stated that Jesus was never unfriendly. But that is not true. What about when He cleansed the Temple? And why did the people answer in John 6:60 "This is an hard saying!"

Answer: Especially then, when the Lord is strict, He imparts to us His friendliness. Think for instance about Titus 3:4, where it speaks about the *kindness* and the *love* of God our Saviour towards man. And how did this kindness appear? Through the sacrificing of His beloved Son!

How else can we unite the terrible suffering of our blessed and exalted Lord, with friendliness of God? Your way of thinking, dear Mr. M., is completely wrong. For the Lord chastises those whom He loves. God has always thought of peace and not of suffering for us, and in that way He approaches us with His friendliness. Often He leads His children in the desert of suffering, loneliness and through bitter disappointments, so that in this wilderness of isolation, He can impart His friendliness to your soul. In this regard please compare Hosea 2:16.

As Drops of Blood

E.G. in H.: In front of me I have your August issue with the article, "Living Prophecy." You state that in Gethsemane, the Lord did sweat blood in His agony. That, however, is not true. For the Lord was not battling with death, neither was He dying, nor did He sweat blood in the garden of Gethsemane. In my Bible I read, "And his sweat was as it were great drops of blood falling to the ground." You must have overlooked the words "was as it were."

Answer: In Luke 22:44, I can read nothing else than what is written. And to make this more clear I will read another translation, "And being in agony he prayed more earnestly and his sweat became as great drops of blood falling to the ground." If from this statement you read that the drops of blood from our blessed Lord in His fear of death are only a symbolic picture, then you do that on your own account. I cannot do that. I see here the opposite; the hard and difficult battle of our Lord, and the depths of His suffering in Gethsemane. This, we can not even grasp intellectually. Only the visible signs permit us to sense the most terrible depths of His battle: "His sweat became as drops of blood."

Especially the words, "as it were" shows us something of the greatness of the sacrifice of Jesus. There are no unnecessary words in the Scripture. Everything has a deeper meaning. When we read "His sweat became as drops of blood" then the Holy Spirit wants to show us even more, according to my understanding, that these were not drops of blood like any other human blood, no not at all, for here the Son of God began to shed His eternal life in His blood, which He later finalized on the cross of Calvary. Of course, He was flesh and blood just as we, but without sin! He had life as we, but His was never ending eternal life. In this light, the statement "as drops of blood" receives a very high meaning. He gave much more than the blood of another person, for He was the life of God.

Furthermore, and this lies on the line with the Scripture Paul writes in Philippians, "And became obedient unto death, even the death of the cross (Philippians 2:8). He was obedient unto death, that is GETHSEMANE, the death on the cross, that is CALVARY.

Have you never thought about it more deeply and realized that God the Father withdrew His protecting hand for a small moment from His Son? And in that moment, all the satanic powers of death fell upon the Lord in order to kill Him. Don't you see, that the Lord Jesus, just shortly before He was to reach His greatest goal of reconciling the world with God through the shedding of His blood on the cross, was dying? This was one of the greatest tests of faith for our blessed Lord. Yes, shortly before Calvary, just before He, the Lamb of God, was to carry away the sins of the world, He was to be *eliminated.* But He stood firm also in this test of faith, for He answered, "Not mine but your will be done." It was the Lord's will to go to Calvary. And His prayer was answered…"Who in the days of his flesh, when he had offered up prayers and supplications with strong crying and tears unto him that was able to SAVE HIM FROM DEATH, and was heard in that he feared" (Hebrews 5:7).

This attack on Jesus was the last and desperate attempt of hell to stop His work of salvation, for Jesus could have died and even shed His blood, but under no circumstances was it to be on the cross. Inspite that the "murderer of the soul" could not know HOW Jesus would defeat him on the cross, he must nevertheless have sensed what would face him at Calvary. Just the night before, when Christ instituted the Lord's Supper with His disciples, and when He gave the cup with wine to His disciples He said, "For this is my blood of the new testament which is shed for many for the remission of sin" (Matthew 26:28). Thus, He was obedient, and I repeat, obedient unto death — Gethsemane, even unto death on the cross — Calvary.

He Descended Into Hell

H.S. in P.: What was the actual purpose of Jesus' descent into hell? We laymen think: as Peter writes, Jesus went to preach the Gospel to the spirits of those of Noah's time in a mass evangelization. And the result was amazing. Let us praise this glorious deed of the Conqueror which His followers may doubtless continue there if not with such success. Surely God wants to save everyone, or does He mean just a small percentage? If that were the case, His will would be very limited and His labors among men poorly regarded. The sin against the Holy Spirit cannot be forgiven in this world or in the next, but are there not other ages to come when forgiveness is possible? The blood of Jesus Christ also cleanses from this sin!

Answer: That Jesus did descend in order to preach the Gospel to the dead is, as you say, a clear biblical fact. No living believer on earth could go and bring the Gospel to the deceased before the Lord's redemptive act. Only He could do that. But after Calvary and Easter the responsibility lies with God's children on earth, which is the reason for the Lord's repeated command: "go ye into all the world!" If children of God only recognized their great responsibility to bring the Gospel to their generation in the whole world, THEY WOULD BE SHOCKED AT THEIR FAILURES BECAUSE WHEN PEOPLE PERISH THROUGH OUR NEGLECT, THEN THEIR BLOOD WILL BE REQUIRED AT OUR HANDS. (Read carefully Ezekiel chapter 3) The doctrine of Universalism is a deadly opiate against the express and repeated missionary command of the Lord to His Church. It seems to me that you yourself are of this persuasion when you speak speculatively about the preaching of the Gospel in the other world.

No Hasty Escape

K.K. in W.: When I read in my Bible about the resurrection of our Lord and Saviour, I am amazed that it says in John 20:7, "And the napkin, that was about his head, was not laying with the linen cloths, but wrapped together in a place by itself." What is the meaning of this?

Answer: The fact that the napkin was not found together with the linen, or the grave cloths, at the resurrection of the Lord, proves in a unique way that the Lord did not, so to say, "escape hastily," He arose in sovereign peace, in a royal manner. Besides, this also shows God's *order* clearly. The napkin and the linen cloths are separated in its proper place, for God is not a God of disorder.

THE HOLY SPIRIT

Is The Holy Spirit a Person?

H.M. in C.: I heard the exposition that the Holy Spirit — and the same goes for the evil spirit too — is a person. What would you say to this? How can a person enter a human heart? This is absolutely impossible. A person is surely a creature. A spirit is intangible, however. It can only reveal itself in some form or other, for instance, in the form of an animal or person. If we try to take hold of such a form, however, it disappears. A spirit can also reveal itself in the form of fire, but a real person can never turn himself into an intangible spirit.

Answer: I would like to ask you a counter-question: is God a personality? "Of course," you will say. We read, however, in John 4:24 and hear this through the mouth of the Lord Jesus, "God is a Spirit: and they that worship him must worship him in spirit and in truth." You are of the erroneous opinion that a person must have a bodily form. This is not so! This is the wonderful thing, that the power to overcome in us is a personality in our person. Jesus Christ in us, He is our hope of glory (Col. 1:27, Eph. 3:17). Thus, the Holy Spirit is also the third Person of the Trinity. Were the Holy Spirit merely a divine influence it could not say in the Bible, "He spoke," or " . . . grieve not the Holy Spirit," or " . . . How is it that ye have agreed together to tempt the Spirit of the Lord?" Ultimately, a personality is not that which we see of it, but that which is concealed in it.

The Unforgivable Sin

A.K. in G.: I had been a Christian for just three months when I read Matthew 12:32. Satan immediately started attacking me by giving me awful blasphemous thoughts. People prayed for me at that time and the fear that I had fallen from grace disappeared. Nevertheless the enemy kept reminding me of that moment for a whole year until one day, having become so furious with this continuous temptation, I wished in prayer that there were only the Father and the Son and no such person as the Holy Spirit against whom one could sin. When I realized what I had thought I was shocked and recognized it as yet another attack of Satan. Since then I am no longer troubled by the previous event but by this new one — worse than ever before. What I need now is a clear answer to the question: Is it possible for a child of God to commit the sin of blaspheming against the Holy Spirit or not? From where do these blasphemous thoughts come? Why do they not come under verse 33?

Answer: Let me make it quite clear from the start: when a person has blasphemed against the Holy Spirit he has absolutely no feeling of remorse about it. That is the judgment on such a person and that is why he cannot be forgiven. Your experience comes from being surrounded by Satan but not possessed by him. That is the painful experience of so many faithful children of God and also yours; they have been given wicked and blasphemous thoughts from demons. The fatal error you make is to mistake these demonic suggestions for your own thoughts, because Matthew 12:31 speaks expressly of people who *willfully* blaspheme against the Holy Spirit, that is, they *want* to. But you have not wanted to. However, the fact that you are overcome to such an extent by this temptation proves that there are some unforgiven inherited sins in your life. The Lord says that He "visits the iniquity of the fathers upon the children unto the third and fourth generation." (e.g. Deuteronomy 5:6). It is therefore important that you confess to the Lord quite simply, "Lord, I humble myself over the unknown abominable sins of my parents and forefathers" (read Psalm 90:8) just as the men of the Bible also did when they acknowledged, "We and our fathers have sinned." At the same time claim the precious blood of Jesus for yourself. Then this inherited line in your life will be broken. The practical outcome will be that whenever some blasphemous thought or other is thrown at you, you will not be shocked, let alone think it is your own fault, but with bold faith you will cast such devilish thoughts far from you by praising the blood of the Lamb.

Spiritual Gifts Today?

B.S. in Q.: For a very long time these questions have troubled me: What do you think of spiritual gifts? Are these possible in the same extent as they were in the time of the apostles? Or were the gifts of the spirit only available then? Here, many have differing opinions.

Answer: I cannot find in the Bible anything that says that the gifts of the Spirit were only reserved for the first Christians. That would be terrible! It would mean that also other promises would not be good anymore, today. Where does this present confusion in this area come from? Satan is the great imitator of God. His activity accelerates in the end-times. Of course he cannot imitate all gifts of the spirit. Of the nine gifts of the Spirit he can imitate about four masterfully. These are: Miracle-working, prophecies, speaking in tongues and healing. We find in these times that there are indeed miracles of God and of the devil, there are healings worked through the Holy Spirit and such from below, prophecies given from the Lord and such which are inspired by powers of the liar. How can one now remain protected from the terrible errors? Walk in the light and in the truth! (1 John 1:7a; 3 John 3:4b). Satan can stand neither the light nor the truth. Whoever walks uprightly, inwardly before God remains protected from the misleading of the cunning powers of lies. For instance, where there is much prayer for gifts of the Spirit, and the Spirit of repentance is still missing, then the Spirit of truth has already left, and the reason and center of prayer is the pious self. Search the giver of blessings and not first of all the blessing. Wrestle to find the Giver, then you will also know which gifts you need from Him. Become obedient to the Victor and the victory will be there, too. For the Word is still valid:

"God also bearing them witness, both with signs and wonders, and with divers miracles, and gifts of the Holy Ghost, **according to his will**" (Hebrews 2:4)

I conclude from this: Whoever will submit himself under the will of God with all his heart, will also pray for the right gifts. Who has an ear to hear, let him hear!

Baptized in The Holy Spirit

A.S. in W.: I am so afraid that when the Saviour comes I shall not be found to have been baptized in the Holy Spirit. I have been praying for this for years, but still have not experienced it, even though I love the Lord with my whole heart and have definitely experienced the new birth, and I also have assurance that all my debt has been paid off and forgiven and that now I may live by faith, because of God's grace.

Answer: You have been misled by those who say you must be baptized in the Spirit, because if you have experienced the new birth as you testify, this can only take place through the baptism of the Spirit. "For by one Spirit were we all baptized into one body...(1 Corinthians 12:13). "No one can say Jesus is Lord, except by the Holy Spirit" (1 Corinthians 12:3). "In whom ye also trusted, after that ye heard the word of truth, the gospel of your salvation: in whom also, after that ye believed, ye were sealed with that holy Spirit of promise." (Ephesians 1:13). It is essential that we, who serve the Lord, should continually be filled and refilled with the Holy Spirit, which comes about by implicit obedience of faith, obedience to the word and prayer. Nowhere does it say in the Scriptures, "Except ye be born again and baptized in the Spirit..." What God hath joined together, let no man put asunder!

Gifts & Fruit

A.K. in B.: After reading the *Midnight Call* for some time now, I must tell you about my convictions: without the serious and honest use of the gifts of the Spirit, I cannot bring forth the true fruit of the Spirit. Also, I have found divine love only among people which have ceased to sin and have earnestly used the gifts of the Spirit. Please excuse my saying this, in case you do not like it.

Answer: You confuse two different things: the GIFTS of the Spirit and the FRUIT of the Spirit. As for the fruit of the Spirit, according to Galatians 5:22, we need this so that the Lord Jesus will be able to recognize us on that day (read carefully Matthew 7:20-23). The FRUIT of the Spirit grows in a person whose life is in submission to the Holy Spirit (compare Galatians 5:18a and verse 25). The Holy Spirit, however, never takes power in a person, when He isn't invited. The voluntary submission of ones life to the Holy Spirit works the fruit of the Spirit. The GIFTS of the Spirit are given by God to whom He chooses (compare I Corinthians 7:7, I Corinthians 3:5b, Ephesians 4:8, I Corinthians 12:11). For what purpose does He give them? For the mutual use (I Corinthians 12:7), or even for self-edification (I Corinthians 14:4). Now, there are children of God who live a holy life, but do not have a special or at least not spectacular gift of the Spirit, nevertheless they bring forth FRUIT of the Spirit. And then there are those who can show "gifts of the Spirit" but no fruit of the Spirit. The first category can stand before the Lord, the latter will not be able to. Therefore it is misleading to say: "without the serious and honest use of the gifts of the Spirit, I cannot bring forth the true fruit of the Spirit." Keep the fruit and the gifts of the Spirit well apart. Then you will divide the WORD OF God rightly (2 Timothy 2:15).

The Filling of the Holy Spirit

W.S. in K.: In one issue of the *Midnight Call,* there was a letter in the correspondence column on the subject of the baptism in the Spirit. I have come across some of the writings of Torrey, Marcus Hauser, etc., and in these the baptism in the Spirit is also mentioned. Other great evangelists are also said to have experienced this baptism in the Spirit. I think something of the kind is reported in the beginnings of the Herrnhuter Brotherhood. There are numerous reports of people who have experienced this baptism in the Spirit. As far as I can see in this matter, there seem to be two main opinions in the Church of Jesus Christ. The one says, as you, that the baptism in the Spirit occurs at the same time as conversion (the new birth). Another opinion says that after conversion there should be a baptism in the Spirit.

And a second question: In a missionary publication I read the following: "There is a judgment awaiting the believers (1 Corinthians 3:10-15 and 2 Corinthians 5:10). They must appear before the judgment seat of Christ, following the rapture. There our innermost, hidden nature will be revealed. To the extent in which we are revealed here, through the Spirit of Christ, there will be no further revelation necessary then. Our deeds in this earthly life, whether godly or ungodly, determine the measure of glory." Will there really be varying degrees of glory in God's kingdom? Would it not be discouraging to know that one could not have part in the whole glory of Jesus?

Answer: The confusion concerning the baptism in the Spirit, is a result of confusing biblical terms. This in itself would not be too serious, because the Lord is not concerned first and foremost with whether we understand biblical doctrines, but how our hearts are before Him. What is so terrible and misleading, is this false dogma of the baptism in the Spirit. Once again, as I have already written, the baptism in the Spirit is inevitably simultaneous with the new birth (cf. 1 Corinthians 12:13, Ephesians 1:13, Romans 8:16 and 2 Corinthians 1:21-22). But the fulness of the Holy Spirit is given to each one according to the degree of his obedience of faith and the commission which he has. This filling with the Holy Spirit has been experienced by many of God's servants, and I have also experienced it many times myself, through God's grace. But if this experience does not repeat itself continually, and ever deeper, our hearts become hardened again, and the fountain dries up. That is why we read repeatedly in the Acts of the Apostles that the believers were filled with the Spirit. (See Acts 4:8, 4:31, 6:3 and 5, 7:55, 11:24, 13:9.) Here Pentecost is not spoken of as a "once and for all" experience, and as a historical event, but as a repeated filling with the Holy Spirit. The false dogma of the so-called "second blessing" harbors great dangers. The one concerned becomes self-confident. He feels himself to be better qualified than other believers who are perhaps more filled with the Holy Spirit, but cannot look back on any spectacular experiences or gifts. But if we want to go the biblical way, and strive and pray for more fulness of the Spirit, in that we allow ourselves to be more deeply sanctified and cleansed, we will be kept from self-exaltation. He who is filled the most with the Spirit of God, is the humblest. Such a man has only one desire, namely to glorify Jesus. The Holy Spirit will discern and penetrate every sphere of his life.

To come to your second question: there are two kinds of salvation. The salvation we receive out of pure grace, because of the death of Jesus on Calvary's Cross (Ephesians 2:8-9), and the salvation we inherit (Hebrews 1:14). Eternal life is for all believers unchanging and the same. There are no degrees here. But the reward is measured out to each man according to the degree of his faithfulness, because God is righteous. Look in the book of Revelation and see how they that overcome are promised seven wonderful things. Look for the seven crowns in the New Testament. Notice the words "heirs" and "reward" in the New Testament. In Romans 8:17 the way is shown us very clearly how we can be joint-heirs with Christ; if so be that we suffer with him, that we may be also glorified with him.

Tongues Movement

R.R. in S.: My wife and I have been believers for some years and with our whole hearts we want to follow the Lamb. For some time now something has been happening in our church, which I am not quite clear about, whether it is of the Lord or not. I mean this praying for the baptism in the Spirit, with its results like speaking in tongues and prophesying. On the one hand we find a reference to it in 1 Corinthians 14 but on the other hand I would like to ask: is the speaking in new tongues proof that a person is now baptized in the Holy Spirit? Is there a difference between a pentecostal spirit and a genuine fulness of the Spirit? How can we discern what is genuine from what is false, according to the Scriptures. I often have an uneasy feeling that there is something wrong in our Church.

Answer: May the Lord save your Church from this false

teaching, because this tongues' movement has done terrible damage. This is because people pray for the baptism in the Holy Spirit without being clear in themselves what the baptism in the Holy Spirit is. Baptism in the Holy Spirit happens at the same time as the new birth, "For by one Spirit are we all baptized into one body, whether we be Jews or Gentiles, whether we be bond or free; and have been all made to drink into one Spirit." (1 Corinthians 12:13). But the fulness of the Holy Spirit is apportioned to each one according to the measure of his obedience of faith and only that Jesus may be glorified; but one false teaching follows the other, each inspired by the spirit from below. They say we must pray for the baptism of the Holy Spirit. This is absolutely wrong. They say that the result of baptism in the Spirit is speaking in tongues and prophecy. This is an even worse error. This doctrine comes to the satanic conclusion that whoever does not speak in tongues is not baptized with the Spirit of God. Defeated is the lying spirit of speaking in tongues. I can hear someone exclaiming: but speaking in tongues is biblical! Very biblical indeed! When Paul refers to speaking in tongues in 1 Corinthians 14 he says in Verse 26b, "Let all things be done unto edifying." And verse 33, "For God is not the author of confusion but of peace."

When we consider the excesses which arise as a result of this tongues' movement, for instance the hysterical crying which has at times threatened to break out in our conferences because of foreign elements, we must oppose this emotional and fanatical spirit in the name of Jesus. Behind it all is the imitator of God, Satan himself, who is able to imitate some of the gifts of the Spirit but not all. But the fruit of the Spirit which is the direct consequence of being filled with the Spirit he can not imitate, because the fruit of the Spirit according to Galatians 5:22 exhibits the nature of Jesus: love, joy, peace, longsuffering, gentleness, goodness, faith, meekness and temperance. **Here** God's will is revealed, because here He finds obedience through faith. Here the Lord gives the gifts of the Spirit **as He chooses.** Where the will of God is operative according to 1 Corinthians 14:40, everything is decent and orderly. If you dear Brother and your wife, walk in the whole truth and love the Lord Jesus with all your heart, and you feel troubled by this speaking in tongues in your church, then you are reacting correctly; because you are perceiving the presence of a spirit which is not from God but from below.

From where does this Pentecostal Movement come, with its speaking in tongues? It came as a replacement for obedience to the faith. Instead of being crucified with Christ, it avoids dying to self. In this lies its great deception, because it is, after all, "biblical." **What will be so convincing about the deception of**

the Antichrist, who will soon reveal himself, which will spread around the whole world? It will be biblical. It says in Revelation 13:13-14, "And he doeth great wonders, so that he maketh fire to come down from heaven on the earth in the sight of men, and deceiveth them that dwell on earth by the means of those miracles which he had power to do in the sight of the beast." Everything about the Antichrist will be biblical, mighty and impressive, but his nature is that of the devil. I have also met people who speak in tongues and prophesy, behind whose possession of the gifts of the Spirit was only carnality, unbrokenness and an antichristian outlook. But I do not want to generalize. In the Pentecostal Movement there are individual burning and honest children of God, just as in the Roman Catholic Church there are also many sincere children of God. The deception is so great in our days, that you are quite justified in asking, "Is there a difference between a pentecostal spirit and a genuine fulness of the SPIRIT AND HOW CAN we discern what is genuine and what is false, according to the Scriptures?" Yes truly, there is a world of difference between the pentecostal spirit and the Spirit of Pentecost; between this desire to possess the gifts of the Spirit without the fruit of the Spirit and without that sign by which Jesus will recognize us and wants to recognize us, ". . .by their fruits ye shall know them." One day He will have to reject those who have the gifts of the Spirit without the fruit of the Spirit. Please see Matthew 7:20-23. You do not need to struggle and try so hard, but only to walk in the truth, with all your heart, because Jesus says, "Everyone that is of the truth heareth my voice." And He says of His sheep, ". . .and the sheep follow him: for they know his voice. And a stranger will they not follow, but will flee from him, for they know not the voice of strangers" (John 10:4-5). Do not follow strange voices which entice and speak so biblically. Resist them in the name of Jesus. God wants to send a Spirit-worked revival in your church. Then there will be repentance, humility and tears and the Lamb will be glorified, and the Holy Spirit will take up to. Have the courage to warn those in your church, wherever it is necessary.

Outpouring of the Spirit

F.W. in H.: Since Joel 2:28-30 has been fulfilled for Israel and that part of the Church of Jesus Christ of Israel, on the day of pentecost, there is one question arising: Is there anything as the pouring out of the Spirit according to Joel 2 possible today or was this reserved only for the beginning of Christianity?

Answer: According to my knowledge the promised pouring out of the Holy Spirit according to Joel 2, is meant first of all for the

Israeli part of the Church, as Peter mentions this in Acts 2:16-21. The three-thousand Jews, which were converted on that day experienced in full measure the beginning of this promise. Here is also true: The Jews first! After this, the Gentiles also received the Holy Spirit. But the historical occurrence of Pentecost itself was for the Jews. In other words: Never again did this pouring out of the Holy Spirit of Pentecost repeat itself. It was a one-time occurrence just as Golgatha, the dying and resurrection of Jesus. Anybody who believes, receives the fruit thereof. I seem to recognize that the circle of Joel 2, is beginning to close itself again in Israel. This means: Special pouring out of the Spirit and revelations are received by those, which come to the body of Jesus Christ as the last ones. All signs point to the fact that as the beginning of the church was Jewish, so will the final part also be from Israel. I do speak specifically about the Church of Jesus Christ, Jews and Gentiles not of the remnant of Israel, which will be converted during the Great Tribulation.

The Holy Spirit During the Great Tribulation

L.B. in E.: It says in God's word: "...he who now restrains it will do so until he is out of the way." You, dear brother have said that it is the Holy Spirit who will be put out of the way. But as there will be people converted, after our rapture, under the most terrible conditions and who will have to pay for it with their lives, God's Holy Spirit must surely still be active on earth, as also in the "two witnesses." I cannot understand this, because many godly men say, that it is the Holy Spirit who must be out of the way.

Answer: You ask how can people be converted during the Great Tribulation when the Holy Spirit, who is the hindrance for the revelation of the Antichrist and according to 2 Thessalonians 2 must be out of the way? — Under exactly the same circumstances as before Pentecost. At that time also, the Holy Spirit was not in believers, but often came upon the believers straight from heaven as we frequently read in the prophets "...and the Spirit of the Lord came upon him." Before Pentecost, the risen Lord Jesus breathed on the disciples and said: "And when he had said this, he breathed on them, and saith unto them, Receive ye the Holy Ghost:" (John 20:22). But the actual uniting with the Lord Jesus through the Holy Spirit first took place at Pentecost. According to our understanding, it will also be like this during the Great Tribulation. Very many people will come to a living faith through the Word which was previously sown in their hearts and which is Spirit and Life and through the working of the Holy Spirit who will then be in heaven.

THE CHURCH

Revival

W.B. in S.: Do you believe there can be a worldwide revival in these last days, or do you feel it is too late?

Answer: In general, God never limited revival possibilities for a lost world. In Isaiah 44:3 He says, "For I will pour water upon him that is thirsty, and floods upon the dry ground." In other words, if the whole population of the world would bow down before the Lord in repentance, then the result would be a worldwide revival. The omnipotence of God has no limits and according to 1 Timothy 2:4, He desires that all men should be saved. The important question however is *who* should be revived? According to my understanding of the Word, the sleeping Church has to be revived and not the world. We do believe as solidly as a rock that God will send a revival in the Church of Jesus. Moreover, we believe on the grounds of the Scripture that revival is to be a normal condition of the Church. We are convinced that the instruction book for the Church, the book of Acts, describes for us clearly the normal condition of the Church, as it permits us to see what a revival in the Church means: "And the Lord added unto the church daily such as should be saved" (Acts 2:47). In other words, according to the measure in which godly revival is present in the Church, the lost people will be convicted and saved. Often one puts the horse behind the wagon by talking too much about a worldwide revival. Worldwide? Yes, but within the Church of Jesus! In this way an uncounted number of sinners will be saved out of this world. But the whole world will never be revived because we are clearly shown the godly principals in Acts 15:14 "...to take out of them a people for his name" or in John 17:14 "...because they are not of the world, even as I am not of the world." The Apostle Paul says in 1 Corinthians 5:10 "For then must ye needs go out of the world." Our Lord Himself expressed this in the high priestly prayer and emphasized these truths in that he said "I pray for them: I pray not for the world, but for them which thou hast given me; for they are thine" (John 17:9).

The truth of the Scripture remaineth steadfast, the world is condemned. We believe assuredly however that if the Church of Jesus Christ would experience revival in the end-times (and that is the will of God) millions of lost souls would be saved from this cursed world which is totally corrupted and ripe for judgment and will never be revived but is approaching unavoidable judgment.

I repeat, we do believe that the Church of Jesus Christ around the world must be revived and we also know that this is the will of the Lord. But I would want to ask everyone who is praying for such a revival: Are you willing to expect a personal revival? Do you want true revelation of your own self? Do you want the deeper cleansing through the Blood of Jesus? I often have a very nagging feeling that those who pray for a worldwide revival amongst the children of this world often and unknowingly reject their own much needed personal revival in their hearts. This however is so vital because the Lord promises in 2 Chronicles 7:14 "If **my** people, which are called by my name, shall humble themselves, and pray, and seek my face, and turn from their wicked ways; then will I hear from Heaven, and will forgive their sins, and will heal their land."

Both Jews & Greeks

R.W. in F.: Paul says in 1 Corinthians 1:24, "But unto them which are called, both Jews and Greeks, Christ the power of God, and the wisdom of God." Are the Greeks then equal to the Jews as a chosen nation? I have always believed that the Jewish people are the only chosen people from among all nations.

Answer: 1 Corinthians 1:24 simply says that the Gospel of Jesus Christ is **valid** for Jews as well as Greeks (Gentiles). This question was strongly debated by the Jewish Messianic believers during the first Evangelical Council in Jerusalem. The first Jews who accepted the Gospel of Jesus Christ were of the opinion that this was meant only for them. But then God sent Paul and Barnabas to the Gentiles, and Peter was sent to the Roman Centurian, Cornelius, to preach to him the Gospel. During this first Council, Peter stated in Acts 15:11, "We (Jews) believe that through the grace of the Lord Jesus Christ we shall be saved, even as they (Gentiles)." That means, as soon as a Jew or a Gentile is converted to faith in Jesus Christ, he becomes a member of the Church and therewith a member of the body of Jesus. They together form a spiritual unity which we call an **organism.** With this however, they lose all other callings or tasks that would have any significance before God. This also is confirmed in Galatians 3:28, "There is neither Jew nor Greek, there is neither bond nor free, there is neither male nor female: for ye are all one in Christ Jesus." Does this mean then that the earthly calling of Israel has been eliminated? Not at all! If that would be the case, then a male would cease to be a male and a female would cease to be a female. The task of the Church of Jesus, whose members are born again Jews or Gentiles is a heavenly one, but the calling of the nation of Israel is an earthly one. I have answered this question in detail in my book entitled "1000 Years Peace." Please read it.

The Mystery of the Church

G.G. in B.: In one article by Dr. Wasserzug, the position of the Church in relationship to Jesus is compared with husband and wife. Then she also speaks in the article about the day of the wedding; the Church is being led into the heavenly reception room and then describes the wedding of the Lamb to the Bride, who has prepared herself for this day. According to my understanding of the Scripture, I thought to be of the same mind with you, namely that the Bride is Israel and not the Church of Jesus Christ? When the Church of Jesus is being united, as His members into one body, she can never be at the same time His Bride but rather would seem to form with the Lord as the head, the body, that of the Bridegroom.

Answer: You are making a great mistake, in that you are wanting to analyze intellectually the mystery of the Church of Jesus. This you cannot do, dear brother. Even Paul, who could claim of himself that the Lord had given him special revelation had to admit, "This is a great mystery; but I speak concerning Christ and the church" (Ephesians 5:32). For this reason we may be a little bit more moderate in this case.

But let me say in brief, how the being and the glory of the Church of Jesus Christ is being pictorially illustrated in the New Testament:

1. The Church is the body of Christ (Ephesians 5:30).

2. She is the Bride of the Lamb (Ephesians 5:27) and from v. 22-33 we clearly see that the entire Church really is the Bride of the Lamb who will be entrusted to Him after the Rapture (Revelation 19:7).

3. She is also being called "an habitation of God through the Spirit" and even "an holy temple in the Lord" (Ephesians 2:19-22).

When you state that the Church cannot be His body, and at the same time His Bride, then your judgment is wrong. Please think back to Adam, the first human being. Where was his wife? With and in him. That is why the Scripture said she was taken *out* of man (Genesis 2:23). And Paul sheds a little bit more light on this wonderful mystery of the Church for us in that he states, "For we are members of his body, his flesh, and of his bones" (Ephesians 5:30). How precious is it to know that when He will reveal Himself we will also be revealed to Him in glory (Colossians 3:4).

Church and State

A.O. in W.: For our home Bible study group we have planned the subject "Separation of Church and State." We have already read some articles about it, and would like to know your opinion also.

Answer: When I am answering this question I am not specifically thinking about your country, Switzerland, for this question is being asked in many different Christian countries. Let me say this: As long as the Church is connected with the State, and is subsidized by tax money of the citizens, we must view this an *Institution of the State.* I remember years ago in a conference with leading clergymen who spoke about the "State, Church and Independent Fellowships." I replied, "Gentlemen, I do not recognize the established Church as the Church of Jesus Christ but rather as a mission field." Nothing has changed this statement. For the Church of Jesus Christ is not an *organization* but it is an *organism;* it is the body of Jesus Christ. As soon as the Church is being separated from the State, it is immediately revealed how much spiritual substance it has. After all, all Christian organizations, churches, independent fellowships and missionary organizations have *within* their *organization* members of the *organism,* that is, born-again persons. Everyone can become a member of a church, without being born-again, but to become a member of the invisible Church of Jesus can only be accomplished through the rebirth. As long as the Church is controlled by the State, people do not need to come to the Church, and still it continues to exist. The same way, for example, are the many European Government Railroads, which lose millions every year but continue to exist because of government support. But as soon as the Church separates from the State it will be revealed what its true content is.

This fact we must view also from a worldwide prophetic-political context: Christianity as a whole represents an Ideology against the Communist Ideology. The West stands against the East and the East against the West. In the very moment when the Communist Ideology will collapse in itself, and that according to Ezekiel 38 and 39 on the mountains and valleys of Israel, then the so-called Christian Ideology will show its true face. According to the Scripture we know that Christianity collectively will be exposed as anti-Christianity. Therefore, blessed is the country, for instance, such as the United States, which has separated the Church from the State. In this way the Church of Jesus Christ is more clearly revealed.

Looking For a Good Church?

S.A. in C.: I have cancelled my membership in my church because I do not receive spiritual food to help me fight an effective battle of faith. I went for some time to a Methodist Church but here the spirit of fashion ruled without opposition. So I continued to search for another church which accepted the Word of God as it is and would do so accordingly. I came to a Pentecostal Church. Here the Word was preached clean and clear. But this church had one catch: there was total confusion at prayer time. One was shouting "Hallelujah," a woman began to prophesy, another began to interpret and at that point I was unable to collect myself reverently for prayer. Is this my own fault or is this whole matter not biblical? I went to another church again but there they taught universalism. I don't believe in this teaching and therefore I felt out of place there too. Now I would like to ask you, where should one get his spiritual bread?

Answer: What shocking confusion and mix-up in the Church of Jesus! This again was shown clearly to me through your letter. From one point of view I can comfort you in this regard; this confusion is almost everywhere. Perplexing and confusing spirits are deceiving the Church of Jesus. You have certainly fallen from the "frying pan into the fire" so to say.

May I suggest, and this in view of the chaotic conditions in many churches: meet with like-minded Christians in your houses if there is no Christ-centered proclamation of the gospel in your area. I believe that with doing so we are on the right path. Even if there is a Christ-centered gospel preaching church in your town, we should nevertheless come together regularly in our houses to seek the face of the Lord through Bible reading and prayer. Behind the Iron Curtain the children of God have to do this also. Large parts of the Western Hemisphere will possibly experience a practical persecution in the near future the spiritual atmosphere forces believers away from the Churches into their homes. This will force us back into the homes as the place to prepare for the coming of the Lord!

God Looks at the Heart!

K.V. in H.: How come the Holy God blesses groups of believers in spite of the fact that they practice sprinkling, that is, the baptism of infants, and are even convinced that this is the will of God?

Answer: I am convinced that God the Lord blesses a person according to the measure of light he has received and is obedient to it, and not according to the measure of the knowledge of others. God looks at the heart and He judges each individual. On the basis of the above mentioned fact, I can have fellowship in the Lord with both groups of believers in spite of the fact that I stand on the ground of the biblical baptism, namely baptism by immersion of the believer. According to historical facts and according to the *cloud of witnesses,* we have had many great men of God who were blessed above measure but nevertheless were convinced that the sprinkling of infants was the right baptism.

I recall Johannes de Heer, a man of God, full of authority, who with his maranatha-message and his more than 800 gospel songs became a blessing for millions of people in Holland and caused great multitudes to come to the knowledge of eternal life through the Lord. In his memoirs he states that before his conversion he was a fanatic Seventh Day Adventist and kept the law and the sabbath strictly. He also mentions several examples where the Lord blessed him in spite of the fact that he was working and living in a false teaching and this only because he was totally honest. Such a blessing of course departs when the person who has received light from the Scripture persistently walks the wrong way and is not willing to be obedient to the deeper light he has received.

SALVATION

Accountability

F.O. in S.: At what age is a person accountable to God?

Answer: We do not set this limit, but the Lord alone. I believe that this age of personal accountability before God will be very variable from child to child, according to the inner ability to understand and grasp the facts of salvation.

What Must I Do?

L.J. in L.: For years I have listened to your radio messages (in German). I envy you for your good relationship with Christ. As for myself, I am not sure of my salvation. I just don't seem to find a contact with Jesus. What must I do?

Answer: First, you should realize one fact; according to the Scripture there is not one single person on earth whom God, in his nature, likes or could accept. The Scripture says, "For there is no difference, for all have sinned and come short of the glory of God" (Romans 3:22-23). And Romans 3:10 says, "There is none righteous, no not one." But just as sure is also the fact that Christ Jesus has been made our righteousness before God (1 Corinthians 1:30)!

You mentioned your long desire to find contact with Jesus. I answer: The Lord has already established this contact long ago in that He sacrificed His only begotten Son for your sins and mine on the cross of Calvary, and so carried away our sins. The way to God is open, according to Hebrews 10:19. God has already given His most beloved also for you (Compare carefully John 3:16).

What must one do to take hold of this gift? One simply has to accept it like a child. For that reason the Scripture says in the Gospel of John 1:12, "But as many as received him, to them gave he power to become the sons of God, even to them that believe on his name." And again the Lord Jesus said, "Verily I say unto you, whosoever shall not receive the kingdom of God as a little child (as a child accepts a present) shall in nowise enter therein" (Luke 18:17).

Thus, dear brother, "L," I am asking you to go down on your knees and pray aloud and in simplicity as a child:

"Lord Jesus Christ, on the grounds of Your words in John

1:12, I receive You now as my personal Saviour and Redeemer. I thank You, that You are cleansing me from all my sins through Your precious blood, as in written in 1 John 1:7. Thank You for giving me the power to become a child of God according to what I have read in John 1:12."

You see, when you do this in faith, then the contact which God has already established through the Lord Jesus Christ, has then also been established from your side. Then you have grasped His stretched out hands. Please read carefully Mark 1:41. Then you may thank Him that you have become a child of God and on the grounds of 1 John 5:3 and you may know that you have eternal life.

Simple And Plain

M.G. in H.: To the question "What must I do to become a child of God?" you always give such a simple answer. A person must believe that Jesus Christ has accomplished it for him at Calvary and thank Him for it and thus receive Jesus as his personal Saviour in his heart. Then He is saved and a child of God. But what if Jesus, who knows our hearts, does not find that person is at all ready to receive His precious divine peace? Supposing this heart has to be cleansed first, recognition, humbling and prayer through many tears? Supposing that heart has to descend to the bottom of the ladder and the burden of sin lie so heavily upon that soul until it seeks refuge under the cross of Calvary? After twenty-five years I still know the day and the hour as if it were yesterday when this miracle happened to me. I would also like to ask you, would there not be many more children of God on the earth if it were that simple? The Lord must receive us and not only we Him.

Answer: Yes, it really is just that simple to become a child of God! But because it is so simple many never attain it. What did the Lord Jesus say? "Except ye be converted, and become as little children, ye shall not enter into the kingdom of heaven" (Matt. 18:3). You described your own personal experience of conversion very graphically, how you broke through to the assurance of faith after much distress, tears and deep repentance. But it is arrogant and presumptuous to want to apply your own **personal** experience to others. The only measure and norm we have is the Word of God alone! Do you not know that in the Bible there are no two conversions alike? Some go first through deep conviction of sin and only break through to spiritual regeneration after this, whilst others only begin to see how corrupt they are in their flesh and only come to true repentance after they have been born-again. Some follow the Lord Jesus for three years and experience miracles, just as Peter did, and are only then truly converted. Others have their Damascus experience like Paul. It is very dangerous to say that it is not that simple! In this way you are questioning the all-sufficient work of Jesus on the cross of Calvary. For many this simple step is the hardest of all because they have to get down from their high horse of self-righteousness and because only those who confess their own bankruptcy are able to receive the Lord Jesus. This, however, is another chapter. The way to become a child of God remains plain and simple just as the invitation of the Lord Jesus is simple and yet so wonderful. "Come unto me all ye that labor and are heavy laden and I will give you rest." Could there be anything more simple than to come?

Conversion And Rebirth

S.K. in H.: Do we have to distinguish between conversion and rebirth?

Answer: No, because after a true conversion follows immediately a rebirth. They belong together. The conversion is the **Yes** of a person to God and rebirth is the **Yes** of God to a person. Compare Ezekiel 38:1. But it often happens that religious experience is mistaken for a conversion, which is no true conversion but only a temporal emotional experience. This does not result into the rebirth. With this we come to the bitter truth of so many "miscarriages" in the church of Jesus Christ. One may ask, how it is possible that brother A or sister B fell back into the world after they were "true believers." They were not born again, but only touched by the Word of God. (Luke 8:13) John says: I John 2:19: "They went out from us, but they were not of us; for if they had been of us, they would no doubt have continued with us: but they went out, that they might be made manifest that they were not all of us."

Confession

J.S. in V.: According to 1 John 5, "Everyone who believes that Jesus is the Christ is a child of God." Must not first the recognition and confession of sins precede the accepting of the Lord, or is this recognition a sign of the new birth. Further I should like to know, must we, according to God's Word, confess our sins before a brother, or is it enough before the Lord alone.

Answer: How is a man born again then? Surely then when he recognizes the corruptness of his past life. The miracle of the new birth happens when a person accepts Jesus Christ as his personal Saviour (John 1:12). Now, no-one accepts the Lord

Jesus who does not know that he needs Him as Saviour from his sins. Secondly, the confession of sins before a brother is for many a great help, but not a condition of forgiveness. The confession of sins must be first of all and above all before the Lord. (Isaiah 1:18, 1 John 17:9, etc.) But when faith is weak, the confession before a pastor can be of great help. See James 5:16.

The Gift of Faith

D.E. in W.: Why are we always asked to have faith, and the unbeliever always condemned, when on the other hand it is always stressed that faith is a gift of God and that no one could believe on his own, no matter how hard he tried?

Answer: You are blocking the answer to your question with your last sentence: " . . . no matter how hard he tries!" This is never true! Of course, faith is a gift of God, and God works "to will and to do." But this gift of faith and the ability to will He gives in that moment when that particular person hears His Word preached with authority. The sinful heart is very skilled to pass on the responsibility of personal commitment. If you believe you are unable to have faith, come, read the Word of God listen to the preaching of the gospel. In this WORD He Himself the Lord, stands before you to give you everything that you don't have: faith, willingness, hope, faithfulness, love, victory, peace, happiness. However, behind your question there beats a rebellious heart, which is not willing. Have you never heard the voice of Jesus, who with tears said and still says: Matthew 23:37-38. "How often would I have gathered thy children together, even as a hen gathereth her chickens under her wings, AND YE WOULD NOT. Behold, your house is left unto you desolate."

Little Children

P.L. in R.: What will happen to little children that die much too young to understand the Gospel!

Answer: The Bible doesn't answer this question directly. But we know that God is just and that a baby or little child is not responsible. We also know from the Scriptures that children of believing parents are sanctified (1 Corinthians 7:14). What the Lord does with these small children we don't know, but we do know that He will do right. So we may trust the Lord completely when our children are called home in their infancy.

Rebirth Process

R.B. in W.: I was asked how one can recognize the procedure of the rebirth. The questioner was of the opinion that the person concerned does not participate at all, be it in regard to faith or in the actual rebirth. God creates this all, without us adding anything to it. I am of a different opinion. What is Yours?

Answer: The procedure of the rebirth is for our eyes and our senses not perceivable; it is a miracle of God. According to James 1:18 we know that He, the Eternal, begat us with the Word of Truth. And furthermore we know that we are born-again not of corruptible but of incorruptible seed. That is written in 1 Peter 1:23. This seed however is the Living Word of God. Also we know that through the experience of this miracle, according to 11 Peter 1:4, we are partakers of the nature of God and we are born of God (1 John 3:9). Besides this we have the rock-like assurance through the indwelling Holy Spirit that we are children of God according to Romans 8:16 and Ephesians 1:13. How this actually happens, however, no person can analyze intellectually. It remains God's wonderful mystery. It is true that the rebirth is an act of God because we read in 1 Peter 1:3, "According to his abundant mercy has begotten us again unto a lively hope by the resurrection of Jesus from the dead." This sovereign act of God is being initiated however through the conversion of the person. Why then are there so many who have been so-called "converted" but have never been born-again? Because their conversion was nothing else but a moment of emotional religious action. Missing was a repentant heart which surrended totally to the Lord.

Over and again we find in the Scripture this two-fold happening; The *yes* of man to God, and the *yes* of God to man. As for instance in Jeremiah 29:12-13, "Then shall ye call upon me, and ye shall go and pray unto me, and I will hearken unto you. And ye shall seek me, and find me, when ye shall search for me with all your heart." The originator of the conversion whoever is not man but God Himself. He laid down this rule before the foundation of the world (Ephesians 1:4). He was in Christ and reconciled the world unto Himself. The conversion of man consists and is built on the ground of the already finished plan of redemption in following the call of God: "Be ye reconciled to God" (11 Corinthians 5:20). If man heeds this call, God the Lord gives His Amen to it, and He leads the caller into the rebirth. Therefore whoever asked, "How can I be born-again?", must do one thing; accept Jesus Christ, the Son of God, with all His heart as his Saviour and Redeemer. Then without question and above all doubts the exalted power of God will lead him into the rebirth just as it is written in John 1:12, "But as many as received him, to them gave he power to become the sons of God, even to them that believe on his name."

The Last Seconds

M.A. in T.: My father died last summer. I'm sorry to say, but he was an unbeliever. My mother accepted the Lord very late in her life and always prayed for my father. She depended on the word in the Bible: "Believe on the Lord Jesus Christ, and thou shalt be saved and thy house." Even after my father had died, she believed, since she had faith and prayed, my father wouldn't be lost. But I cannot believe that.

Answer: Your question is being asked many times. I can only tell you what the Bible says, for instance in John 3:36 and 1 John 5:12. With the Son we have eternal life, without the Son we are lost forever; But whether your father is lost, you cannot assert, for you do not know what happened in his last moment. Maybe this story will help you:
"A mother prayed and struggled with tears for her only son who was a slanderer and curser. In faith she asked for his conversion and was full of confidence for his salvation. Then he was drafted into the army. He served in the cavalry. His mother kept praying. Shortly after she received notice that he died in battle. Despair grabbed her and she asked herself: Were all my prayers for my child in vain? Did I trust in vain in God's promises? A terrible darkness fell on her soul. There, in a tearfilled night, she saw her son appearing in a white garment in her bedroom. He said: "Mother, your prayers are answered. The distance from the stirrup to the ground was just enough to give myself to the Lord." You can learn from this, that a split second is enough, to call on the name of the Lord. I advise you and your mother therefore: leave now everything to the Lord, even your dead father.

Excuses

T.L. in H.: In an old issue of the *Midnight Call* you told of a mother whose son was converted through her prayers when he fell dying off a horse and called on the Lord and was saved. Don't you think this is a danger to those that say: Well then I have plenty of time to be converted, perhaps on my death-bed, after all we must remember the grace of God to the thief on the cross!?

Answer: No, for 1) when God gave that young man in the last second of his life the chance to call on Him, it is very clear that he had no opportunity to do so before, because he didn't have enough light to see the necessity of conversion. And God showing him in his sudden death this light proves to us the sovereignty of God. 2) If someone seeks to relax upon this, it shows that he has, through the preaching, already felt the need of conversion. And God showing him in willing, he only tries to quiet his conscience which is aroused. People who consciously resist the urging of the Holy Spirit are in greatest danger, because with every "no" towards the Lord, their hearts become harder. (compare Exodus 7:13, 22; 8:32,) Jacob Better said on his death-bed: If God should heal me once more, I would tell people: "On the death-bed, one cannot be converted anymore." Surely he meant those people, who resist the Lord continually, even though they know of Him. These have seldom a chance to repent when the period of grace runs out and they lie on their death-bed (compare Ecclesiastes 12:1). 3) The grace of God, as the thief on the cross experienced does not exist any longer in this sense, for the thief was the very first who received grace in his very last moments. Before and after him never again was a person in the same position. Therefore: "Behold, now is the accepted time; behold, now is the day of salvation . . . To day if ye will hear his voice, harden not your hearts," (II Corinthians 6:2, Hebrews 3:15).

Conversion

E.K. in W.: One question always troubles me: How can a preacher maintain that it is only possible to be converted once; he cannot see into a person's heart and know if the person concerned, as a result of the Word preached, has not received new light!?

Answer: Your question is ambiguous. There is a conversion which takes place once and for all and cannot be repeated. On the other hand there are people who are converted ten or twenty times. What is the reason for this? The conversion which takes place ONCE is an absolute, unconditional "Yes" to Jesus Christ and therewith to God the Father. Then the Lord pronounces His Yes and simultaneously gives that gift of eternal life which can never be lost again. He has turned from his way, been converted, and therefore will live (Ezekiel 33:11). Such a person can never again be converted because otherwise he would be crucifying the Son of God anew (Hebrews 6:6). On the other hand there are countless "conversions" which are only half-hearted, emotional or with conditions as the Lord says through the prophet Hosea, "They return, (i.e. they are converted) but not to the most High." (chapter 7:16). To this sort of conversion the Lord does not answer with His Yes, that is, He does not respond with regeneration or re-birth. True conversion takes place simultaneously with the re-birth. But if re-birth does not follow the conversion the "decision for Christ" was not a complete surrender.

What is the reason for these half-hearted conversions? They come from half-hearted preaching of the Gospel. Paul said to the Corinthians, "For though ye have ten thousand instructors in Christ, yet have ye not many fathers: for in Jesus Christ I have begotten you through the gospel" (1 Corinthians 4:15). Preachers of the Gospel have such a responsibility! If for instance young people are moved by emotional means, with music or songs which stimulate them to tears, to make "a decision for Christ," by those whose lives are not fully dedicated to the Lord, then there is no power present for the re-birth of those who wanted to enter the narrow gate. If on the other hand the man of God preaches without any compromise judgment and grace and the whole of God's plan, the sinner breaks down and is able to grasp the outstretched, nail-pierced hand of Jesus with his whole heart and is born again ONCE and FOR ALL to a new and lively hope (1 Peter 1:3). Everything else is not only emotional junk but also dangerous deception. Thousands are walking around who have made "a decision for Christ" but who are not born-again. Their new life did not break through and they are bastards and not children because the father who conceived them spiritually was himself sick and half-hearted. Those among my readers who have to confess: "I am a spiritual miscarriage; I am not born-again even though I made "a decision for Christ," I can tell you most assuredly that you can be born-again this very minute on the grounds of that Word in Jeremiah 29:13, "And ye shall seek me, and find me, when ye shall search for me WITH ALL YOUR HEART." In other words, kneel down and say, "Lord Jesus, I give myself wholly to you now with everything I am and have unconditionally. I want to belong to you whatever it costs." And when you thank Him for the forgiveness of your sins through the precious blood, then God has already given you the re-birth. He that hath ears to hear, let him hear!

God Has No Grandchildren

T.G. in K.: Writes among other things; he cannot digest psychologically the religious up-bringing in his childhood to this day and that he still suffers from it.

Answer: It is important that you free yourself spiritually from all pious tradition from that which has been handed down for generations. I mean it in this way: The Lord leads each of His children individually. Your parents have brought you up in the fear of the Lord. Now swim BY YOURSELF against the current. Now YOU believe in the Lord. You have discovered now — as you wrote yourself — that you cannot live on your parents' faith. On the contrary, in an unexplainable way you have even been repulsed by it. Don't your parents walk uprightly before the Lord? I'm sure they do, but as soon as you take on their faith without finding your own personal relationship with the Lord it will become spiritual inbreeding. Suddenly everything becomes repulsive to you. All at once you do not want to hear of faith anymore and yet you yearn for redemption and you want to follow Jesus. Then the moment has come when you without being influenced by anyone in your surroundings — parents, brothers, sisters, or others — you have to surrender to the Lord. Then you will be formed by the Lord and no longer by your surroundings. Then you will become dependent upon Him and no longer upon other people. This is the transitional state in which you find yourself right now. So cast yourself with all your soul upon Jesus and He will prove Himself in you as the very personal Redeemer who understands you into the deepest parts of your soul and transforms you with His gentle, deep love into His own image. When you have had this wonderful personal experience and have come away from the faith of your parents, then you will thank God on your knees that you still have parents who always have pointed you to Jesus.

Victory in Jesus

G.C. in B.: I cannot believe or grasp the fact the Lord Jesus died for me and I am without hope and without any aim in my life. How wonderful it must be for people who have a personal Saviour and even know that He is soon coming back to take them Home. A long time ago I found out that my uncle and my great grandfather practiced witchcraft. I myself go to church but still have no peace or joy; instead my heart is usually full of contradiction and rebellion. I often have the feeling that even my free will is captive.

Answer: Your free will is NOT captive! The free will of man is his nobility. You may be persecuted, and threatened by satanic powers and doubtless also your sinful nature troubles you, but you still have a free will. You only need to call out loud in the presence of the Lord, "Lord Jesus I am going to follow You!" Do not say, "I would like to," or "I ought to," but say, "I am going to follow You!"

Please understand me — I am not denying that you have the FEELING that your will is no longer free or that you FEEL as if you are being tossed about. But however weak and miserable and bound you may feel yourself to be, your free WILL IS THAT WHICH NEVERTHELESS, ENABLES YOU TO BE ABLE TO DECIDE FOR YOURSELF WHETHER OR NOT YOU WANT TO BELIEVE. This free will which ACCORDING TO YOUR FEELINGS is enslaved, can prove its freedom by crying to God. That is why I could ask you and beseech you not to let yourself be influenced any longer or in any way by what you feel, or even by set convictions which the devil suggests, like for instance, "You are no longer able to WANT to." That is one of the greatest lies which comes from hell, and causes many people to sink into destruction even though they could have been saved. I ask you once again to call out loud, "Lord Jesus I am going to follow you." Then begin to thank Him for saving you from all the inherited demonic or sinful bondages and all your guilt, through His precious blood. The victory of Jesus Christ over all the darkness in your life is unlimited. Praised be His name in all eternity!

Jesus Came to Save

E.D. in K.: Though I am against the doctrine of universalism, I do ask myself: is eternal punishment not too much, even for a person who has the sin of a whole life upon him? Just imagine a cancer-stricken person, what he suffers in just one hour. Or just one hour of the torture of a martyr! It is asked of us people who are weak, to show mercy, couldn't God, after say one hundred years of executed vengeance be satisfied?

Answer: You are looking at the eternal damnation from the wrong point of view. Man doesn't BECOME lost, he IS already lost! The natural proud heart fights against this fact with despair. God does not let anyone be lost, on the contrary He gave His dearest, that He had, His only Son, so that all who believe in Him should not perish. Man, therefore is in a much worse state than it is commonly believed. He is lost through the inherited sin. Now someone might say: but can I help it that I was born in this state? No! You cannot help to be born that way, but it is your fault if you remain in that condition! For Jesus is here, to save you! So the problem is exactly the opposite: it is not God who curses the people, but people condemn themselves into all eternity by not accepting the free gift of salvation.

Will All Be Saved?

E.E. in S.: Doesn't Romans 11:32 teach very clearly that at the end all men shall be saved?

Answer: No! The Bible does not teach "universal salvation." When the little word "All" is mentioned here, then all those are meant, who believe. Believers of the false doctrine of universalism act as if they had a deeper knowledge. But it doesn't take a deeper knowledge to defend this teaching, because it rests on understanding and therefore on psychic ideas. One says, God is love, God wants that none should perish, God reconciled the world with himself, therefore: all men shall be saved. Besides, one couldn't imagine a hell anywhere on the new heaven or the new earth. But it is not at all important what you can imagine or not but only what the Word of God says. When will you finally start to fear His word, which speaks of eternal glory and of eternal damnation. Everywhere, this false doctrine of universalism creeps in, spiritual death follows. I know this from my own observations. But, they say, this teaching is proven with the Bible. One could prove any of a number of false teachings through Bible verses, when one takes these biblical statements from their context and founds on them this special teaching disregarding many other biblical statements. Only the COLLECTIVE TEACHING of the Bible is important. The Scriptures cannot be broken apart (John 10:35). Besides, just as truly as God is the eternal love, He is also eternally unchangeable, holy and righteous. Today, now is the accepted time of salvation. Whosoever refuses the redemption paid with the blood of the Redeemer, brings upon himself, eternal unending darkness. The wrath of God REMAINS on him (John 3:36).

Born Again — Lost Again?

M.H. in H.: There are many differing opinions on the question, can a born-again person be lost again?

Answer: A person who is **truly** born again cannot be lost, because the Lord Jesus expressly said, "Neither shall any man pluck them out of my hand," and "No man is able to pluck them out of my Father's hand." The question, however, is wrongly put;

it is even dangerous, because many Christians without Christ call themselves a regenerate who in actual fact have never surrendered their hearts to the Lord Jesus. They have merely become conformed to the **outward** New Testament standards. They are "converted," have been baptized, belong to a church, sing and pray with the others, but as far as their fruits are concerned they are not children of God but of Satan. If I were to say to such Christians in name only, "Peace, peace and no danger — nothing can happen to you, you are born again," I would be a lying prophet. To people who deceive themselves and passify their awakened consciences with the dogmatic phrase, "A born-again person cannot be lost" I can only say, "You are on your way to hell with your imaginary heaven. Be converted with all your heart and you will be saved!"

The question, can a born-again person be lost, comes from the degeneration in discipleship. We should be careful not to give a degenerate answer. The only right answer to this question is a counter-question, **What** is a born-again person? It is a person who loves Jesus Christ with all his heart and who has only one passion: how can I please my Lord better, how can I progress in sanctification? For such a person, the question as to whether a born-again person can be lost is senseless. Of course, someone is sure to say at this point, "But I have known people who used to be Christians and who have fallen right away and are back in the world." Answer this with 1 John 2:19, "They went out from us, but they were not of us; for if they had been of us, they would no doubt have continued with us: but they went out, that they might be made manifest that they were not all of us."

Never Was Saved!

T.W. in S.: My brother is today completely in the world and a unrepentant mocker. And yet, he once was a child of God. Is he now lost?

Answer: Your brother never was a child of God, but only an imitator. We have to stop calling every person a child of God who had some moving religious experience in a gospel meeting. The important part is not the experience but the fruit (Matthew 7:20-24). That's why it is so misleading to count those converted. Through experience this has become clear to me. As for your brother, undoubtedly the word in John proves right: "They went out from us; but they were not of us; for if they had been of us, they would no doubt have continued with us; but they went out, that they might be made manifest that they were not all of us. (1 John 2:19). That's why you should pray for your brother without ceasing!

Predestination?

E.B. in K.: Is it predestined where man spends eternity?

Answer: You do not express yourself correctly. God has known from the beginning, even before the foundation of the world, where man will spend eternity. Based on this fore-knowledge He has fixed man's election. For God there is no time. He is eternal, which means, for Him there exists no past or future, all is eternal present. This is the way He has also seen you, before the foundation of the world was laid. In this connection, please read carefully Romans 8:29 and note the sequence, "For whom he did foreknow, he also did predestinate to be conformed to the image of his Son, that he might be the firstborn among many brethren." First He foreknew you and me, and then based on this He predestined us and this in Jesus Christ the beloved (Ephesians 1:4). Now you will say: "then all my trying would not help me, because it is already predestined, where I will spend eternity." This is not so however, because God's fore-knowledge does in no way hinder your sovereign free will. He still calls today "Whosoever will, let him take the water of life freely" (Revelation 22:17). Jesus still calls: "Come unto me" You can come now. And when you come to Him through the narrow gate, you may turn around afterwards and read over this gate on the inside: "Chosen, before the foundations of the world."

The Shepherd's Voice

E.S. in H.: I am often uncertain if I really hear the Shepherd's voice. I have difficulty in discerning whether certain thoughts come from my own heart or from the Holy Spirit. With this comes the doubt whether I am really born-again.

Answer: Jesus said to Pontius Pilate, "Everyone who is of the truth hears my voice." (John 18:37). So you do not need to strive to recognize His voice, but to examine yourself before the Lord: Am I of the truth before Him? That is, are you willing to accept the truth of Calvary for your own life? This is the truth that makes us free! And everyone who is of the truth will always hear the voice of Jesus and recognize it in the midst of all the confusing voices, and cry with the writer of the Song of Solomon, "The voice of my beloved!" (Song of Solomon 2:8).

SANCTIFICATION

SATAN Defeated

J.K. in A.: In one of your articles I read "The devil is defeated, we do not concern ourselves with the devil and his power, for he has been defeated on the cross of Calvary!" Can you please base this statement on the Scripture? If someone is defeated and his power is broken then he is powerless and not dangerous anymore! But how then can the Apostle Peter write to the members of the Church and warn them in 1 Peter 5:8-9, "Be sober, be vigilant; because your adversary the devil, as a roaring lion, walketh about, seeking whom he may devour: Whom resist stedfast in the faith." Please notice also in this regard what Hebrews 2:14 says.

Answer: The admonition of 1 Peter 5:8 compels us to be sober, to be watchful in maintaining constantly the victory in Jesus in faith. This is exactly what Paul meant in Ephesians 6:11. Paul does not say that we should "fight against the attacks of the devil," but rather that we "stand and become strong in the Lord!" In Hebrews 2:14, we have the clear statement that the victory of Jesus Christ is an absolute victory and includes everything, that even death, for a child of God is not death anymore but a passing through to eternal life.

With this, do we deny the battle of faith? Under no circumstances! We are on the battlefield, but we are not fighting *towards* the victory of Jesus, but we are fighting *from* the already achieved victory of Jesus! We are not striving anymore for an "ideal" of the victory, but we are right in the midst of this victory. For this reason we can, in faith, talk about the victory as a present reality: "But thanks be to God, which giveth us the victory through our Lord Jesus Christ (1 Corinthians 15:57). You may ask, "Why then does the devil rule in this world?" Answer, that we through faith demonstrate the victory over Satan and his power and in this way bring honor to Jesus' name.

The World

I.S. in D.: It is said that we should not conform to this world. What do you understand by "world"?

Answer: What the Bible means by world you can find written in 1 John 2:16, "For all that is in the world, the lust of the flesh, and the lust of the eyes, and the pride of life, is not of the Father, but is of the world." That is the world. If you love Jesus, then you do not ask how close can I remain to the world and still be a Christian, but, how far can I get away from it to serve Him better?

Fear Of The Lord

L.F. in L.: What exactly is the fear of the Lord?

Answer: Only those who love the Lord with all their hearts know what the fear of the Lord is. True fear of the Lord is a product of all-embracing love for Him. This is awe at His holiness, fear of grieving Him, fear of departing from His ways. It is this very fear of the Lord which is lacking in the Church of Jesus Christ today. Why? Because many Christians love themselves instead of Him, the Lord, alone. Where, however, churches are gripped with the fear of the Lord, there is revival. The fear of the Lord has great promises, "The fear of the Lord is his treasure" (Isa. 33:6). Here the fulness of God is released. "The fear of the Lord is the beginning of knowledge" (Prov. 1:7), which means that with the fear of the Lord I also receive divinely endowed wisdom, "The fear of the Lord is to hate evil" (Prov. 8:13). "The fear of the Lord prolongeth days" (Prov. 10:27), "The fear of the Lord is a fountain of life" (Prov. 14:27). (See also Prov. 15:16, 33; 16:6; 19:23 etc.)

Surrender

G.L. in K.: We are always being told to surrender ourselves to the Lord completely; self must be done away with. We are never told how to do this, however. Our "self" is still there.

Answer: You do not have to do anything. You cannot. Have you been trying to squash your "self," your proud ego? It always recovers. In the most spiritual things and in all religious activity, self plays a big part unconsciously. You must reckon with the fact that it has already happened. What? Paul says, "**I am** crucified with Christ." Doing away with self, to put it in other words, is nothing other than taking the death of Jesus Christ seriously. As surely as He died on the cross, we may know that our old man is crucified with Him (Romans 6:6). This is not mere theory, but it has practical results. Self does not want to go this way. Again and again, pride, self-assertion, irritation, criticism, anger, etc., break out, but the Scriptures say, "Put off concerning the former conversation the old man, which is corrupt according to the deceitful lusts" (Ephesians 4:22). With these words we are told to take Calvary and being crucified with Christ seriously. When you speak of how to do this, it shows that you are of the opinion that you have to exert yourself and this is what self does, our personality. **You do not have to exert yourself, but surrender yourself.** How does this happen? In that you give up yourself as Jesus did. He said of Himself, "No man taketh it (His life) from me, but I lay it down of myself" (John 10:18). Then you may praise the Lord, despite all the provocation of the flesh and all the indignation of self, "I live; yet not I but Christ liveth in me" (Galatians 2:20).

Victory, Then Defeat?!

D.T. in K.: How do you explain this: After I had a real victory over a certain sin, suddenly there was defeat?

Answer: When the Lord makes His victory manifest in you once or twice, then He can do it always, because He is the same, eternally. Why then the sudden defeat? This comes from the "feeling of power," which you permitted in your heart after the victory. Because the enemy could not overcome you in your weakness, especially since you trusted completely in the victory of Jesus, he tried it in the opposite way — successfully! He pulled you "up" inwardly very gently, instead of putting you "down" into despair. He planted in you the seed of spiritual arrogance, which brings forth self-reliance and with this the next temptation was a won battle for him: he didn't find a watchful praying child of God but one "to whom nothing can happen anymore." Therefore "let him that thinketh he standeth take heed lest he fall" (1 Corinthians 10:12). The secret of lasting victory is: in a real consciousness of weakness to be independent on the Lord completely. Only this way you will have victory in the victory. To say it even clearer: What was your defeat? Was it that you sinned anew and in so doing grieved the Lord? No! It was your former self-confidence in the flesh which you placed right after your victory. The consequence: the renewed "must to sin." That's why you should humble yourself before the Lord and prayerfully hold fast on Galatians 2:19,20: "...not I, but Christ in me..."

Temple of the Holy Spirit

W.G. in R.: In the Bible we read, "Be ye holy; for I am holy" or "Know ye not that your body is the temple of the Holy Spirit." I hear so often that disciples of Jesus have died of cancer. I do not understand how a body which is the temple of the Holy Spirit can at the same time be eaten away by cancer. I know that we do become ill; Elisha also became ill and died. But there is a living bacillus in cancer. Is this bacillus not satanic?

Answer: We must see this clearly: as God's children, we are free from the **guilt** of sin, we are also free from the **power** of sin, but as long as we are here on earth we are not free from the **presence** of sin. If we were free from the presence of sin, our bodies would be incorruptible, for the wages of sin is death. Why does the Lord leave us here on this earth in this condition? So that His strength is made perfect in weakness and our body in actual fact, despite its sinfulness, through the obedience of faith can be a temple of the Holy Spirit, where there is no room for sin or guilt. Illness is the direct or indirect result of sin: indwelling sin. Cancer is certainly a special curse in this century. One in four people in Switzerland dies of cancer. If a child of God becomes ill with cancer and the Lord does not heal him or her in answer to the prayer of faith, this believer undergoes judgment and compensates in his flesh, through suffering, that which is lacking in the Church. The temple of his body is in no way profaned. Do you think that the Lord Jesus was profaned when He became a curse and hung on Calvary's cross, or when His body was broken in torment? The wonderful thing is, that whoever rests in Jesus is turned into blessing, darkness into light. One of my friends, a blessed man of God, through whose prayers many were healed, was stricken with this terrible disease. He strove in prayer for whole nights, but the Lord said, "No." He told me that he often thought on the word, "He saved others, himself he cannot save." But what did he cry out shortly before he went home? "What a happy man I am!" Was he then profaned through the disease of cancer? On the contrary, he was made perfect through suffering, sanctified and glorified.

God's Blessings

S.O. in E.: Why is it that the work of some children of God is more blessed than others?

Answer: This could have two reasons: FIRST OF ALL one child of God may consecrate himself more to the Lord than the other. The Lord said in this connection a clear word: "He that believeth on me, as the scripture hath said, out of his belly shall flow rivers of living water" (John 7:38). There are many who do not want to believe according to the Scriptures. That is, in complete obedience act according to the Word. A **second reason** is spiritual optical delusion. What do you call "Blessing?" Does an Evangelist, perhaps, preaching to a full church, have more blessing than does an old mother, who cries in her room for lost souls? Never! God has altogether different measures. Concerning this, we can never determine who's work is blessed greater. Man sees what meets the eye, God, however, looks at the heart. In eternity we will probably be surprised as some children of God will be crowned, for what the Lord could work through them, that appeared to do nothing in our eyes. The Lord shall hold ready His glory for all that served Him with sincerity.

Victory Easier For Some?

R.J. in B.: Is it not easier for a Christian who is naturally friendly and kind, to follow the Lord, because he has less temptations? Perhaps he has other weaknesses but is it not to his advantage when he "inherits" such Christlike characteristics — which everyone expects of a Christian?

Answer: In no way! You must not mistake those innate characteristics of charm and friendliness with true likeness to Jesus. The former only produce emotional, human feelings. It does produce drawing power but can never draw to the Father and the Son. The characteristics of Jesus though, which come from the conversion of a previously proud, imperious person convince the sinner in his heart of his own corruption. I would even make the opposite statement: it is an advantage when a person by nature has all the negative characteristics and then becomes changed into the same glory of the Lord visibly even as by the Spirit of the Lord (2 Corinthians 3:18). A disciple of Jesus like that has a much greater and more obvious testimony to the power of Jesus in His life than a person who was always a friendly type. In the former the change is apparent whereas in the latter it is veiled except if he truly allows his natural being to be sanctified through obedience and faith.

Temptations

L.H. in P.: In our Bible Study meeting we came upon the question about temptations being God's will or not. The brother leading it said that they are not God's will but the Lord permits them. James 1:13 says, " . . . God cannot be tempted with evil, neither tempteth he any man." Our Lord Jesus was tempted (Matthew 4). Was this then not God's will? Jesus was obedient unto death. In my opinion the Lord's will is over everything that happens in the life of a child of God. What do you say?

Answer: There are two sorts of temptations — divine and satanic. If you want to know what satanic temptations are then look at the temptations of the Lord Jesus in Matthew 4. God would never do such a thing, which is what James clearly states. God never tempts anyone to evil.

In contrast to this the positive type of temptation comes from God. This is said for instance in Genesis 22:1, where it says, "And it came to pass after these things, that GOD DID TEMPT Abraham." Why? So that the genuineness of his love, of his dedication to the Lord and his faith could be proved. Of Israel it is also said, in Deuteronomy 8:2, "And thou shalt remember all the way which the Lord thy God led thee these forty years in the wilderness, to humble thee, AND TO PROVE THEE, TO KNOW WHAT WAS IN THINE HEART, whether thou wouldest keep His commandments, or not." David recognized this too, as he exclaimed in Psalm 26:2, "Examine me, O Lord, and prove me; try my reins and my heart." We see from this that there were two types of temptations — on the one hand the divine temptations which when endured unite us more closely to the Lord, and on the other hand, the satanic temptations which separate us from the living God when we give in to them.

Punishment For Sins

U.S. in C.: Do we punish ourselves or does the Lord punish us when we have sinned? A friend of mine put it this way: "When a child, inspite of warnings of his parents plays with fire and as a result sutters injury, he is punishing himself for his disobedience." How do you define this?

Answer: Both ways apply. He who does not believe on the Son has already judged himself as the Lord saith in John 3:18. Whoso committeth sin causes his own eternal destruction for again the Scripture says, "The wages of sin is death" (Romans 6:23). And Proverbs 13:13 saith, "Whoso despiseth the Word shall be destroyed."

On the other hand however, we recognize in the Scripture the great faithfulness of the Father, who tries everything through loving admonisions, but also through hard punishment, to draw His disobedient child back to Him. The question of punishment or mercy over the sinner is in the deepest sense, a conflict within God. It reveals a high tension between His holiness and righteousness on the one hand, and His unspeakable great love on the other hand. This is for instance clearly revealed in Hosea 11:8, "How shall I give thee up, Ephraim? how shall I deliver thee, Israel? how shall I make thee as Admah?" But behold, when God reconciled the world unto Himself in Christ, this conflict was wonderfully solved in that His righteous judgment was put upon His Son, instead of us. That was the only way the love of God could establish the way, through the redemptive work of Jesus Christ on the cross of Calvary, to our hearts. Thus, when the Lord punishes, His heart's motive is always love, "For whom the Lord loveth, He chastiseth" (Hebrews 12:6).

Therefore, we have reason for thanksgiving when a sinner comes under the judgment of God, instead of being left to the enemy, which would mean he will judge himself through sin. I believe that was the reason why David chose the judgment of God when he was confronted to choose from three different judgments after he had sinned. He was requested to choose; either three years famine; three months under the destruction of his enemy, or three days under the sword of the Lord. David said, "I am in a grave state, let me fall not into the hand of the Lord for very great are His mercies but let me not fall into the hand of man (1 Chronicles 21:13). By this he meant, "Lord do not reject me for my sins to my own destruction but judge thou me."

Falling Back

H.K. in R.: The trouble after revival and after the Lord's Supper is falling back into sin. — "The spirit is willing but the flesh is weak." Through this the conscience is continually troubled and we cannot rejoice about being a Christian as we should. The devil tries in many ways to make us backslide. Are there people who do not sin anymore? I do not think so, for all have sinned and come short of the glory of God. The history of Israel is full of backsliding, God's forgiveness, new beginnings and relapses. In this connection a Christian needs an open helpful Word in which the preacher of the Gospel includes himself also.

Answer: Your attitude is wrong. We must not reckon with falling back into sin but rather reckon unceasingly with the victory of Jesus! In this way we are able to say with the apostle Paul, "Thanks be unto God who giveth us the victory through our Lord Jesus Christ" (1 Cor. 15:57). It is impossible for us to live without sinning because our flesh is sin. "I know that in me (that is in my flesh), dwelleth no good thing" (Rom. 7:18). We do not need to do or think anything bad, and yet we are sinners from our birth. This, however, is the wonderful victory of Calvary, the work that

Jesus Christ accomplished: this, my corrupt flesh, is judged, condemned, crucified and dead with Him. The attitude of faith which pleases God is this: we know that the old man is crucified together with Him (cf. Rom. 6:5). To lament, "we always fall back again" pleases the devil to no end. You will now say, "But what if I do fall again?" Then stand up again immediately in the name of the Lord Jesus! If you are suddenly overtaken in a sin then humble yourself immediately under the judgment of Calvary. The blood of Jesus Christ cleanses from all sin, ever deeper, ever clearer. "If we walk in the light, as he is in the light, have we fellowship one with another and the blood of Jesus Christ his son cleanses us from all sin" (1 John 1:7). By this I do not mean we should abuse the precious and holy blood, simply fulfilling the lusts of the flesh and then habitually asking the Lord to cleanse us in His blood. Certainly not! The godless man sins regularly but for a child of God sin is an accident. Jesus is Victor!

Sanctification — Active or Passive?

H.R. in A.: I continually hear, when in a particular circle of very spiritual people, that each one must penetrate into the perfect law of liberty, which is, however, a secret. How is this possible in actualy practice? With my whole heart I desire it; but recently I have often had to face the fact that, as our minister says, "I can not." He maintains that 99% of our sancitification is "passive," i.e. that God does it in us without our doing anything ourselves. When he said this I disagreed with him, because Paul says something quite different: but now in practice, I unfortunately often find him to be correct. Where is the door to liberty?

Answer: Sanctification is neither a passive nor active work on our part. Holy is the man for time and eternity, who is born-again (1 Corinthians 6:11 and Hebrews 10:10). This is the eternal and unchangeable position of the believer in Jesus Christ before God. He is now acceptable to God in Him, Ephesians 1:6, This is the sure foundation of our justification by faith, on which we stand. This is your **position.** Taking **in faith** this position of an already accomplished salvation we shall **in fact** progress in sanctification. Sanctification which is complete at the new birth will become a growing fact through the daily obedience of faith. And what is this daily obedience of faith? It is no "self-betterment" through moral effort, but a personal affirmation of what God says in His Word, when He says that in me, that is in my flesh dwelleth no good thing, and that the imagination of my heart is evil from my youth. This word draws us to the place where we stop trying to make ourselves better: it draws us to Calvary. As soon as a person affirms Calvary with its judgment of his corrupt flesh, he is sanctified. This means he is crucified with Christ, has died with Christ, has been buried and resurrected with Christ to a new life. Please compare Ephesians 2:6 and Romans 6:1-11. At this point the impossible and illogical begins to happen: my end is my beginning. The completed judgment brings reviving grace into action. I am now sanctified and therefore continually being sanctified. "For this is the will of God, even your sanctification," (1 Thessalonians 4:3). All this is through and to Him who says, "Without me ye can do nothing." When you therefore ask: "Where is the door to liberty?" Jesus Himself gives the answer in John 10:9, "I am the door: by me if any man enter in, he shall be saved, and shall go in and out and find pasture." In this way, daily sanctification is a simple matter, because it is already accomplished and increasingly penetrates every area of our lives as long as we abide in Jesus.

Perfect in Eternity?

K.M. in O.: When I live in self-denial I say "yes" to death. In other words; I surrender that which the Lord Jesus does not like within me. This is how I understand it. Now my question: When I am dead physically I cease to sin. Have I then reached perfection with this, that is when I am in eternity? What then will happen to a person who does not practice self-denial? Will he too see the Lord face to face? Or what differences will there be?

Answer: The process of sanctification starts only then, when we according to Romans 6 count ourselves crucified with Christ. Then the change into the likeness of Jesus begins. The perfection refers to our going home, to the fact that we advance from faith to sight. But will eternity be enough for us to come closer to the image of the Lord? The Lord is not only in His existence but also in His character and being unlimited! So we must remember that being saved we are never placed into a "static" condition when we enter into glory but into a dynamic one, so that 2 Corinthians 3:18 reaches all the way into eternity. I must add, however, that this fact, according to my understanding, is already in effect here on earth for those who live in sanctification but not for those that live their lives in disobedience; for as the tree falls that's the way it lies. In other words: He who submits himself to the wonderful process of sanctification, will experience its continuance in eternity; but whoever remains a Christian by name only throughout his life, will remain the same in eternity; he is lost forever.

Sin After Rebirth?

E.P. in G.: The statement in 1 John 3:9 bothers me very much:
"Whosoever is born of God doth not commit sin." I am born
again, but I cannot say, that I do not sin anymore. How can I understand this passage?

Answer: Just as it is written, "WHOSOEVER is born of God."
1 John 5:4 says this even clearer: "For WHATSOEVER is born of
God." What in you is born of God? Your Spirit, and this new-
born Spirit is perfect, holy and righteous, it cannot sin. But what
isn't born of God within you? Your flesh! This can still sin in
spite of the rebirth, for God will not renew our flesh. There is
only one way in which the Spirit can blossom in all of Christ's
glory and that is constantly saying no to the flesh. In other
words, "I am crucified with Christ." According to Romans 6:11
you may in faith believe that in all desires of the flesh, you are
dead to sin.

Why Do Innocent Suffer?

J.K. in H.: Why does God permit so many innocent people, I
mean those who believe in Jesus, to perish in disasters together
with those who do do not believe in Jesus? Why do accidents
happen to believers?

Answer: Who are you to judge who is guilty and who is innocent?
The Scripture clearly teaches "that all have sinned and come
short of the glory of God." Why it is that one is taken into the
judgment of God and others are spared, lies within the sovereign council of God. Never should any man assert of himself
to be a council to God because the Scripture says "Nay but, O
man, who are thou that replies against God" (Romans 9:20).
Rather, thank the Lord on your knees that He has protected you
from such accidents and catastrophies which may have been
needful for the other person to call him to possible repentance
because judgment and grace are closely united. If you are in
the midst of such judgment of God thank the Lord now in faith
for it with a humble and repentant heart. He will then crown you
again with loving kindness and mercies (Psalm 103:4). This of
course is not valid for such who have previously and continuously rejected the grace of God. Such will only receive judgment
after they have rejected the offered grace. Nevertheless many
children of God may experience this judgment but in a different
way: through judgment to glory!

CHRISTIAN LIVING

Finding the Will of God

M.M. in B.: What is your scriptural position toward children of God who use the Holy Scripture as if an oracle? I know of believers who if faced by a decision simply open the Bible and expect in this way an answer from the Lord. These believers claim that they have a permission from the Lord and He even gives them visions such as, for instance, David and the prophets who received an answer in that way from the Lord.

Answer: You are speaking of two different things, of the **Word** and of **visions.** Very often the Lord guides our attention to a particular promise in the Scripture which we in faith claim for ourselves for a certain situation of temptation or trial. Very often I have experienced the Word of God in this way and received new strength and assurance! Through His Word, the Lord confirms Himself and His promises to us in a wonderful and immeasurable way. We do reject however; the so-called Scripture drawings by which one draws one scripture after another until he receives a Bible verse which emotionally suits him. That is a wrong way.

In regard to visions the following: Many believers, especially sisters walk through life burdened under those visions. Their life is guided by visions and dreams. Through their soul, that is through their emotion, they are being guided through hallucination and inspiration from below and are being deceived to see all kinds of things and interpret visions, thoughts and dreams. The Scripture however says in Jeremiah 23:28, "The prophet that hath a dream, let him tell a dream; and he that hath my word, let him speak my word faithfully. What is the chaff to the wheat? saith the Lord." As far as David and the prophets are concerned, yes God did speak at sundry times and in divers manners (Hebrews 1:1). To us however; in the New Testament He did speak and He is speaking through His Son, and the Son of God is the Word which was made flesh. Has not God told us **all** in Him?

Win People for Jesus

N.E. in H.: We are a group of young people and wish to intro-
duce other people to Jesus. We have established many contacts
and always try to lead people into a discussion. But it is sad to
say, we always experience over and again that a discussion
does not lead up to its intended goal. How can we do it better?

Answer: I am very glad that you try to win people for Jesus
Christ. That is the most important task of a born-again person.
There is one thing you definitely should avoid, and that is an
open discussion. That may be very advisable in politics, but
not in connection with the Word of God. Not for nothing does
Paul say in 2. Timothy 2:14, "Of these things put them in remembrance, changing them before the Lord that they strive
not about words to no profit, but to the subverting of the hear-
ers." And he adds in verse 16, "But shun profane and vain bab-
blings: for they will increase unto more ungodliness." Further,
in verse 23 he admonishes his young co-workers again, "But
foolish and unlearned questions avoid, knowing that they do
gender strifes." How serious these admonitions are, we can
sense from his words in 1. Timothy 6:4, here he calls these discussions, "doting about questions." The German Bible says
the "pest of questions." Which then results in strife or words.
He then closes his letters with the words, "Oh Timothy, keep
that which is committed to thy trust, avoiding profane and vain
babbling, and oppositions of science falsely so called." Besides,
Titus writes the same, "But avoid foolish questions and gene-
ologies and contentions and striving about the law, for they are
unprofitable and vain" (Titus 3:9). And in 1. Cor. 1:20 we read,
"where is the wise, where is the scribe, where is the disputer
of this world? Has not God made foolish the wisdom of this
world?"

Something different of course is the defense of faith against
false teachings. To express this biblically, "And take the helmet
of salvation and the sword of the spirit which is the word of
God" (Eph. 6:17). Or in another place, "Fight the good fight of
faith" (2. Timothy 6:12). Correct defense of faith, therefore,
can only be done with the Word and this in the power of the
Holy Spirit. There is for instance, a difference: One can dispute
with false teachings (such as Jehovah Witnesses, Mormons,
etc.) and getting locked into a question of who is right and who
is wrong, or if one can say in authority, "it is written." And
when the false teacher quotes scripture verses out of context,
then we answer "again it is written." That is defense of faith according to the Scripture!

Water Baptism

P.S. in A.: According to Matthew 28:19, Mark 16:16, Acts 2:38 — and there are other appropriate texts — baptism, in my opinion is an act of obedience and a public testimony that I wholly belong to Christ. Or is my opinion wrong? This is not to say that I think I can earn my place in heaven therewith; I believe myself, and am saved through the grace of the Lord Jesus Christ, who has washed me white as snow from all sin with His precious, holy blood. At our church little or no value is attached to baptism. This often grieves me. Those who are baptized are regarded rather as being peculiar. Why is it in the Bible? The Bible is God's message to us. How is Romans 6 to be understood then?

Answer: Jesus said to John the Baptist, "It becometh us. . ." He was referring to John, who baptized, and Himself, who was baptized, because He wanted to be identified with sinners. The baptism of John was a baptism for the forgiveness of sins in preparation for the coming of the King. John, of course, was the one who prepared the way. The baptism which was practiced later on, however, is to be distinguished from the baptism of John, cf. Acts 19:3 please. This baptism has a much deeper effect. I do not mean the water of the baptism in itself, but **that to which the one being baptized testifies.** In Romans 6:3-4 it is clearly stated that a person who is baptized testified by his immersion in the water that he is dead and buried with Christ, and in coming up out of the water he testifies that he is risen with Christ. When a community of believers who believe on Jesus Christ, His crucifixion and His shed blood, repress this biblical truth, súch a community may be blessed for decades, but sooner or later it will disintegrate, because they did not want to go the whole New Testament way. What is the reason that so many truly regenerated people are not baptized? There are a few reasons: either they have been born again through a very central biblical truth and now think this is sufficient, or else they come from a church which practices the baptism of infants. This, however, is no more than a remnant of Catholicism. Whoever reads the Bible unprejudiced and without any preconceived opinion will see clearly that baptism is a testimony to what has taken place in a person, and not vice versa. Whatever the reason may be for a person not being baptized, he misses a great blessing because baptism is a command of the Lord. It is not only a witness therefore, but an act of obedience.

Sabbath

G.G. in N.: Where in the Bible do we find proof that God the Lord has pleasure in our worship on Sunday, and that we should keep this day holy?

Answer: Is your question an implication that we should keep Saturday as the Sabbath? The Lord Jesus rose from the dead on the first day of the week; on the first day of the week He appeared to the disciples; on the first day of the week they broke bread in the houses, and on the first day of the week the Church in Corinth brought together their offerings. That is why we like to rest on the first day of the week and it is not that we "must" but we "may."

How to Become a Missionary

O.R. in S.: Please tell me exactly how and if a person can become a missionary. Thank you for your trouble.

Answer: By becoming a child of God! To be a child of God is to be a missionary; these two things are inseparable. If we bury our talent, we will never to able to say when we stand before Jesus one day with empty hands, "You didn't call me, Lord." On the contrary! The Lord will ask us what we have done with our calling which we received as God's children. With compelling clarity and gravity, the Lord says in Ezekiel 3:18 that if we do not warn the wicked, He will require his blood at our hands. For some reason, over the years, a division has arisen between being a child of God, and being sent by God, because people have the idea that only those are "missionaries" who have given up their earthly profession, been ceremonially consecrated and sent off overseas, leaving a prayer-letter address behind. Nothing of the sort! Certainly such people, if the motive behind all this is Jesus alone, are consecrated people, but this in no way detracts from the "sending" that every single believer has. When Jesus said in His High-Priestly prayer "As thou hast sent me into the world, even so have I also sent them into the world." He was also thinking of His other blood-bought ones. The calling is there for all believers. "How" is determined by the Lord. Whether full-time or part-time, everything we do, whether we are businessmen, nurses or bus-conductors, should serve as means to the end that our high calling be fulfilled. Should you see yourself led to fulfill your calling in full-time service, we will gladly obtain further information for you.

God or Mammon?!

H.H. in M.: I made my decision for the Lord Jesus many years ago. For some time now, I have been a widow and receive a pension. Now, I made the acquaintance of a widower, whom I love and who wants to marry me. If I get married again, my pension will be withdrawn. Now I am in a great discrepancy and ask you for advise: Is it permissable for my friend and I to live together as if married?

Answer: You cannot live on two sides. Do you want to live in adultery, only because of the pension? You cannot serve God AND mammon! Marriage is holy before God. It should be performed before the face of God. Leave this way of destruction immediately; marry that man, if he is born-again, for what will it profit a man if he gain the whole world and loose his own soul? If you weigh off obedience of faith against money, you make a big mistake. Your true motive should not be a financial advantage but the holy will of God, who in heaven reserves an incorruptible and undefiled inheritance for all who follow Jesus. (1. Peter 1:4).

Precious Souls

J.W. in L.: My colleague, for whom I prayed, found peace with God through the precious blood of our Lord and Saviour, Jesus Christ. At my invitation, this brother then brought his wife to me, and we all listened to your record, "The Message of the Cross," and the wife of this brother was also converted. As this couple own a tape recorder, the brother taped this record and played it back at the next opportunity for his own brother and sister-in-law who were visiting them. Within a few days these two also found peace with God. Through the message on this record then, four souls found the Lord Jesus within a short time. Don't you think this is wonderful? We have no lively fellowship here however, no examples. We have to encourage and strengthen one another now through reading God's Word, praying and singing. But on my part there is a hindrance here. By nature I am shy and retiring, and I pray daily that the Lord will take these inhibitions from me, and I believe that He will do this. I would be very grateful for a few hints on how we could arrange our meetings.

Answer: We rejoice with you that precious souls have found the Saviour. Greet these new brethren heartily with Philippians 1:6. And you, dear brother, with regard to your inhibitions, can be fearless and of good cheer. When you consciously and in faith stand before the Lord and not before men, you will be able to renounce all fear of man, in the name of Jesus. Where the Spirit of the Lord is, there is liberty. I would like to give you personally the word in Hebrews 10:35-36, "Cast not away therefore your confidence, which hath great recompence of reward. For ye have need of patience, that, after ye have done the will of God, ye might receive the promise." It is important now that you do God's will.

Where do you go from here? Come together in your houses, and let a brother take over the leadership of the meeting each time, which should be opened with a simple prayer. Then open your Bibles, and begin to read one book or one epistle. I would suggest you begin with John's Gospel. Read a chapter together, and let each one voice his thoughts on it, with a fervent prayer in your hearts that the Lord will open His Word to you, through the Holy Spirit. He will do this, because it is promised us in Psalm 119:104-105 and in verse 130. Read also in this connection Psalm 19:8. When you have spent a little time in Bible Study, kneel down and pray together. Thank the Lord for the redemption through His blood, for His precious Word, and for His presence, because even if you are only a few you may know that His promise is true that "Where two or three are gathered together in my name, there am I in the midst of them." Then begin to work in prayer and to make intercession for others. In prayer we have four things to do: ". . .supplications, prayers, intercessions and giving of thanks" (1 Timothy 2:1).

"Faithful is He That Calleth You"

W.W. in D.: I would like to ask you the following about the situation of a young man: he is the only son of a widow who needs his care desperately; she is ill, alone and poor. He received, however, the call to the mission field very clearly and knows, that it would be disobedient if he didn't go. What do you advise in this situation?

Answer: It is written in I. Thessalonians 5:25, "Faithful is he that calleth you, who also will do it." That means: the young brother cannot go to the mission-field, as long as his mother is not cared for. If he is sure of his calling, he may wait in the assurance that the Lord will "do" it and show a possibility that his mother can live without his care. He should in no way leave his mother without money and care for it says in I Timothy 5:8, "But if any provide not for his own, and especially for those of his own house, he hath denied the faith, and is worse than an infidel."

Women in Men's Apparel

G.G. in A.: In a back issue of your magazine I read that it says in the Bible that a woman should not wear men's clothing, i.e. slacks. I don't understand this fully and decided to ask you: —
1. Is it sin if I as a sincere Christian wear slacks?
2. I personally think that it looks better for a young girl to wear slacks than a mini skirt. What do you think about lengths of skirts?
3. Somewhere in the Bible it says, "He that believeth on me, out his belly shall flow streams of living water." What is meant by "streams of living water?"
4. What do you think about dancing? May I go dancing?
5. Is it a sin to wear lipstick and other cosmetics?

Answer: It is an abomination in God's eyes when women or girls wear men's apparel (compare Deuteronomy 22:5) and you are not on the right path if you look on slacks as a preferable alternative to a mini skirt. All that can be said about length of skirts is: it should be as long as not to provoke the masculine world. The statement about the rivers of water comes from our blessed Lord and Saviour. He says in John 7:38, "He that believeth on me, as the scripture hath said, out of his belly shall flow rivers of living water." If you wonder what it means then read verse 39 where it says, "But this spake he of the Spirit, which they that believe on him should receive : for the Holy Ghost was not yet given; because that Jesus was not yet glorified." These rivers of living water simply result from being filled with the Holy Spirit. As for your last two questions, I would like to ask you a counter question: How can you serve the Lord Jesus better: with or without dancing, with or without lipstick etc.? In everything you do, keep your eye on the biblical compass in Colossians 3:17, "And whatsoever ye do in word or deed, do all in the name of the Lord Jesus, giving thanks to God and the Father by him." As far as cosmetics in general are concerned, it is terrible how women disfigure themselves until they walk around like living, embalmed corpses! They seem to be unaware that they make themselves much more offensive and ugly than they were before.

With this we are closing all further correspondence concerning slacks, (also the possible future question on this theme) because the spirit of fashion has in the meantime commanded that slacks for ladies are no longer fashionable, but skirts instead. And behold, all the ladies who on the one hand resist the Holy Spirit, blindly listen to the fashion director. The demons of fashion have dictated and that's that! Truly their "glory is their shame" (Philippians 3:19)!

Women in Church

F.M. in Z.: On the occasion of a Bible lecture we were urged to go to the prayer meeting which was then announced, so that God's Word would find more acceptance here also. In our meeting, however, it is not customary for sisters to pray aloud. But since that time our hearts have been exercised as to what the Scriptures really say about this. In 1 Corinthians it says that sisters should be silent in the churches. But does this apply to prayer meetings? Could you explain to us what the Bible means? The Bible also clearly teaches that sisters should not pray with their heads uncovered, because it is a dishonor to her otherwise (1 Corinthians 11:5). Paul seems to attach special value to their knowing this.

Answer: Even if it is not customary for women to pray in your meeting, it is not biblical because 1 Corinthians 11:5 says clearly that a woman may pray and even prophesy. When Paul says, in another place, that women should be silent, it was only from the point of view of their talkativeness and their desire to have the greatest say, in the church. Whoever makes a rigid rule that sisters may not pray in a meeting is greatly mistaken. Furthermore, without being prejudiced, one senses this when present in such meetings. The Spirit of God is hindered. There is a feeling of rigidity and restraint, because a number of those gathered — members of Christ's Body — are not allowed to pray. Nowhere do the Holy Scriptures forbid a woman to pray. And as for your statement that women should not pray with uncovered heads . . . I would heartily agree with you, only the head covering spoken of in 1 Corinthians 11:15b is not merely a scarf or hat but, "her hair is given her for a covering." In the K.J.V. margin it says, "Her hair is given her for a veil." If a sister has short hair because of ill-health, she should cover her head with a hat. But if a sister has long hair, she already possesses the natural head covering.

Biblical Position of Women

B.H. in C.: I recently had a heated argument with a woman because she claimed that there is not one single verse in the Bible that would forbid a woman to be politically active and stand in equal position with men. Women, she says, were for centuries subject to men. May I ask you to give me the Bible verses fitting in this situation.

Answer: The position of a woman in marriage is clearly given in the Bible. Please read to this Ephesians 5:22-27. Also, her position in the Church is clearly pointed out: "Let your women keep silence in the churches" (I Corinthians 14:34). Paul not only means that women should not speak in tongues in the Church but that they should abstain from all gossiping, which is a nuisance in the churches unto this day. Besides this, Paul shows how a woman can be active in her unbelieving surroundings and that is "in the meek and quiet spirit." "Without the word" (Compare 1 Peter 3:1-4).

I know however that all this does not very well fit into the "year of the woman" but the Bible doesn't have to bow to the emancipation of the woman but vice versa: women and also men have to live according to the Scriptures! By the way, woman is not created to rule over man much less to master him, but as we read in Genesis 2:18 " . . . an HELP meet for him." There is no Scripture however that states that woman in her submissive position should be a slave: her task on the other hand consists in serving him in love and that of the man in loving service (compare again Ephesians 5:22-25).

The position of the woman in the Church is described in Philippians 4:2-3. Paul testifies here that Euodias and Syntyche are true warriors of the Gospel and he praises in Romans 16:1-2 also the service of Phebe in the church of Cenchrea. The risen Lord gave the first commission to testify of His resurrection to a woman (John 20:17).

Of a political activity for the woman we find nothing in the Bible. Some might say here, that Deborah was a judge. That is true, but she was working for the "theocracy" that is the Kingdom of God on earth. It has always been like that, we can trace it to the present day: when a woman leaves the boundaries given by God, she immediately becomes a tool of the enemy (compare Isaiah 3:12, where the political activity of the woman is presented as a judgment for the nation.) When, however, the woman remains in the limits given by God, the Lord works great things through her. Many times He especially uses a woman as a key-person. So it was a woman who was the first to proclaim the resurrection of the Lord Jesus Christ. Paul started a whole new work when God opened the heart of the first person in Europe: a woman by the name of Lydia (Acts 16:14). Then we can see in the Old Testament, it was Esther who in God's hands became a tool to save her nation! Also the fervent prayers of another woman: Hannah, which she sent up to God for a son were so decisive that this son, Samuel, brought about an important blessed change in the history of Israel. So we see: If the woman remains within the limits set for her by God, the results will be eternal blessing.

Fighting in Wars

A.H. in S.: Does this not amount to disobedience to the Lord, when brothers in Christ fight with weapons in wars against "enemies" amongst whom are also Christians?

Answer: This is one of those questions which "gender strife" because children of God confront one another here like bitter enemies. In my opinion, this is because they are confusing two things: through the new birth a person becomes a citizen of heaven but through the natural birth he is a citizen of a country. Being a citizen of an earthly country, however, has its consequences. A citizen does not only have rights (such as the use of public means of transport, telephones, water supplies, etc.) but also duties. Military service is one of these, I believe all arguing would come to an end if people would consult the Bible. Apart from Romans 13:4 which says that a ruler does not bear the sword in vain, it is relevant to see how John answered the repentant soldiers who came and asked him what they should do. According to many people's views today, he should have said, "Refuse military service immediately!" But John says in Luke 3:14, "Do violence to no man, neither accuse any falsely; and be content with your wages." This is the same man who pointed to Jesus and said, "Behold the Lamb of God, which taketh away the sin of the world." He accepted the Lamb and accepted the military duty of a soldier. How is this possible? "It is impossible" say many dogmatists. But with God all things are possible. God is able to bring His children through the entanglements of war and to preserve not only their bodies but also their consciences, and to protect them from contamination and guilt. In this way they are led individually to be obedient to rulers and yet to serve their Lord. Many a soldier or officer who has been through a war can testify to this.

Giving of Tithes

S.W. in A.: What is your opinion concerning the giving of tithes according to Malachi 3:10? Is the "storehouse" the Church, to which the tenth should be given?

Answer: The children of Israel HAD TO give the tenth because they were under the law. The tenth was the least that God asked. But we MAY give the tenth of our income, and in that moment, when we glady bring the tenth to the Lord, we will experience the Old-Testament promises of blessing, "and prove me now herewith saith the LORD of hosts, if I will not open you the windows of heaven, and pour you out a blessing, that there shall not be room enough to receive it." My personal opinion is that the tenth should be the LOWEST MINIMUM which the New Testament believer gives, since God in His Son has given to us such an unspeakably great gift. For it is true, the more one gives to the Lord, the more blessings one will receive.

WHERE the tenth should go is entirely up to the individual; there are no regulations. The Lord says, **"Bring ye all the tithes into the storehouse,"** that is into the house where the living Word is preached, where the Gospel is being spread and the Church of Jesus Christ is built. Every child of God has to let the Spirit lead him. God's 'storehouse' is, however, without a doubt, also the nation Israel from which in the future streams of life and glory will flow into all the world (compare Romans 11, 12 and 15).

Counting the Cost

G.B. in L.: I am taking the liberty of coming to you with my troubles. I have been a child of God for a few years and want to remain one with my whole heart.

Two years ago I met a young man who is a Catholic. We became good friends and this friendship developed into mutual love. I knew, however, that God could not give His blessing on this love, so I separated from him and went abroad for a year. I told him that I had chosen to follow Jesus and that there could never be a future for us together. Nevertheless he continued to visit me during my stay abroad. Now I have asked him to stop visiting me because I want to belong to my Saviour completely. Since my decision I have undergone such severe temptation and it often takes an incredible effort to go to work even. Please pray for me. I have given myself anew to the Lord and also my friend who is "seeking," but I know that Jesus is much more precious to me than the deepest love for a human being.

Answer: May the Lord give you much grace to remain firm in this new decision and never to enter into a marriage which would be against His will. As long as the young man is Catholic and not born-again, you do not belong together. If you were to give in, a very unhappy marriage would be ahead of you.

Now you are probably wondering how you can remain firm. I would like to give you the following advice:

1. If you see that your acquaintance does not make a clear decision for Christ, then STOP PRAYING FOR HIM, because by praying for him you are prolonging an emotional relationship which in time will prove impossible to resist.

2. Be consistent about refusing all further contact with him.

3. Seek the face of the Lord often — through Bible reading and prayer.

Taking the Lord's Name in Vain

G.T. in G.: Shouldn't we warn people who curse, of the sin they are committing with their cursing?

Answer: Without a doubt! It says: "When I say unto the wicked, Thou shalt surely die; and thou givest him not warning, nor speakest to warn the wicked from his wicked way, to save his life; the same wicked man shall die in his iniquity; but his blood will I require at thine hand." (Ezekiel 3:18). But even more we should stand up energetically and face the cursing of believers. There are children of God, who throw around expressions like "Oh Gee" or "My Gosh" etc. The "Oh Gee" means "Oh Jesus" and "My Gosh" stands for "My God." It is written: "Thou shalt not take the name of the Lord thy God in vain; for the Lord will not hold him guiltless that taketh his name in vain." (Exodus 20:7). Also the Word in 1 Peter 4:17 proves true: "For the time is come that judgment must begin at the house of God."

Insurance

I.L. in D.: According to your opinion, is it right for Christians to sign up for insurance like life, death, liability...etc.

Answer: "Let every man be fully persuaded in his own mind" (Romans 14:5). When you have no inner freedom to insure yourself but you want to rely completely on the Lord, then the Lord will deal with you according to your faith. But do not condemn the other brother or sister who think they should insure themselves. Personally, I have insurance on this earth only what I HAVE to according to the law. For all other, present and eternal things I keep my insurance-policy carefully in Romans 8:38-39: "For I am persuaded (insured), that neither death, nor life, nor angels, nor principalities, nor powers, nor things present, nor things to come, nor height, nor depth, nor any other creature, shall be able to separate us from the love of God, which is in Jesus Christ our Lord."

Giving Thanks

I.S. in N.N.: Should a brother pray before a meal in a restaurant? Is he not merely an offense to other people therewith?

Answer: What a question! Of course one should pray before one eats! What is that to you whether there are unbelievers in your presence or not? Live as though you were alone in the world with the Lord. It sounds very pious to say "Is he not merely an offense to other people therewith?" But you should rather say, "I

am afraid to pray before other people." This is where the trouble
lies! I would like to ask you to read the words of Jesus in this
connection very carefully, **"Whosoever therefore shall confess
me before men, him will I confess also before my Father which
is in heaven"** (Matt. 10:32).

Autopsy

D.C. in B.: What is our reaction to be, as believers, when a
relative dies in a hospital and a request is made to perform an
autopsy, in order to determine the disease or cause of death?
My father suffers from cirrhosis of the kidney, but is now in
relatively good health again. For the specialists, this is a miracle
of helping. HE WILL NOT SUBMIT HIMSELF TO FURTHER
EXAMINATIONS, HOWEVER, ALTHOUGH HE WOULD MAKE
AN INTERESTING STUDY FOR THE DOCTORS. This is not
because of religious convictions, mind you, but because it
would not be pleasant. In the case of my father having to go into
a hospital on account of this or another disease, and were he to
die there, the question of an autopsy is sure to arise.

Answer: With all consideration for Medical Science, I would
never offer my body for purposes of research, on the grounds of
the Word of the Lord in 1 Corinthians 6:19, "Know ye not that
your body is the temple of the Holy Ghost which is in you, which
ye have of God, and ye are not your own?" This temple of the
Holy Ghost turns to dust, but remains until the resurrection. In
this temple of the body, the spiritual seed is concealed which
cannot be analyzed materially, but out of this the Lord will form
the glorious body, the resurrection body. For this reason, we
reject the removal of organs after death.

Unequally Yoked

F.G. in H.: I am, by the grace of God, His child. Now I have met
a young man and we love each other. But he will have nothing
to do with my faith. I think however that once we are married I
will win him for the Lord through faithful prayers and being a
good example.

Answer: This you don't do but the opposite could take place. He
will pull you away from the Lord, especially since you are
disobedient when you marry an unbeliever. Doesn't the Bible
say clearly in IICorinthians 6:14-15: "Be ye not unequally yoked
together with unbelievers: for what fellowship hath
righteousness with unrighteousness? and what communion
hath light with darkness? And what concord hath Christ with

Belial? or what part hath he that believeth with an infidel?" Therefore I warn you earnestly not to get married to an unbeliever. If you are disobedient to God's Word you will suffer pain after pain. The Lord has something better in store for you if you can only wait.

Cremation

R.N. in S.: Your tract on cremation (not available in English) was very interesting. I am in total agreement with it. But in regard to the resurrection of the body, I cannot understand it. When the spirit-soul leaves the body to the predestinated place, (as can be seen from the words of Jesus to the criminal on the cross, Luke 23:43; also in the story about the richman and Lazarus, Luke 16:19-31), I believe that over there one will already have a spirit-body. Why then, is it still necessary to have a resurrected body?

Answer: What do you, for instance, think about the Scripture in 1 Thessalonians 5:23 where it speaks of the undividable unity of the body, soul, and spirit, and emphasizes, "And the very God of peace sanctify you wholly; and I pray God your whole **spirit** and **soul** and **body** be preserved blameless unto the coming of our Lord Jesus Christ"? Or, what do you think of 1 Corinthians 6:19-20, "What? know ye not that your **body** is the **temple** of the **Holy Ghost** which is in you, which ye have of God, and ye are not your own? For ye are bought with a price: therefore glorify God in your **body,** and in your spirit, which are God's." In spite that the body is given over to corruption, and it dies, this very same body will be resurrected in power and in glory, this is very clearly stated in 1 Corinthians 15.

Whosoever does not want to recognize it in the light of these Scriptures which are impossible to misunderstand and so clearly reveal that cremation of a body is an abomination before God, such a person is very hard to help.

PRAYER

In The Name of Jesus

R.L. in A.: What does it mean to pray in the name of Jesus? Should you conclude each prayer with — in Jesus' name? We don't say at every opportunity — in Jesus' name — although it says in the Bible, "And whatsoever ye do in word or deed, do all in the name of the Lord Jesus." This would seem to me like taking the name of the Lord in vain.

In Daniel 7:2-5 and Revelation 13:7 we read that the saints are delivered into Satan's hand. Do we as David did in view of these passages, who thought in his heart that one day he would still fall into Saul's hands? I only want to please the Lord but I am often so oppressed by the enemy who tries to tell me that he can slay me even at heaven's door.

Answer: Do you know what it is to pray? It is nothing other than coming into the holy presence of God. We may never draw near to Him, however, in any other way than through the Lord Jesus Christ, who said, "I am the way, the truth, and the life: no man cometh unto the Father, but by me." There is no other way. We only have boldness to enter into the holiest by the blood of Jesus (Hebrews 10:19). Anyone who tries to enter in any other way is called a thief and a robber by the Lord in John 10:1. Now this does not mean that he who forgets to mention the name of Jesus in prayer or prays **directly** to Jesus will not be heard. No, what matters is our attitude and the knowledge of that which the Lord told us repeatedly and emphatically, "Verily, verily, I say unto you, Whatsoever you shall ask the Father in my name, he will give it you" (John 16:23). We have absolutely no right to ask the Father for anything except on the grounds of the shed blood of Jesus and in His name.

To your second question, Daniel is speaking of the saints who are delivered into the hand of the Antichrist and converted during the Great Tribulation. The Church of Jesus Christ will then be with the Lord already.

Pray For Revival

H.B. in S. Many believers say that to pray for revival in our time is useless. We cannot prevent God's pre-determined judgment through our prayers in this direction. Are you of the same opinion?

Answer: No! I fear that believers who deny the possibility of revival are somehow not willing to be revived themselves. The Lord has expressed His will concerning revival very clearly. I would call to your mind Isaiah 44:3, "For I WILL pour water upon him that is thirsty, and floods upon the dry ground . . ." And the Lord Jesus says in Luke 12:49, "I am come to send fire on the earth; and what WILL I, IF IT BE ALREADY KINDLED?" Paul says in Ephesians 5:14, "Awake thou that sleepest, and arise from the dead, and Christ shall give thee light."
The fateful conclusion of many believers that there can be no revival arrives from the fact they consider revival as something extraordinary, but actually revival is the normal condition of the Church of Jesus Christ. God is not a God of the dead but of the living! Many Christians have fallen prey to the false idea that revival is something spectacular, something unusual, but revival is nothing other than when we believers break through from outward appearance to reality. Revival is the actual fulfillment of the Word of the Lord, "He that believeth in me, as the scripture hath said, out of his belly shall flow rivers of living water," so that what Jesus said comes to pass, "He that abideth in me, and I in him, the same bringeth forth much fruit." Who dares to narrow down these promises of the Lord or to limit them to certain times? The excuse that the Lord will not give another revival is a poor one; it is even the proof that God is WAITING to send a revival. The true reason for the lack of revival is that everything spiritually is so dry and dead, hard and stubborn, but in view of this apparently hopeless situation the Lord calls, "I WILL pour water upon him that is thirsty, and floods upon the dry ground."
There is yet another reason why many do not want to believe in a revival. Revival must begin IN US, for this reason the Lord says through Hosea 10:12, "Sow to yourselves in righteousness, reap in mercy; break up your fallow ground: for it is time to seek the Lord, till he come and rain righteousness upon you." Read also Jeremiah 4:3, Whoever breaks up in his fallow ground and removes the stones of sin and disobedience from his heart will experience a personal revival which will spread to others.

Prayer Meeting

D.Y. in T.: How should a prayer meeting be conducted? Ours isn't a prayer meeting anymore, but a Bible discussion session with about 10 minutes prayer and 50 minutes Bible study.

Answer: This is a dangerous, malicious trick of the enemy, that he permits a prayer meeting to turn into a Bible-discussion hour. One should keep the introduction to the prayer meeting as short as possible and down to the point. The most important prayer requests should be said clearly, but then the time should be used for prayer, and this should be; short, direct and in faith. Bible-class you can hold at another time. A well conducted prayer meeting can become a spiritual power house, which receives powers from above, and is far-reaching even to the mission-fields around the world.

Pray Boldly

H.M. in Z.: I have so often heard in prayer meetings that we may pray importunately. I always feel a bit uneasy when I hear people pray "Lord, do it right now . . ." Are we to dictate the Lord to do something? From my own experience I have learned to pray: Lord, You know all about it; have mercy, or forgive, or help. Should we not ask God reverently, like a good mother or father teaches the children to say: Please may I have this or that?

Answer: The reason you are offended by these direct prayers does not lie in the prayers but in your own inner attitude. The Lord Himself encourages us to pray boldly through the parable of the man who went to his friend at midnight and woke him up saying, "Friend, lend me three loaves," for it then says, "Though he will not rise and give him, because he is his friend, yet BECAUSE OF HIS IMPORTUNITY he will rise and give him as many as he needeth" (Luke 11:8). The Lord does not want that sort of passive praying, "Lord you know this or that . . . " He rather wants us, while praying to grow in faith and become more bold. You are only claiming the first part of the threefold promise of the Lord Jesus in Luke 11:9, "Ask, and ye shall receive." But that is not all that the Lord says; He continues by saying, "Seek and ye shall find" and even more than that, "knock, and it shall be opened unto you." Could it be that you are of the mistaken opinion that we can change God's mind through our weak prayers and our bold perseverance? This is not the case. God is the eternally unchanging One. The opposite is the case: the more perseverantly and urgently — the more importunately too — we pray in faith, the more WE ARE CHANGED because through our faith God is able to answer our prayers and bless others.

You expect too little from the Lord if you only get as far as saying in prayer, "Lord, You know everything." With assurance I can tell you that the Holy Spirit wants to pray with utmost urgency through you (Romans 8:26), so that the mighty arm of the Lord is moved and He then receives all the praise and glory. People who pray bring about miracles!

The Holy Spirit Prays Through Us

H.M. in X.: I have often heard it said, "Prayer moved by God's arm creates wonders. It helps man." Does God not already know in advance what His plans are? He surely knows what He will do. This question of prayer has burdened me. There was a family with a sick child. The parents went all over the place and called all the believers to pray to save the child's life. The child was kept alive, but turned out to be mentally retarded. God already knew what would happen. He knew that the child would be retarded if the child would stay alive. Why then did He answer that prayer?

Answer: You must never think that through our prayers God's disposition in regard to a matter will change. Rather it is the opposite: We are being changed, when we pray genuinely and in faith. Then we are being led into the disposition in which God Himself can finally deal in His way with us and bless us. For He is always the one who blesses and helps. But our heart is hard. Yet, through constant prayer, it is changed and becomes receptible for God.

The victorious prayer is a great secret. Basically speaking, we are not actually praying but the Holy Spirit prays through us according to Romans 8:26. It is very easy to disregard this wonderful truth and unwittingly ignore the soft, still urging the Holy Spirit. Most of us, who belong to the Lord have experienced this, as I often have: One is being called to a sickbed and has suddenly a great inner liberty to pray for his or her recovery and instant healing. In another case one is called to a sickbed and knows assuredly from inner conviction that the Lord is about to take this child triumphantly home to Himself.

The Lord has promised that the Holy Spirit will lead us into the full truth. I am afraid that those believers you mentioned have overlooked this hidden fact, in that they have stormed heaven with prayer for the healing of this sick child, where obviously God had found "some good" in this child (1 Kings 14:13), and wanted to take him home to Himself. According to experience, we know that the Lord, who is faithful, answers prayers and this sometimes even according to one's desires, but then one has to carry the consequences. Nevertheless, and this I would like to emphasize, let the parents of this retarded child not resign in despair, for through this poor child they will be drawn deeper into the presence of the Lord. In this connection let them hold themselves to the promises of Romans 8:28.

Prayer Directed to Who?

M.D. in B.: Many people think that according to the Bible we should not pray directly to Jesus but only to God, in the name of Jesus. How should one answer this?

Answer: The Lord Jesus expressly told us that we should pray to the Father in His name. Compare John 14:13-14, 15-16b and 16:23-24. That is why the Lord Jesus continually pointed to His Father. God is the goal and His Son is the way which leads us to this goal (John 14:6). This was the only reason for Jesus' suffering as 1 Peter 3:18 puts it, "For Christ also hath once suffered for sins, the just for the unjust, **that he might bring us to God."** Should we not go this way then? After all there is no other way! Through the blood of Jesus we have boldness to enter into the holiest, that is, into the immediate presence of God, according to Hebrews 10:19. Jesus Himself taught us to pray, "Our Father, which art in heaven . . ." Paul too teaches us the same and says, "I thank my God through Jesus Christ" (Romans 1:8 and 7:25). Nevertheless, we acknowledge that Jesus Christ is the Lord (Romans 10:9). We put on the Lord Jesus Christ (Romans 13:14). Through Jesus Christ we have received the grace of God. Are we therefore not to pray directly to the Lord Jesus Christ? He Himself says in John 12:45, "He that seeth me seeth him that sent me." Especially in times of trouble and when death is approaching we may call on His precious name. At the moment when Stephen was going to God in glory he called out "Lord Jesus, receive my spirit" (Acts 7:59). And the same Paul who says in Ephesians 3:14 that he bows his knees unto the Father of our Lord Jesus Christ, speaks in 1 Corinthians 1:2 of those who call upon the name of Jesus Christ our Lord. In 1 Timothy 1:12 he himself thanks our Lord Jesus Christ. He even goes further than this and says that we should not only thank and call upon Him but our whole lives should also be filled with His name — "For me to live is Christ" (Philippians 1:21), and "Whatsoever ye do in word or deed, do all in the name of the Lord Jesus" (Colossians 3:17). To summarize we could say: we may call upon the Lord Jesus Christ directly, but we can only draw near to God through Jesus Christ and only then can we say, "Abba Father."

Praying to the Holy Spirit?

I.K. in D.: In a Christian magazine the question was asked, "To whom should we pray? To the Father, or the Son or the Holy Spirit?" Part of the answer read as follows: "The New Testament gives a clear answer: No where is there a verse which speaks of praying to the Holy Spirit." This last sentence shocked me. What do you say.

Answer: The statement in the magazine you mention is quite correct. We do not pray to the Holy Spirit but rather the Holy Spirit prays through us (Romans 8:26). Jude, in his short epistle, also says that we should not merely pray but "Praying in the Holy Ghost" (verse 20).

We pray through our Lord Jesus Christ to the Father. The actual prayers are taken by the Holy Spirit for us with groanings which cannot be uttered, to God, but we never pray to the Holy Spirit (cf. John 14:13-14 and 16:23-24).

An Unbeliever's Prayer

J.B. in N.: Can God answer the prayer of an unbeliever, as he prays, for instance, for the healing of his sick sister?

Answer: God can do anything, therefore, this type of question is already inclined to limit God's unlimited power. Only unbelief could ask this way. HOW God answers the prayer of a person lies within His sovereign will.
Does God hear the unbeliever? Of course, for the promise of Psalms 50:15 is true and without condition. "Call upon me in the day of trouble: I will deliver thee, and thou shalt glorify me." Especially this verse if proof of the fact that God will listen to those that do not belong to Him yet and hear them in their need, **so that they may praise Him through their conversion.** But whether the Lord will do this in every case is again another question. The eyes of God are like flames of fire. He examines the hearts. He also knows the motive of the prayer of the unbeliever and when He chooses to, He will perform gracious miracles for the sake of the unbeliever because of his unbelief, so that he will no longer blaspheme His holy name (compare John 10:38 and 14:11). For the latter there is hope, for when an unbeliever starts to pray, he comes close to the living God. He is not far removed from the Kingdom of God anymore. Since, according to 1 Timothy 2:4 "Who will have all men to be saved and come to the knowledge of the truth." He, in His marvelous mercy hears the cry of the unconverted, so that they might be converted.

Prayer for the Dead?

K.A. in J.: Would you please tell me where in the Bible it is written that one should not pray for the dead, when on the other hand there is talk about fellowship with the upper world?

Answer: I talked often with people, who through the work of the Holy Spirit denounced in repentance an adulterous connection, but then kept on praying for that person, with whom they had sinned before. The terrible consequence was: The sinful binding came back and darkness and unhappiness befell them, because it was prayed without permission. If prayer is made for a person whom one doesn't want to give up, then one is bound to this person. If you keep praying for a person after he has died, you step over the border which God does not permit to be overstepped. (Luke 16, 16-31) You are brought in touch with the deceased physically through this praying for him. For by asking God for him you are at the same time asking for him and this is an abomination unto the Lord. (Deut. 18:11-12). Besides all that, by praying for the dead you bring yourself into a spiritistical realm and expose yourself to the inspirations of other spirits and with this also become spiritually bound.

The Lord's Prayer

E.S. in H. We belong to a church where the new preacher asks the congregation to pray the Lord's Prayer together. We are not accustomed to this and according to our knowledge it contains something which we find incompatible with other verses of Scripture. It says, "Forgive us our debts as we forgive our debtors" and "Lead us not into temptation." We do not find anywhere in the Bible though that God leads us into temptation. Is this not tempting God when we ask Him to forgive us as we forgive others? My husband and I simply do not like to pray this prayer. Please give us some light on this.

Answer: Please do not forget that the Lord's Prayer is the prayer that the Lord Himself taught us and therefore it is the most perfect prayer there is. It is not tempting God when we ask Him to forgive our debts as we forgive our debtors, but it implies rather that if we ourselves are not prepared to forgive we may not expect forgiveness from Him. His love can only be fully experienced by those who give love themselves.
Concerning your question about "Lead us not into temptation" James says, "God cannot be tempted with evil, neither tempteth he any man." This is to be understood as follows: Let us not fall into temptation. Help us to be victors in Jesus Christ. Incidentally, it is interesting to know that the Lord spoke the Aramaic language and the Aramaic text of the Lord's Prayer says at this point, "Lead us so that we do not into temptation."

Praying Aloud

M.Z. in E.: I go to a church where the brother who preaches asks people to pray aloud (i.e. before the whole congregation). He says, "You do not have to pray here, but if you feel led to you may pray." I cannot get rid of the feeling that he is waiting for me to pray. We do not do this in our Evangelical Church, and I think that it is not given to everyone to be able to pray in front of others. What do you think? Prayer is surely the conversation of the heart with God. But does one also have to pray aloud?

Answer: The Saviour Himself said that private prayer is necessary where we can close the door behind us and stand in the gap for lost souls. How important, however, is also united prayer with others! The Lord has promised special blessings in answer to communal prayer! Please read for yourself Acts 4:24. We have here a prayer meeting of God's children who are together with one accord. The answer to their prayer comes immediately. "And when they had prayed, the place was shaken where they were assembled together; and they were all filled with the Holy Ghost, and they spake the word of God with boldness" (verse 31).

Chapter 2:42 also speaks of persevering, united prayer and in verse 47 we have the answer already, "And the Lord added to the church daily such as should be saved."

The trouble is, you see, that so many children of God are "private" Christians who neglect prayer fellowship with others out of spiritual laziness or pride, i.e. feelings of inferiority because they think they cannot pray beautiful prayers. Therewith they are neglecting, however, the greatest source of power which the Lord has given to His Church.

Of course, one cannot expect a person who has not been born-again to pray in the presence of others. But if you have been born-again then you have the Spirit of sonship (Romans 8:15-16). It is the same Spirit who prays through us (Romans 8:26). Then you can take part in the prayer meeting with other like-minded children of God, not where it is conducted in a hysterical, disorderly way, but there where the prayer requests are brought before the Lord in a businesslike manner and yet in holy reverence.

Prayer is Not in Vain

K.B. in C.: I was moved by your article in the June issue titled, "Praying in Practice." Now I am wondering why my prayers to God for revival have not been answered, inspite of my praying in faith and in the name of Jesus. You wrote in this article, "if the promise is true" (and I don't doubt that) "knock and it shall be opened unto you." Why then have I not experienced an open heaven and a mighty breakthrough of revival? This is also a personal question for my life.

Answer: Be not dismayed, be comforted for two things are true:
1. The Lord is leading us, even then when we don't notice it.
2. Our prayers are always answered, even if we don't see it yet.

Furthermore, our prayers have yet an ultimate fulfillment, for they are the smoke of incense which after the Rapture will be poured out on earth and will cause voices, thundering, lightening and earthquakes (Revelation 8:5). In other words, not the visible result as an answer is always decisive, but the fact that the Lord does answer, even if the answer is still hidden, still invisible. The heros of faith of Hebrews 11 grasped this fact. They had seen the fulfillment afar off, they believed, they prayed, but they did not experience the physical fulfillment thereof. They were comforted, however (Hebrews 11:30), for they knew God was faithful, it was impossible that God would lie!

Thus, your prayers for the place and the people among where the Lord has put you, are not in vain. The opposite is true for He said, "Before they call, I will answer." His answer is on the way! It makes no difference if the answer comes now, tomorrow or later. It does in no way change God's eternal faithfulness. Therefore continue courageously in prayer on the grounds of His promise!

Praying While Holding Hands

T.J. in M.: A church here in Italy which preaches the Word of God started a new habit. Often during prayer or during songs everyone is holding each others hand, which is supposed to emphasize the unity of the Church, it was explained to me. What do you think about it?

Answer: To hold each others hand during a prayer meeting is accompanied by great dangers, because who is forming this chain, this unity? Obviously, the members of the Church of Jesus. But who can know if among this group there are some Judas'? And here the Scripture warns, "Touch not the unclean"! Furthermore, the Lord Jesus said in John 4:24, "God is a spirit, and they that worship him must worship him in spirit and in truth." We are convinced that the spirit of worship and intercession is hindered when one tries to help or further the unity through bodily contact.

Prayer Chain

J.T. in U.: A new style has come to our church which I cannot follow inwardly. It is called the "prayer chain." This is how it works, one starts the prayer then stops without saying "amen," and the next one continues until all who have come to pray have prayed, then there is a period of silence until someone says "amen." Is there a Scripture which either confirms or rejects this style? Until today I was of the opinion that after every prayer there belongs an "amen."

Answer: Prayer fellowship has a great promise when prayed in unity (Acts 1:14, 2:1, 2:45, 4:24, etc.). But this prayer meeting must not be ruled by a spirit of the masses, for prayer is an individual act, and cannot be done collectively and closed with one "amen." It is important to be an individual prayer, because the Spirit of God prays through the individual believer. When a brother or a sister prays, then all others pray with him, and with their spirit and with their mouths say "amen" to that which has been prayed through the Spirit, by the one who was praying.

From our Lord's point of view, we believe that such a prayer system is an insult to His personal love of each individual. When the Scripture says, "For God so loved the world," in order to emphasize that no one is exempt from the love of God which was established through the giving of His Son, but our Lord does emphasize however, that He loves the individual person, "Yeh, I have loved thee with an everlasting love," (Jeremiah 31:3). "Therefore with loving kindness have I drawn thee," (Jeremiah 33:3). In Isaiah 2:19 He even said, "I will betroth thee unto me forever." Of Soloman it is written, "And the Lord loved him," 11 Samuel 12:24. For these reasons we reject the collective prayer meetings which close with one "Amen."

FAMILY LIFE

Our Children

A.T. in S.: The behavior of children of God is often preached in our church. But my question is, how should we bring up our children who are either too young or have not yet experienced a new birth? We cannot always agree with what is done in schools and kindergartens today. Or do we take the wrong attitude? You yourself have many children: how are they brought up concerning cinema, dancing, sport, theater? And what do you think about their studying?

Answer: Indeed, we have twelve children and are very happy. Incidentally, if the firstborn follows Jesus, those who come after will find it easier. How does one manage this? We should rather ask how God manages it! He, the Lord, brings it about in the following way: when parents pray perseveringly for and with their children and when these parents, because of their love for their children, teach them to be obedient, unsparingly, then He begins to work mightily and early in such children's lives, for children's hearts are naturally inclined towards heaven. They develop a very acute sense of what belongs to the world and what to Jesus, so that they do not lust after the empty things of the world. Although they go through their crises and temptations, they are surrounded by an invisible protective wall because they are sanctified through the faith of their parents (1 Cor. 7:14). Should they study? Of course they must learn. If in your home, "As for me and my house, we will serve the Lord," is put into practice, they are immune from any pernicious school influences. To summarize I would say that as long as you consistently set up the family altar through reading the Bible together and praying together and as long as you bring up your children in the biblical sense, as described above, you yourselves as parents are being obedient to the Lord and you will then experience that your children will obey you too. All true parental authority is founded in the authority of God. If parents do not obey God they cannot expect their children to obey them; however, the contrary is a glorious reality!

Letter to Parents

Answer to Parents: Over and again we receive letters from parents who ask us to pray for their children who are showing signs of rejection towards the Gospel. To this I would like to say something basically: I do not believe that it is the higher way of faith to expect help exclusively from the prayers of others; that means more or less, God should act on the increased prayer of other children of God for our own children. Of course prayer is the most powerful weapon we possess if we have not failed to do *first* the most important; namely to find the origin of the cause of this rejection and eliminate it. Have you parents for instance, ever thought about why and how this situation came to be? Did you bring up your child from its youth in the fear of the Lord? I do not mean in Church, Sunday School, etc., but in the *fear* of the Lord. Did you parents bring up your children in prayer and did you teach them to be *obedient* which is so vital and important? Is this the area where you have failed? In most cases that is the reason because by their fruits ye shall recognize them. The rejection of your children points to a vacuum which was left open previously in his or her life. And that is exactly the place where the deep reason for the rejection of the Gospel of your child lies. Recognize and accept this before the Lord now and repent over it with all of your heart. Only in this way will the Lord change, through His Spirit the thoughts and attitudes of your son or your daughter. The change of your children begins with you! If you are willing to accept this and pay the consequences the Lord will intervene in His time in a wonderful and powerful way!

Young Children and the Devil

G.Z. in E.: Should one tell young children about the devil or not? One evening before the children went to bed, I sang among other things a chorus which speaks of Satan's waiting to devour us. Afterwards my eight year old Mark asked who Satan is. I told him that Satan is the devil. Then as I came to my five year old daughter she asked the same question, but not being satisfied to leave it at that, she wanted to know more and more about the devil. I told her that the devil was originally an angel in heaven who wanted to be greater than God, and so he could not remain in heaven. She still wanted to know more, so I told her more. All this troubled my daughter so much that after half an hour she came and said she could not sleep because of the devil.

Answer: You did not act very wisely in this matter. We do not present our children with the devil, but we magnify Jesus in their eyes. I can well understand that your daughter could not sleep, and the devil will have had great pleasure in this. Show your children how great and wonderful Jesus is, and that is sufficient. The only great, mighty and glorious One who is to be loved and feared is the Living God through the Lord Jesus Christ. The devil is not to be feared; because he has been conquered through the blood of the Lamb (Revelation 12:11).

Prodigal Son

G.G. in S.: After my son decided to follow Jesus, we had a time of prayer together each evening, till he began to go out with a non-Christian girl. He himself is not yet 20 and the girl has just left school. From the beginning I told him, that according to God's word it is not allowed. He does not realize that he has come to love the world. Instead of leading the girl to Christ, and separating for a while as we advised, she has pulled him downwards. It even went as far as his giving up his cherished career and going away to live with her, (she looks after her father) where he has found himself a job as a handy-man seldom coming home any more.

Answer: I have prayed for your boy. That is our strongest weapon. If he, at his age, now loves the world and goes with a non-believer, there is nothing more you can do other than to humble yourself before God for all your neglect in his up-bringing and repent over all your prayerlessness. And this humbling of yourself with repentance will give you power — priestly power to intercede for your son because you have very definite promises which also include him.

What are Our Children Being Taught?

M.B. in M.: I am worried about my children who are being taught in school that the Biblical teaching of the creation of man is only a myth, that man descended from apes, and that the original story of Adam and Eve falling into sin is not true, etc. Besides this, I am occupied with another problem; Jesus describes "death" repeatedly as "sleep." But I also find other expressions which seem to prove existence immediately after death. Please give me some helpful information.

Answer: In general terms, the entire school system and method of the Western World is well into Apostasy. To answer our "educated" children, as you say, can only be done one way. If science contradicts any statement of the Bible, we know, nevertheless, that the Bible is correct under any circumstances! Besides, we know from experience that science and especially natural science has been correcting, renovating and changing their theses at least once every decade. Therefore, a person who holds to the guidelines of the so-called "scientific acts" is actually standing on very thin ice. He is like a weaving weed, for nothing has proven to be more unreliable than the "wisdom of the world" (1 Corinthians 1:18-21). On the grounds of these Biblical statements, it testifies to a primitive spirituality without comparison, if one relies on such foolish and humanistic conclusions, instead of relying on the infallible Word of God. For this reason I have no inner desire to go any further into detail in this matter. It is too foolish and dumb. You can believe that your children, if they are brought up right, have an inner sense, which tells them what is really true and what is not. We never had to explain or clarify to our children, and never had to "liberate" them from the teachings of their school. The opposite is true. My boys often came home with loud laughter and told us, "listen, they are trying to fool us in school; they tell us that man comes from the ape!" That is a healthy reaction of a child who has found the Lord.

Your personal question on the problem of death seems to be more important to me. The expression "sleep" in the New Testament means that the body after death — in contrast to when it is alive — remains motionless and lies there as if asleep. How long? Until the first or second resurrection. The spirit however, of him who was a believer is immediately in paradise with the Lord in glory. To this the Scripture testifies more than clearly in 11 Corinthians 5:1-6.

Sex-education In School

A.O. in H.: I have been moved inwardly to enclose the "Open Letter" which I have written to help if possible, Christian parents in their battle for their children. There is much damage being done on the level of sex-education among children because parents are often ignorant of what is happening in many schools with their children. I am a school teacher myself and have therefore, a certain knowledge in this field.

Answer: Gladly we are publishing here three points of your very important letter:

"Even if some schools have the right, according to certain laws to give sex-education to the children it is still our task to bring up our children in modesty and exhortation in the Lord. Sex-education often disregards God's law and order. In God's eyes, outside marriage sexual relationships, homosexuality, lesbian love, masturbation, unchastity, etc. are sin! The detailed lecturing on these subjects before the class destroys the feeling of shame in the children, entices their sexual desires, and prompts them to practical acts, which is exactly what parents don't want. We want to protect our children in this time of lawlessness in that we admonish them and get a good example before them.

Our weapon in this battle is the Word of God (Ephesians 6:10-17). To oppose the very cunning and camouflaged weapon of the devil and of many people we are in need of the godly weapon arsenal. Our battle against sex-education is to protect our children, and we must help them before damage is done. The assertion that this type of education is not harmful to children or youth, or that sex-activity outside marriage is also totally false. Statistical facts speak against it. In Sweden for instance, where sex-education has been practiced for over 20 years, it has had the following results:

   a) pregnancies of girls under 14 up **900**% (1965-1972)
   b) abortions by girls under 15 up **200**% (1968-1974)
   c) veneral disease by children under 14 up **900**% (1950-1972)

If we want to free our children from this kind of "education" and to educate them from the godly point of view in a healthy atmosphere, and according to the individuals need and development, then it is worthwhile to pray and work. We then can go to the teacher or principal and on hand of the Bible ask to free our children from this certain type of education. During this time the child could be in another class and receive some useful education. This of course, would only apply to countries who have incorporated into the Law of the Land religious and moral conscience freedom. Many parents have already won this battle through the grace of God. In this case, we stand with open conscience before God and call out with Peter, 'We ought to obey God rather than man' (Acts 5:25).

Every normal human being is shocked and repulsed when he recognizes what is being shown and taught to these children, who are often still innocent, and how their tender soul is being polluted by sex-education. The most holy and intimate relationship which God has entrusted to adults, which symbolizes the deep and sacred unity of Christ with the Church, is being shamelessly revealed to children, who do not have the ability to grasp it, not to mention their immaturity which disables them to digest this education properly. But this, by many governments, legalized "education" inevitably pollutes the souls of those young people. For sexuality is only then sanctified if it is expressed within and through the bonds of marriage. When however, this is being exposed to the unqualified and minors it will only lead to the decay of those young people. But shamelessness is increasing today. Professor Joachim Illies, a Natural Scientist, expressed it with one sentence, "A person without shame is a crippled soul." He furthermore stated that, "It is high time in this our insecure world to ask for certain limits and orders which are valid for us at all time." Then he continues, "Responsibility is much more than shame. But the future of all of us is being threatened by the victors who know no shame. If we don't oppose in this field strongly, only shame will remain in the end, shame who knows no victor." Another scientist expresses his view with these words, "Shamelessness is the expression of a weak mond."

We are living in the last period before judgment, fornication and sodomy are being more or less legalized. But it tears one's heart to see these innocent children being drawn into the mire of decay. Therefore, we are thankful for this open letter. The Lord bless your work. May He come soon to take His Church to Him!

Finding a Life Partner

R.K. in N.: My daughter is eighteen years old and is a Christian. She is presently occupied with the question of finding a partner but does not seem to do anything. She is of the opinion that God has chosen her partner even before the foundation of the world and that she should not choose her future husband herself. I am of the opinion that she can choose freely, only of course if it is according to the will of God and her future husband would be a believer also.

Answer: Here we have one opinion against another. I am of the opinion that your eighteen year old daughter, as far as she belongs to the Lord, can relax with patience in view of finding a partner for life because in this case she has already surrendered her will to the Lord. She even can afford to say "no" to someone whom she would feel is not the partner according to God. She can patiently wait until the right man, according to the will of God, comes her way, the same way she rightly asserts the partner has already been chosen by God for her.

Besides, I cannot avoid having the impression that you as a mother are acting a little soon and are worrying unnecessarily in regards to the fact that your child should have the right partner for life. It is much better to encourage your daughter to remain free, after all she is still so young. The Lord Himself will take care of this in His own time and will fulfill this important matter as it is written in Ephesians 2:10 and Psalm 37:5.

The Pill

W.G. in E. "The pill" has become a catchword. Everyone knows what is meant by this term without any explanation. We read about it everywhere, even in Christian literature. Please would you give this theme a little space in your Correspondence Column in *The Midnight Call*?

Answer: The much-discussed pill is conducive to immorality and has no place in a marriage. It empties the marriage, which is of God's institution, of its highly exalted and holy value. If a person does not want children, he should not marry, and if a person is unable to have children for health reasons, God will give grace for him to walk the higher way. A person who takes the pill as a contraceptive is saying with this that God has made something not right. He is doing the same as those who tinker with the contents of the Bible, or like the astronauts who want to get away from the earth. The earth is not enough for them. Ultimately all this, including the pill, comes from rebellion against the living God. Married couples who make use of this pill will receive a curse instead of a blessing. Already there are voices testifying to this curse.

Divorce

N.N. in S.: Is divorce a sin, when the husband is really the one to blame? When he cannot stand his wife anymore in body and soul and gets her into despair through slander, theft and then lands in prison?

Answer: According to the Word of God divorce is only possible when one part is an unbeliever and breaks the marriage. Please read carefully 1. Corinthians 7:10-13, Matthew 5:32 and Luke 16:18. Whoever re-marries as a divorcee as long as the former marriage partner is still living, becomes an adulterer, whether blamelessly divorced or not. Upon such a second marriage lies never the blessing of the Lord even when a believer marries another believer and says he was led this way be God: for the Lord never leads contradictory to His unfailing Word. In Malachi 2:16 it says, "For the Lord, the God of Israel saith that he hateth putting away: for one covereth violence with his garment, saith the Lord of hosts." Therefore I advise: anyone who cannot stand it with him or her anymore, for reasons of adultery, to pray earnestly and wait to see if the Lord won't change the curse into blessing. Search with all your heart — by humbling yourselves in prayer — the way of reconciliation. But if this way remains blocked, then hear the Word of the Lord: "And unto the married command, yet not I, but the Lord, Let not the wife depart from her husband: But if she depart, let her remain unmarried, or be reconciled to her husband." (I Corinthians 7:10-11). In this connection I want to warn all pastors and preachers, who for any reason attempt to re-marry divorced people! If you are a born-again servant of the Lord, don't you see, that by this action you disregard the Word of God and lose all authority?

Family Planning

K.V. in H.: Would you please help young married Christian couples in view of their questions in regard to family planning?

Answer: We have in the Scriptures 3 very plain statements which answer the question of family planning:
1. The Lord God said, "Be fruitful and multiply and replenish the earth" (Genesis 1:28).
2. "Lo, children are an heritage of the Lord" (Psalm 127:3).
3. From the Gospel of John we learn that children are procreated according to the will of man (John 1:13).
Through the so called "Modern attitude" toward family planning, one has lost these immovable truths. When the Lord commanded, "multiply and replenish the earth," He did not add a warning about over-population. God the Lord knows what He said and when he said that children are a gift of God then they are according to James 1:17, "a good and perfect gift."
With this inner attitude we have accepted our twelve children with thankful hearts from the Giver of all good gifts. The fact that the will of man is expressively mentioned in the Scripture indicates that Christian couples should seek to walk in the light of the Lord, even in regard to marriage duties (Psalm 32:8). In this inner and holy attitude the couple will know when the Lord wants to give them the gift of a child. Thus, they will have inner joy and liberty in all things.
The basic reason man does not want children, or only a few, is found in the end-time attitude, "they all seek their own." 11 Timothy 3 adds to this "that in the last days perilous times shall come and man shall be lovers of their own selves." Often it is the case that such married couples who do not want children experience the fulfillment of the Words of Jesus "But for him that has not shall be taken away even that which he hath" (Matthew 25:29). Which in this connection, means after they have decided against children for a long time, they will find that they cannot have any when they would want them.
From my personal experience I can testify together with my wife of the deep blessing it is to be permitted to raise a large family for the Lord. And what an immensely wonderful inner joy it is to experience that these children, when they are grown up, begin to love the Lord and to follow and serve Him!
May this be an encouragement to all believers who did not want children or forcefully limited the number of children, to renounce this egotistic attitude in the name of Jesus. If you have received children, thank Him on your knees for each one He, the Lord, has entrusted to you. For every child is an eternal being, which should be something to the praise of his wonderful grace for all eternity!

Women's Lib

B.S. in O.: From a Biblical point of view can one call the world-wide Women's Liberation a good thing?

Answer: The worldwide Women's Liberation Movement is a typical sign of the endtimes. It is the breaking through of the limits of order set forth by God. In a sense it is the spirit of anarchy, the spirit of the lawless-one who is at work here. Women, who in this connection let themselves be deceived, are stepping over the border God has put down, and therewith lose their unique femininity. The result is that in our days we have many "men-women", creatures who act and appear repulsive but are unable to realize it themselves. That is the reason they are running around in men's clothing. They are wanting to become "men" but later on cry and lament because they are experiencing an unhappy marriage!

In Ephesians 5:22-33 we are being shown in a wonderful way the position of the wife towards the husband. It is a picture of the relationship between Christ and His Bride. Women's Liberation is nothing other than the destruction and tearing apart of the Godly frame and order, which is caused by the underlying spirit of the Antichrist himself.

But let the men not triumph, for this is not a license to be a tyrant! Husbands are often of the opinion, due to their misunderstanding of the Scripture, that because they are the head of the marriage they are permitted to suppress at will their wives. How often and deeply have I felt sorry to have met sisters whose appearance radiates nothing but fear and anxiety. The husband as the head of the family must never forget that his position is a *spiritual* one, and not a physically commanding one. The husband, as the head, practices *serving love* and the wife willingly practices *loving service.*

Just recently I heard that in Germany, the Government occupies itself with a *Children's Liberation.* Several so-called educated men and women are not talking about the necessity for a *decision making* for children in the family. The parents, especially the fathers, should not have the authority in the future anymore. Basically speaking, the spirit of anarchy which rejects all authority and government is about ready to reveal himself in a person. That person is the Antichrist.

The Husband's Role

H.H. in M.: How far should a husband really rule over the wife?

Answer: Although we already discussed this question, it seems important enough to go over it once more, because among believers there is in this area many misunderstandings. What do we read? **"For the husband is the head of the wife"** (Ephesian 5:23). This points to a profound oneness of two personalities. They are relying upon each other. The head cannot exist without the body or vice versa, the body is nothing without the head. When the husband is the head, he is not worth more or better than his wife. It could be that his wife is more intelligent and sanctified than he. The difference lies not in the valuation of the personalities but in the difference of the positions. For instance, even though Mary, the mother of our Lord, was more important in the history of salvation, than her husband Joseph, the head angel of the Lord came to Joseph, where the family was concerned not to Mary, not even to Jesus. How precisely should the husband use his authority in the marriage? By ambitious ruling and commanding? Never! Then he is only a tyrannical dictator. His authority should be expressed in serving. In serving because he loves. This is the right execution of authority which is not influenced by the self-love but by the benefit of the other. How then does the husband have to be the head of the wife? Please read on in Ephesians 5:23: " . . . even as Christ is the head of the church: and he is the saviour of the body." Now look at the administering of authority of the Lord Jesus, as the head, which is expressed in the following two verses: "All power is given unto me in heaven and in earth" (Matthew 28:18) and "The son of man came not to be ministered unto, but to minister, and to give his life a ransom for many." (Matthew 29:28). In the offering of His life, He performed his majestic authority in heaven and on earth. When the husband accepts this right position, then also the wife is brought into her right position. Gladly, she will submit herself to him, because she loves him and recognizes him as her head. Gladly she will let him lead, because she knows, he loves her and seeks only her best.

Marriage in The Lord's Will

H.D. in P.: In 1 Corinthians 7:39 we read "The wife is bound by the law as long as her husband liveth; but if her husband be dead, she is at liberty to be married to whom she will; only in the Lord." I understand it this way; we can choose our own partner for life as long as he is a Christian. Or can it be against God's will even then when two believing persons get married?

Answer: Of course it is possible to enter a marriage against the will of God even when both partners are believers. Especially the child of God has to seek the will of God through prayer in this very important step. "For we are his WORKMANSHIP,

created in Jesus Christ unto good works, which God hath before ordained that we should walk in them" (Ephesians 2:10).
Many, who had not the patience to wait for the leading of the
Lord in this vital question, ran blindly into life-long unhappiness.
In this connection, I think especially of the last-minute panic out
of which many a sister was married to a man because she was
obsessed with the thought of missing the last opportunity. Afterward, however, when it is too late, she begins to sigh, if I
only hadn't! Therefore let all the candidates for marriage quietly
and patiently pass before your eye and don't hesitate to give
them a friendly "NO," if you are not sure, that the Lord says:
"This is he" (1 Samuel 16:12). And even when all around you
one after the other gets married and you alone remain, even
then wait upon the Lord. "Every good gift and every perfect gift
is from above, and cometh down from the Father" (James 1:17).
However, one needs a sensitive listening and spiritual ear. Too
often one follows the impulses of the soul and just plain human
impulses in this all important decision and confuses them with
the will of the Lord. Many have a bad conscience and pray in
this manner: "Lord, if it is not your will, prevent it." But let me
tell you: the Lord does not prevent the things from happening if
we desire them at all cost — with the only exception that before
such a step we have placed our will entirely into His will. Then,
however, we can claim Isaiah 30:21 and Psalms 32:8 and last but
not least John 16:13.

Another Woman

N.N. in T.: My husband had an affair with another woman for
several years, of which I know. When I asked him to be honest and
to make things right again, he denied it and made me look jealous,
especially since I had no direct proof of his affair. With the help of
the Lord I have tried love, goodness and calmness to bring him
back to me and I have continually prayed for his conversion
thinking that if God would permit this, there must be a reason for it.
Early this year, however, I felt that I was at the end of my strength.
After long consideration, I decided to force my husband into a
discussion by presenting him proof. A few months ago, in a
peculiar way, I came across a letter from the "other" woman. I paid
her a visit and asked her to leave my husband. She denied
everything and made fun of me. My husband does not want to leave
me, because he really is very conservative. He assured me that he
had broken off with her and deep inside is glad he did. I noticed,
however, many dishonesties and just cannot trust him anymore. My
heart is constantly trembling. I feel that I cannot bear to be cheated
any longer. What should I do? What is wrong with me?

Answer: One thing you have to keep in mind: if your husband really had an affair with another woman, then your marriage-vows are already broken. In this case you are already divorced. I cannot see clearly in your letter, if you have definite proof of it. If you are, however, very sure, that it is so, then you can help your husband in two ways:

1. you can start to pray more earnestly for him.
2. you can tell him, that you will leave him for the time being until he has broken off with the other woman completely and everything has been cleared up. This you should only do if you have proof of his adultery in the past and present.

What I advise you may sound very cold but it is the best way. I do realize, of course what you suffer as a wife, but don't we all go through sorrow into the glory of God, when we are true children of God. And who knows, how your husband might suffer inwardly, because of his sin.

Do you have prayer-fellowship with each other? Because, if there is no fellowship in prayer or the wife withdraws herself from her husband (comp. I Corinthians 7) it is easy for a husband to become an adulterer. These dangers are especially great in our time. Therefore, I would heed these two advises, provided of course, you are SURE, that he committed adultery, that it is not only your suspicion. Pray earnestly for him and tell him very clearly that you will not demand a separation because the marriage is already destroyed it can only be healed again by thorough repentance on his part and denunciation of any other such binding. Then you should examine yourself before the Lord, where you have failed him, where you for instance have not encompassed him in heartfelt love and prayers for him. The cleansing power of the blood of Jesus over your wrongdoing will enable you in faith to pray with authority for your husband.

She Wants To Be Reconciled

L.M. in N.: My daughter married a man whom she met in a church choir years ago. She is a Christian and at that time her husband was also. They now have four children. However, her husband has now met another woman and wants a divorce. My daughter does not agree to the divorce and wants to be reconciled to her husband, particularly for the sake of the children. I think our Lord and Saviour is mighty enough to bring good out of all this.

Answer: With God nothing is impossible! You should point out to your daughter first of all that this marriage was not in accordance with the will of God. Many Christian girls rush into a marriage which is not the Lord's will without realizing what they are doing. When your daughter — presuming she really is a child of God — repents over this disobedience she will receive more power and joy in prayer to pray for her straying husband. Moreover, you as mother will also be able to break through in prayer to the throne of grace. In other words, the adultery of your son-in-law is the result of the deeper cause of disobedience in your daughter. When this cause has been removed through repentance and the cleansing blood of Jesus, the results will abate and everything can be made good. The Lord truly is able to turn the curse into a blessing!

Repent

W.K. in A.: What shall I do? My marriage is hell. My husband promised me prior to our marriage that he would go with me to church and give me complete freedom in my faith. But later everything was different. He is an enemy of the gospel and we have terrible arguments.

Answer: The first thing you should do is, in God's presence, recognize how great YOUR sin is (see other question). To see, in this, your sin is much more important than to overcome the difficulty. When you see your disobedience then really repent before the Lord and accept in faith the forgiveness. Afterward you will suddenly see how everything has changed already. Not your husband but you! You will bear all aggression much better. You can be still. The love of Christ becomes active through you towards your husband. God is then able to let you experience Deuteronomy 23:5b.

Pray for Husband

S.E. in B.: Please pray, that my husband will be converted!

Answer: A very frequently discussed subject in the *Midnight Call*! But I know an even better and more biblical way, by which your husband will be converted. Read once very carefully 1 Peter 3:1: "Likewise, ye wives, be in subjection to your own husbands; that, if any obey not the word, they also may without the word be won by the conversation of the wives." Have you understood correctly? "Without the word!" — by their walk (conversation) they win their husband!

Fornication

H.F. in K.: In the D.G. Church, several people have been excluded from participating at the Lord's Supper. The reason: two young people who were engaged had sexual relations before their marriage. The leading brethren excluded them based upon the fact that they had committed the sin of fornication. I have carefully analyzed and thought about this matter and have come to the conclusion that in this case no sin of fornication or adultery had been committed. I think in this case Exodus 22:16-17 is valid. According to this Scripture it would have been sin if they would have not married and would have separated.

What are your views?

Answer: We must give credit to the elders of that Church who acted decisively and consequently. Most churches would not dare do that today. When the Lord says in Exodus 22:16-17 that "He shall surely endow her to be his wife," He does in no way exclude the fact that fornication had been committed. Or do you want to make the Word of the Lord powerless when He says "whoso marrieth her which is put away does commit adultery?" Moses suffered the people because of the hardness of their hearts and permitted divorce. But this act in no way changed the laws of God. It was and remains a sin. I do not belong to this denomination, neither do I know if I would feel at home with them. Every part of the Church of Jesus has its own structure and ways, but that does not matter. The main thing is that Jesus Christ the Crucified remains the *only* one in the *center* of their proclamation. I would not dare to criticize the elders of that Church in that they chose such a strict way. As a matter of fact, I did not read in your letter if these two young people repented of their sin. I am deeply convinced that if they had humbled themselves and repented genuinely in the presence of the elders they probably would have been excluded from the Lord's table only for a period. Whoever calls sin good however, will be struck by the Word of the Lord through the prophet Isaiah, "Woe unto them that call evil good, and good evil; that put darkness for light, and light for darkness; that put bitter for sweet, and sweet for bitter" (Isaiah 5:20). Such people we cannot help. They exclude themselves from the fellowship of the saints. Don't you see how far we have gone, how powerless the proclamation of the Gospel in our Churches has become: and this only because fornicators, idolators, and liars are permitted in our midst! We want to say "no" to sin decisively for we have the Lamb slain for us, Jesus Christ!

Take Her Back Again

E.K. in H.: I am a believer and have a brother who is also a believer. He has a wife who is many years older than he. She is senile and only talks nonsense and makes his life a misery. He would like to divorce her and remarry. This is not biblical, is it?

Answer: Your brother married this woman and he cannot simply say now, she is much older than I and senile, so I will divorce her. She is his wife! If your brother is a believer, he should know from God's Word that a divorce on these grounds is out of the question (cf. Matt. 5:32 and Luke 15:18), let alone a remarriage. Should he do this nonetheless, he is being disobedient to God's Word and this is sin. Disobedience leads away from the center of God's will and results in unhappiness. I would give your brother the opposite advice. He should take his wife back again, from whom he has been separated for two years already, despite her shortcomings and faults, and he should pray with her and bless her in prayer. If he is indeed a child of God, then according to Romans 5:5 the love of God is poured out in his heart through the Holy Spirit. When he comes into God's presence together with his wife, you will see what happens. The Lord will do great things in both of them.

Engaged or Married — Does it Matter?

A.P. in X. Some time ago two young people were married at our church, both were in our youth group and from good Christian families. Some people who attended the wedding service in the chapel maintained that the bride was expecting, and sure enough four months later the son and heir had arrived. I had the opportunity of hearing the opinions of a few young people from the youth group about this. They said the young couple intended getting married in any case and that it is not so serious that the wedding had to take place a little earlier than planned. They said "in the Bible there is no verse which gives clear instructions in this matter or even forbids premarital relations. People are not so narrow-minded today as they were twenty years ago.

I am profoundly shocked at these statements, coming as they did from my church and as I myself have two children of marriageable age.

Is the opinion that a girl should enter into marriage pure so completely old-fashioned? Do the veil and headdress symbols no longer have any significance? Should not we parents and preachers speak with the young people on this subject? An acquaintance of mine from another part of the country confirmed that the morals there had also become very loose. What do you think about this?

Answer: An engaged couple is not a married couple! A pregnant bride is not a bride but a married woman, or else she has become pregnant through prostitution. An Israelite girl who was not a virgin at the time of her wedding had, as the Bible says, "wrought a folly and must be stoned." We read this in Deuteronomy 22: 13-21. It is a feeble excuse that marital relations are allowed before the wedding ceremony when the young man concerned is going to marry the girl in any case. Experience tells us that there is no guarantee of this. Apart from this, the wedding in such a case is not a wedding but a farcical lie, because the white dress in no longer white. The marriage which takes place before the face of God has been impudently anticipated. The child which is subsequently born is an illegitimate child. It is noteworthy what the Apocryphal book of Wisdom, chapter 4:6 says, "For children of unlawful beds are witnesses of wickedness against their parents in their trial." Therefore, I say to all young, engaged couples: take care that you enter marriage pure through the power of the Lord and those of you who have sinned must seek cleansing and forgiveness through the blood of Jesus, before the face of the Lord.

Remarriage

T.E. in O.: A man who believes himself to be a Christian attended our church for a long time. I do not know whether his first marriage was a step of faith, but it ended in a divorce. As a single man, he certainly had difficulties and problems. People realized this and helped him. He accepted the consequences and visited Bible Studies and services regularly. He also testified that he had found the Saviour. Now, however, he does not want to remain single any longer and intends to enter into a second marriage. This acquaintance of mine went to a minister, taking his future wife with him, with the intention of obtaining the Lord's blessing on his marriage. His experience was, however, that he was abused and told that he was a sinner. I think, if a sinner has recognized and confessed his sins and wants to live in faith now, it is judging and an offense to refuse such a man the blessing of the church.

Answer: We are not concerned here with rejecting or judging anyone, as you suggest in your letter. Neither does it matter what you or I or the minister in question thinks, **but rather what the Bible says!** Turn to Matthew 5:32 please. At the end of this verse it says, "Whosoever shall marry her that is divorced committeth adultery." There is no mention made here of whether a person was a Christian at the time of their first marriage; the way is simply shown which God has prescribed for man. When a divorced person remarries, he is breaking a clear commandment which God has given, and he must accept the consequences of this. (Please read also Luke 16:18 and 1 Corinthians 7:10-11). God does not bless such second, ungodly marriages. This brother, whom you say has come to the cross, should be told this. He is not being rejected or ostracized with this, — on the contrary, he is being helped. Human compromising on this so earnest matter is very human, but inspired by Satan. When Peter wanted to keep the Lord Jesus from the cross, the Lord said to him, "Get thee behind me, Satan." It is not helping this brother to agree with a second marriage or even to have it legitimated by the church. On the contrary, he is being helped towards destruction. You will ask now, "What about his difficulties and problems?" The answer is in Ephesians 3:20! The Lord can do over and above all he asks or thinks. Through intimate fellowship with the Lord, He, the Lord, is able to carry him through and make everything alright.

Saved in Childbearing?

B.M. in L.: What is the meaning of 1 Timothy 2:15, where it says, "she shall be saved in childbearing?" Does it mean that the woman will be saved by bearing children?

Answer: This question must be understood in the entirety of the question of the woman's position in the Scriptures. Paul is saying here, "a married woman should not continue to trespass, as did the first woman, Eve, but rather she should take up the position as a mother, and a mother does bear children. Of course, Paul had no intention of saying that the woman would be saved by bearing children, because the condition to be saved is the same for men and women. Please read also the second part of verse 15, "If they continue in faith and charity and holiness with sobriety." You see, to help you understand this we could read the text in a different succession: "the woman shall be saved if she continues in holiness, in faith, in love with sobriety and in this position bear her children."

ENCOURAGEMENT AND EXORTATION

Be Strong in the Lord!

S.M. in B.: I feel so weak and often so discouraged, even right now again. So often have I failed in my life, and obviously have saddened the Lord.

Answer: Even so be comforted! The Bible says "If thou faint in the day of adversity, thy strength is small" (Proverbs 24:10) You may answer, "But that is my problem, I am not strong, I am weak." Then listen, you can seek refuge in your weakness and powerlessness in the strong Redeemer. That is what Paul means in Ephesians 6:10 "Finally my brethren, be strong in the Lord and in the power of his might." The Prophet Micah, calls to us "I walk in the power of the Lord of Hosts." And David sings in Psalm 27 "The Lord is the strength of my life." Therefore, cease now to look at yourself, at your inner sad conclusions, but rather cling to the strong Lord, safely in the arms of Jesus! Oh how very deep and infinite is His understanding of those He has bought with His own blood. He knows all your worries, all your deep and inner miseries and your hidden fears and weepings. Therefore be not dismayed, He will carry you, He will bring you through!

Anxiety!

E.Z. in U.: Whenever I get into a conversation with other people about the world situation I find that they have great fear of the future and reveal hopelessness. As soon as I mention in this connection, the judgments of God, there is immediate inner opposition within them. Certainly our time is marked with fear. In my case, during my youth, the church services and revival meetings were based on a "blackmail" principle: Fear had to drive sinners to the altar. In my parents' home there was often discussion about the Great Tribulation and the anti-Christian empire. My father as well as my mother were full of fear, and in

this atmosphere we grew up. Our Lord Jesus says "I have overcome the world," but He also says "in the world ye shall have
tribulation (anxiety)." If He has overcome the world, has He not
overcome our anxiety also?

Answer: Anxiety is certainly a sickness of our time. And the
Lord Jesus did speak about it as you mentioned in your letter.
However you are mixing up these two concepts. 1. Fear is a
natural defense action of our soul against approaching danger.
2. Anxiety consists mostly of miswarnings of the soul of danger
which in reality does not exist. There is, of course, a positive;
a saving fear. Just this morning I read in my Bible, "The fear of
the Lord, that is wisdom; and to depart from evil is understanding" (Job 28:28). You are to blame however, that you, in order
to ease your conscience have mixed up the terrible fear or
anxiety with the "fear of the Lord," which was implanted into
your soul during your youth in these revival meetings. According to your writing it seems to me that your parents did not rest
sufficiently in the fulfilled works of Christ, but they did fear the
Lord. When a person becomes fearful under the conviction of the
Holy Spirit, then it becomes a *saving fear.* He fears the Lord and
humbles his proud ego in that he abases himself. In this way
God meets him in Jesus Christ as the Father who loves him.

The tragedy however, is that of the new "fear-sickness," of
which millions of people are suffering today, and has nothing to
do with the fear of the Lord. This kind of fear or anxiety has actually no motive. And it originates in the invisible world. To say
it plainly; we are living, in our days, during an invasion of the
powers of Hell. This invasion comes from the father of lies, and
practically embraces all people who do not walk in the truth —
and these are many. That is the reason for so many "soul-sick"
people (emotionally sick) and they perish from this anxiety
which has no cause. This type of anxiety has taken hold of their
soul and causes the person to panic. It forces the person to react
unnaturally, unusually, and irresponsibly. How long? Until
this person comes to Jesus, who totally frees him of his fear-
neurosis. The person liberated from this type of fear later ad-
mits in shame and tears, that he feared the unknown things, the
threatenings of the powers of darkness, which in reality are
powerless, for Jesus Christ, on the cross of Calvary has defeated
them. Therefore I am calling with great assurance to everyone
who is overshadowed by this fear to grasp the pierced hand of
Jesus! Cling to it tight! Then you will rejoice with the great
multitude of the redeemed: "Thou art my hiding place; thou
shalt preserve me from trouble; thou shalt compass me about
with songs of deliverance" (Psalm 32:7). Then you will have
come out of this fear into the *fear of the Lord,* and the peace of
God will fill your soul.

Walk in the Light!

O.P. in Q.: Is this attitude right: that a child of God doesn't need the daily prayer for forgiveness, because the forgiveness of his whole debt has been paid once and for all?

Answer: This attitude is wrong. But it is also wrong to think that one could just keep on sinning, because every evening one would ask for forgiveness anyway. Both are very wrong! Those that say we need no more forgiveness, should read 1. John 1:8, "If we say that we have no sin, we deceive ourselves, and the truth is not in us." According to our POSITION, a child of God is righteous and without blemish before God (1 Corinthians 6:11; but according to the CONDITION; he has to realize this in practical faith. The Bible calls this purification and sanctification (1 John 3:3); 1 Thessalonians 4:3. To the careless ones, who want to hide behind their weakness and do not want to let go of their sin but instead use the blood of Jesus every day because this is more comfortable than resisting sin — I want to warn: Do not abuse the Spirit of grace! Do not hold the blood of Jesus as an unclean thing! This you do, when you are not ready to let go of sin. But this is the way: Walk in the Light, then you will learn to claim the blood in faith for your deeper purification and sanctification (1 John 1:7) and not only for superficial cleansing, which would lead to pious hardening of heart, if it would not go deeper.

Reviled for Jesus!

T.H. in F.: I have very much trouble; so that I sometimes become confused, and almost go crazy with wrongful accusation. I have to suffer because of my faith.

Answer: Jesus says in Matthew 5:11-12a: "Blessed are ye, when man shall revile you, and shall say all manner of evil against you falsely, for my sake. Rejoice, and be exceeding glad: for great is your reward in heaven." Look behind the person, who reviles you, the enemy, who wants to destroy the peace in your heart. The more closely we are bound to the Lord the more we become independent of that which people do and say good or bad against us. I am not so much interested what people say or think about me, but what God thinks of me. Besides, it is not the worst fruit of which the wasps like to eat. In times of such adversity it helps to read out loud Exodus 14:14, "The Lord shall fight for you, and ye shall hold your peace."

God's Love

H.K. in R.: Even though I have prayed for more love to God, I have not received it. He still does not have the first place in my life.

Answer: You are praying in vain. If you have already been born-again to a living hope, then you are praying for something which you already possess. This is what Romans 5:5b says, "The love of God is shed abroad in our hearts by the Holy Ghost." Therefore, this love has been given us! Why then cannot this wonderful love of God, which includes the whole of the world, become operative through you? It is because in some specific sphere of your life you are disobedient, you are holding on to a particular sin and therefore you are suffering from prayerlessness. Stop asking God to give you love! You could ask for this till you are a hundred years old and you would never be answered because God does not give what He has already given to the fullest. You should repent of your sins of omission and sins of commission. Then you will see how this wonderful love of God in your heart will break out again and the Lord will no longer need to say to you. "Thou hast left thy first love."

Sickening Self-assertion

E.L. in L.: Dear Brother, please pray for me that I may be freed from Satan. Do I not, in the first place, need to be freed of my sinful self, from my perverse, hasty, neurotic and conspicuous self? I fight against my conspicuousness but in vain. No one likes my company and I sense withdrawal and rejection on the part of others. I am also given to gossiping without being able to help it and cause my family much annoyance. The greatest evil though is my disobedience to the Lord, and also unbelief, anger, envy, mistrust of others — because I always imagine that people are talking about me.

Answer: O dear! What shall I pray for you? You are already free! You have given me such an exact description of yourself that I can tell that you already know the truth about yourself. The Lord Jesus said, "The truth shall make you free!" It is now time that you started to look unto Jesus as it says in Hebrews 12:2, "Looking unto Jesus." By looking in this direction your cursed self-contemplation stops; your corrupt uncontrollable gossiping will be silenced; your unbelief and malice disappear, envy and mistrust will no longer have any room in your heart. All this takes place by looking up in faith to Jesus! You see, that uncontrollable desire to gossip, the envy and mistrust in your heart, all come as a result of your sickening self-assertion because you do not accept the self-recognition which is already present within you. Because of this you find yourself in the vicious circle of the ego. When this is the case even the best preaching is of no help to you. What you must do now is to bring this crystal-clear recognition of your own self to Jesus. Stop trying to compare yourself with others, because in this way you will remain proud, malicious and mistrustful. Compare yourself now with Jesus' Being, with the Lamb, by looking up to Him. When you do this, the last resistance within you will be broken. I am not praying that this will take place, but rather I am thanking the Lord that it is taking place, because you have recognized the truth about yourself, " . . . and the truth shall make you free!!"

Constantly Tortured

E.D. in F.: I am being pursued and constantly tortured. Especially at night I am under the impression that I'm being worked over with some kind of harmful rays. I pray to the Lord for help but nothing happens. What shall I do?

Answer: There are many thousands of worn-out Christians which are befallen by this persecution, hallucination. But I see two causes here. On one hand it is an emotional weariness whereby the enemy finds a good ground for his deceptive insinuations. The complaints are always the same "I am being persecuted by rays; I am being watched" etc.
The only help is first of all; recognition that you are dealing with an emotional sickness. I repeat: 1. Emotional weariness. 2. Demonic depression (not possession). When you recognize this then you will be able to thank the Lord for His victory and His precious blood which can re-new everything.
In any case, I can assure you that you are neither under the influence of some kind of rays, nor are you persecuted by people. But we are all offended, we who are children of God, but not by flesh and blood, but by the powers of darkness (Ephesians 6:12). These dark powers have been victoriously overcome by the Lord Jesus on the cross of Calvary (Colossians 1:15; Ephesians 1:20-22). In this assurance we can wipe out all fiery darts of the wicked one with the shield of faith (Ephesians 6:16).

Mechanical Christian

N.D. in X.: I have been in the Lord's service for one year now, but for a long time I have been concerned how I can become a true servant of Jesus Christ. I see with sorrow how I do many things mechanically, and I have become such a lukewarm Christian who just goes on working for the sake of it. I know it can't go on like this. I am a hireling who has not much genuine love and interest in people, but rather seeks his own. I have so often cried to the Lord on my knees because of this, but have usually gone straight back into the old routine. I am particularly troubled by my indifference towards others. I am so often disobedient to my Lord. This is surely the root of my trouble. Often the Bible is a difficult text book in which I brood over the verses, or else I have no desire to pray. I am caught up in a mad rush, trying to do as much as possible, but this is all wrong. How do I get out? Often I just do not have the courage to obey the Lord, and so I get more and more miserable. I am so upset by things which did not bother me before. I often lack the necessary patience with people. I have a great longing that the Lord will revive me, humble me, and break me so that obedience and love for the Lord will result.

Answer: Only a follower of Jesus can be a true servant. When you ask "How do I become a true servant of the Lord Jesus?" listen to the answer He gives you in John 12:26 "If any man serve me, let him follow me: and where I am, there shall also my servant be." To be a true servant then, the Lord does not require any special exertion on your part, except that you follow Him, "...let him follow me." Here we come to the question, "how can I follow him?" Only in a pure condition (Revelation 14:4). Here the undefiled are spoken of " ... which follow the Lamb whithersoever he goeth." And in verse 5, " ... and in their mouth was found no guile." This is following the Lamb in practice, you see. All your indolence and indifference will disappear the moment you are cleansed from every stain of the flesh and spirit by the precious blood of Jesus, and continually **walk in the whole truth before God.** This is the meaning of the statement in verse 5, " ... and in their mouth was found no guile." No more lying in prayer such as "Lord, take away my sins" which you do not want to let go, but confess to Him truthfully your whole deceitfulness. — "Lord, this is what I am like, so corrupt, so twisted, so impure and perverse." In this way, you accept God's Word as being the truth, and it will then reprove and correct you. Then you have truly come into the light " ... and the blood of Jesus Christ His Son cleanseth us from all sin" (1 John 1:7). With this you have already begun to follow Jesus, in denying yourself and accepting Him. Then it is merely a careful remaining on the narrow way, close to Jesus, second by second, heartbeat by heartbeat.

In following the Lamb, you will come across deep eternal wells of living water, which you did not know of, " ... and of his fulness have all we received, and grace for grace" (John 1:16). "...the river of God, which is full of water" (Psalm 65:9).

All this indifference, indolence and prayerlessness, however, are hiding these wonderful sources from you. I would like to ask you to begin right now following Jesus by accepting the cleansing from all sin through the blood of Jesus.

World War III

N.E. in F.: Everytime I read about the coming III World War, I get very scared and frightened. I have been a refugee twice before and now at my age I don't think I have sufficient strength to overcome this fear.

Answer: If you are a child of God your anxiety is totally groundless. Let me say this very plainly and clearly: The Lord has always endowed His children, in times of great need and trouble, with a wonderful capability of making oneself invisible for the enemy. David expresses this with the following words, "For in time of trouble he shall hide me in his pavillion: in the secret of his tabernacle shall he hide me; he shall set me up upon a rock" (Psalm 27:5). Or in Psalm 57:1b "in the shadow of thy wings will I make my refuge, until these calamities be overpast." Besides, the book of Revelation speaks in a wonderful way of the fact that the Lord holds back judgment until the last of His servants be sealed. That means, until the elected be sealed with the Holy Spirit who have accepted Jesus. To this fact a great and uncounted number of children of God have testified with their experience throughout the centuries as to how the Lord has protected them in a wonderful way. For example: Just before the allied troops arrived in a French city in 1945, it was heavily shelled by the enemy. But somewhere in this city there were children of God assembled who prayed to the Lord that he may protect this city from the catastrophe of war. They did this in a spirit of humbleness and repentance and the miracle did happen. The city did not receive one direct hit during that barrage of the enemy. The American General, of the later arriving troops, testified that he had never experienced such a thing during all of the war; an untouched city! Therefore we do not bring joy to the Lord if we begin to be fearful of possible wars and rumors of wars. We are hidden in His hand and no one can pluck us out.

Weak

B.H. in W.: In one of your crusades in April 1965 I received the Lord Jesus as my personal Saviour and testified to the fact publicly. Afterwards a counselor advised me to read the Bible daily. I followed this advice, and the Bible has become my faithful companion. At that time I was sixteen years old. One year later I found my way into a young men's prayer group in which I still take part today. During these three years I have heard a great deal, but I have actually experienced very little with Jesus. I have to testify as Paul did, "O wretched man that I am, who shall deliver me?" In the past I have experienced that "in me dwelleth no good thing." I envy people who can confess Jesus freely because they have been freed from themselves; I can't. But sometimes I am so deeply troubled because of this inability to witness that I can hardly endure it. At this point it becomes evident to me that I am basically unwilling. My question to you is: How do I get to that point when it is no more I but Christ that lives in me? How can one be so possessed by a love for Jesus and experience victory over his own flesh and his sins? Will you tell me in practical terms what I have to do, please?

Answer: Your deep inner trouble is not that you've experienced little with Jesus, as you put it, but that your faith in Him, the Lord, has not grown. Even if you did have many experiences, signs and much help, these things would never be of lasting value. The presence of the Lord alone can help to carry you through. This happens through faith. By faith in what? In the Lord and in all His promises. If you were to "experience" much, you would not be able to have faith, and you would become an emotional and unstable person. For that reason the Lord allows us to experience little of what we think would be good for us. He wants us rather to experience His **presence.** Because whoever comes to God must believe that He is (Hebrews 11:6). The heroes of faith who are described in Hebrews 11:13 and 39 did not have these experiences which you speak of. But they had the Lord and that was sufficient. Their faith went from strength to strength. Why is it then that your faith is not strengthened and therefore you have come to a crisis? Because you take too little time to seek the face of the Lord, through Bible reading and prayer. The Bible is full of wonderful promises for those who want to seek the Lord with all their hearts. Here He reveals Himself to you. This is more than a miracle, more than an experience; it is infinitely more than emotional feelings. But exactly how, I cannot explain. Go into your room alone and take time to pray, especially in the mornings, because the Lord says, "...ye shall seek me and find me when ye shall search for me with all your heart" (Jeremiah 29:13).

In Prison

H.W. in D.: I am in prison and have to remain here for sometime yet. My heart is full of guilt and sin and I know that no-one can help me. I am a backslidden child of God, for I have left the straight and narrow way and I am at the end of my strength. My many previous convictions make me unable to believe that I can ever be free of my guilt. I know that without Jesus I can do nothing. Once when I had a Bible in my cell I began to read but the words were unintelligible to me. Then as I read John 10 the Lord Jesus opened my blind eyes and I began to praise Him for it. Soon, however, I began to worry about myself again. To follow Jesus became more and more difficult. Maybe I have become the victim of an unclean spirit like Jesus spoke of, which after seeking a resting place returns to the man bringing seven other spirits more wicked than himself. I no longer enjoy reading my Bible and praying. I would like to put everything right but it does not work. Instead of doing good I do evil. Can you pray for me that I may come back like the prodigal son? I know that a life even outside prison is meaningless without Jesus.

Answer: When you begin to look at yourself and your past and the tendency to do evil, you may well despair. Then there is indeed no hope for you and when you are free it will start all over again until you are back in prison. What kind of a life is that? Truly, in your life it is just as Paul says in Romans 7:19, "For the good that I would I do not: but the evil which I would not, that I do." And then he cries in verse 24, "O wretched man that I am! who shall deliver me from the body of this death?" But in the next verse he says, "I thank God through Jesus Christ our Lord." Why this sudden thanks? Because — and this applies to you **now** — Jesus Christ accomplished all that on the cross at Calvary for you and for me. He carried away all your sins, your guilt and He took your sinful nature upon Himself. In 2 Corinthians 5:21 it says, "For he hath made him to be sin for us, who knew no sin; that we might be made the righteousness of God in him." In other words, outside of Jesus Christ there is absolutely no hope for you. Like all other people, you are desperately wicked on account of your human nature, but in Jesus Christ you are perfect before God. You must stop trying to be better. Your good resolutions that it will be different when you are free will not help you. What will help you and make a new man out of you is a conscious surrender of your life to Jesus Christ! Surrender means to give up something that you have tried to hold on to. For instance a sinking ship which is kept afloat as long as possible and then surrendered to the waves and sinks. You have tried for a long time to keep above water but you have seen that you are unable. Surrender yourself **now** to the ocean of God's love and you will sink in it. This means that your sinful nature will be judged on the grounds of the death of Jesus on the cross, and you will be able to say with Paul, "I am crucified with Christ: nevertheless I live; yet not I, but Christ liveth in me" (Galatians 2:20).

It is false to think that through moral effort you can improve yourself (and I see from your letter that you have already come to that conclusion). The opposite, however, works wonderfully and gloriously: if you surrender your life to Jesus Christ by a clear, free-will decision. He will say of your life, "Behold, I make all things new." In this way, your time in prison will turn into a blessing for you because you have much time to be still and have close fellowship with the living God through His Son, Jesus Christ.

First Love Lost

H.S. in A.: With deepest sorrow I have to admit that the worst thing that can ever happen to a born-again person has happened to me: I have lost my first love for the Lord. I never knew it could happen. Converted in my youth with deep peace and great joy in Jesus, I experienced miracles! But now this first love is no longer in my heart. Without this love of Jesus I cannot live. I must be newly ignited and want to burn for the Lord. Everything else is otherwise pointless. What shall I do? Can I ever recover again this love and deep peace?
My second question: When the Lord says to me in Mark 10:21, "Sell whatsoever thou hast," does it mean our business also?
Answer: The Lord has not given you the recognition of your loss of first love so that you sink in despair but in order that you return to Him. That is such a simple matter and yet so sublime. Acknowledge what God has shown you in His Word, "Thou has left thy first love." When you acknowledge it you are humbling yourself and confessing your sin. At the same time the cleansing power of the blood of Jesus will clean from the sin of omission (1 John 1:7) and you will have returned to your first love whether or not you feel it. It will be a glorious fact again. As for your second question: When the Lord required that young man to sell all that he had and follow Him, it was because that young man was bound by his riches. This same challenge applies to all of us in that we should use for the Lord all that He has entrusted to us whether it is our profession, business, money or the like. In other words, if your husband earns his living with his business then it must serve only as the means to that end, i.e. first the Lord and then the business.

Nothing But Pious Flesh

E.C. in G.: The way I am now, I often think, it is all nothing but pious flesh. And sometimes it appears to me, as if my life is nothing but one big lie. That makes me very weak, for if that is so, I could not hear the voice of the good shepherd. "He, who is of the truth, will hear my voice," says the Lord.

Answer: What a blessing! You are wrong if you think you could not hear the voice of Jesus. In your condition the voice of the Lord can be heard clearest. For the spirit of truth, which the world cannot receive, succeeded to lead you into all truth, namely into the whole uncompromising truth about yourself. Now you must say yes and amen to what the Lord has shown you about yourself through His Spirit and His Word. Also say yes to the Lamb, that has bled for you. When you look with horror and terror into the depth of your own flesh, you are very close to the Crucified One, for you are able then to say yes to the judgment of the cross over all sinful and lost flesh! But this is the victory! For in this judgment you are being united with Him, who is your holiness, and then you learn to understand with amazement: not I but He! God does not look for my good deeds but for His in me. The Lord bless you!

Sadness and Despair

J.A. in Z.: I feel nothing else but sadness and despair. I am seventy years old and a suffering woman with many sicknesses and illnesses: stomach, gall bladder, heart, kidneys, etc. I just cannot bear it anymore.

Answer: No one will despair who trusts in the Lord! Through faith in Him, the Lord, who does not lie, rejoicing comfort and confidence will issue forth! Please do not observe too much your physical ailments, rather thank the Lord that He has given to you in black and white the proof that "he hath borne our griefs, and carried our sorrows" (Isaiah 53:4). Cease praying to the Lord that He may take away this or the other ailment and begin to thank Him for the glorious fact of the redemption through His precious blood. Giving thanks will protect you from inconsistency and praising him will draw your throughts upward! You have permitted the enemy to pull you down far too much, but the Lord is patiently waiting for you. (Please compare Isaiah 30:18). Now, does that mean that all of a sudden you will be redeemed from your physical sufferings? Not at all! For the Lord does much more! He will strengthen you in a wonderful way that when you suffer physical tribulation you will hold on to the fact, "He is stronger than all the powers of the enemy." And you will be able to exclaim with Paul rejoicing "For when I am weak, I am strong." Should the Lord however take away the symptoms of your sickness, then He just gives it as an extra bonus, to recuperate your faith, so that you will be able to withstand new temptations more victoriously. I am already convinced that the Lord has helped you in a kingly manner.

Jesus Cares!

W.B. in W.: We are very lonely and have no one to care for us. Both of us are old (71 and 75). We are refugees from Poland and therefore we are looked upon as stepchildren. And because we are believers, people ignore, reject, and even mock us.

But now my question: We have two daughters, one is married and the other is not. The one who is not married is 47 years old and works at a Christian Rest Home as a cook, some two hundred miles away from us. She is of the opinion that her service is more important than caring for her parents. She thinks that whoever puts his hand to the plow and looks back is not fit for the kingdom of God. I replied however, then we should change the commandment, "thou shalt honor thy father and thy mother." What is your opinion to this?

Answer: First of all, rejoice over the fact that you are being rejected and suffer because of the precious name of Jesus! For Peter explains: "If ye be reproached for the name of Christ, happy are ye; for the spirit of glory and of God resteth upon you" (1 Peter 4:14).

In regard to your daughter, however, I am asking you to judge your child mildly. It lies within the very nature of a human being that when he is grown up he wants to leave the home of the parents, even if not married. That, of course, does not void the responsibility of the child towards his parents if they are in need of help. In your case, however, it is encouraging, for you have a heavenly Father, who let it be written down for you, "Casting all your care upon him; for he careth for you" (1 Peter 5:7).

Please consider also that your daughter may presently be in an inner conflict, in that she sees her calling in this Christian home, and is now wrestling with the question, "must I go back to my parents or not?" I repeat, you may present this entire situation to the Lord. He will do all things well, for He said, "Even to your old age I am he; and even to hoar hairs will I carry you" (Isaiah 46:4). When our children can not care for us anymore, the Lord will! He is faithful until the day He takes us home. That is our strong comfort!

No Inner Joy

M.M. in P.: Can you give me some advice? I do not have the carefree joy of a child of God, but often suffer from depression and at times anxiety; these are perhaps the result of bad nerves because when I am under any strain, as for instance during the pre-Christmas rush with all its obligations, or when a journey is planned, or when I have any decisions to make, this state of anxiety arises, accompanied by sleeplessness. I completely lack the characteristics of a regenerated person.

Every morning in prayer I make intercession for an 88-year-old lady who was once involved in card-playing, but who vehemently resists correction.

Answer: I believe you are a child of God, but that through your parents and forefathers you are somehow affected by powers of darkness. These, however, have no right to you, because Jesus has paid the full and precious price of His blood for you too. I would ask you to seek the face of the Lord all the more through Bible reading and prayer. In this way you will be inwardly strengthened; at the moment your inner man is not strengthened and satisfied, but spiritually starved. This is why you lack the signs of the new birth, although the germ of life is present, and on the basis of your acceptance of the Lord Jesus and your willingness to follow Him you may hope for grace (cf. 1 Peter 1:13). — At the same time you should immediately cease to pray for a person (in this case the 88 year-old lady) who has been involved in fortune-telling and who violently resists correction and does not want to repent. Such intercession contaminates your own soul. The Lord has other tools for such people who are bound through occult sins. **You** simply need the Lord's presence. In Ephesians 3:17 is written that wonderful word, "That Christ may dwell in your hearts by faith." Despite all feelings and experience you may hold onto this fact: "Jesus lives in me." If you hold fast to this in faith, this fact will become operative in your emotional life. Do not pay so much attention to what you feel then, but rather to that which the Scriptures say. Lay your hand upon it in faith and give thanks continually. Fight the good fight of faith, and you will experience wonders.

Slandered

G.S. in L.: I know that Jesus commanded us to forgive our enemies seven times seventy times. Now, for some years, I've brought a woman before the Lord in prayer. She is very difficult, for she gossips about me. When I first heard about it, I asked her for forgiveness, in case I had done something wrong or hurt her unknowingly. It seemed she was satisfied after that. But a few weeks later she got ready for an even greater blow. I have told everything to the Lord, but my heart was still very heavy. Now I meet her on the bus frequently and she would like to make friends. Very much, I pray that I may have love for her. But I cannot be friends with her anymore, or what do you think?

Answer: The Lord Jesus says, that we should be happy when people say all manner of evil against us FALSELY (Matthew 5:11). Are you sure that this woman lies? Then it is not you who suffers harm but the one who starts the rumors. However, you were not wise in starting the conversation by asking for forgiveness. It would have been much wiser to take the woman aside and to say: "Please, tell me honestly what it is that bothers you about me, so that I can repent." The wrong accuser, according to Psalms 15, is expelled from the presence of the Lord. So, you have a pastoral duty towards that acquaintance, not, however, in the sense of justifying yourself - for as you stated you are innocent of the things which this woman says about you but to help her.

I believe that if you take this inner position before the Lord, it will be a greater relief to your heart. But if, inspite of your exhortation, the woman again chooses the way of slander, then break off any relationship with her decisively and pray for her in secrecy.

Old Peoples Home

S.L. in Z.: I have been living in an old people's home for seven years. I have an eighty-two year old neighbor who knits furiously whole outfits and reads only newspapers and trashy literature. She does not greet me when she sees me and only shouts at me when I want to show her a little kindness. This often depresses me. We are told, "Love your enemies, bless them that curse you," but how can I do this?

Answer: Love will find a way! The incomprehensible, unfathomable love of God, of which Hebrews 9 speaks, has obtained eternal redemption for us. Do not forget that our position was absolutely hopeless and Satan had a right to us. He was able to stand before God and claim: he belongs to me, he has sinned, for, "He that committeth sin is of the devil; for the devil sinneth from the beginning." God found a way. Which way? He offered Himself up in His Son, Jesus Christ. I am convinced that your 82 year old neighbor is desperately unhappy. She is trying to work it off by knitting and by being abusive.

My practical advice to you is to begin to pray fervently, to surround your neighbor with a fiery wall of prayer. One day an opportunity will arise of talking to her and this old, tormented soul will open to the Lord. Please do this and let us know what you experience; our God fulfills the desire of them that fear him: he also will hear their cry, and will save them! May the Lord bless you!

Satan's Attacks On The Old

A.B. in H. This dear brother in the Lord wrote, among other things, that the attacks of Satan increase as we grow older.

Answer: Courage, dear brother! The last part of the way is often the darkest. When the morning draws near, it is still night. The nearer we get to home, the louder the dogs bark. But Jesus is Victor! His grace is sufficient in life and His grace is sufficient in death. By His hand He leads us into a better country.

Death Fear

H.H. in T.: Presently I am without joy and the fear of death keeps coming over me. Added to this I have no deep knowledge of the Scriptures although I read the Bible every morning and evening. Often I wonder if the Lord Jesus has not forgiven me of my confessed and my secret sins as he has forgiven others. One fault I am aware of and I want to confess this to you and the Lord: as I am very sensitive to noise, and doors are often slammed here I just act according to "As you do to me I do unto you" yet I know what it says, "Recompense to no man evil for evil." So it is disobedience when I do it all the same. For this reason I sometimes doubt whether I will even be able to go with the Lord Jesus when He comes. Am I perhaps not even born-again or have I not really been converted? I really want to be a child of God.

Answer: The Lord has forgiven your sins because you have confessed them and asked Him for forgiveness. You can claim this in faith on the grounds of 1 John 1: 7&9.
In old age the soul becomes weaker and through this the resistance in the spirit meager. Then unbelief often creeps in. The enemy comes with all sorts of unimportant things and tries to make our redemption unsure. Just imagine, the devil is trying in your case to deny that mighty, immeasurable gift of salvation through the blood of Jesus through the banging of doors and other annoying things. Please don't listen to the father of lies who is always trying to deceive God's children in cunning ways. Instead open your Bible and look at the positive side where it says — and this applies to you — "We HAVE redemption through His blood" (Ephesians 1:7). We ARE God's children" (1 John 3:1). "Christ HAS given himself for us" (Ephesians 5:2). Thank the Lord for this and you will see that the little foxes disappear from your vineyard and you will be able to sing, "Sing, oh sing of my Redeemer, With His blood He purchased me, On the cross He sealed my pardon, Paid the debt and made me free."

"My Flesh and My Heart Faileth"

M.L. in G.: In my distress I am turning to you. I have confessed my sins but it was not meant sincerely. I am 67 years old and can no longer remember things. This depresses me very much and I often kneel down but cannot pray anything. Is this a demonic power perhaps? You will tell me to pray now, but how and what?

Answer: I have prayed for you. As I read that you cannot remember things, and you are physically weak, the words of the Psalmist came to my mind, "my flesh and my heart faileth: but God is the strength of my heart, and my portion forever." (Psa. 73:26). The Lord even hears your sighs, the unspoken words. It is written, "Before they call upon me will I answer." Please read also the precious truth of Hebrews 11:6, ". . . he that cometh to God must believe that He is, and that He is a rewarder of them that diligently seek Him." That is all. Draw near to Him in holy reverence, through the blood of Jesus, and believe that He is. He will do the rest. It does not depend upon your words, but upon the attitude of your heart. It is also written, "We know not what we should pray for as we ought: but the Spirit itself maketh intercession for us with groanings which cannot be uttered" (Rom. 8:26).
There is also a great secret in simply thanking in childlike manner for the redemption through the precious blood of Jesus, and that you too are redeemed from the power and guilt of sin and may now belong to Him. When you do this you will be happy and it will no longer be an effort to pray. Your life will be a prayer then. Reach out with all your heart to Him who really is! Do you believe that He is? Do you believe that He is near to you now? "Seek ye the Lord while he may be found, call ye upon him while he is near." He is near you. I repeat once again: it depends upon the attitude of your heart. "For," the Lord says, "ye shall seek me and find me, if ye shall search for me with all your heart." Therefore, what you say, cry and sigh is of secondary importance. He wants your *heart.* Do you understand this now? Please begin to practice this. Say to the Lord quite simply, "Lord, Thou knowest all things, Thou knowest that I love Thee." May the Lord bless you!

Out of the Frying Pan...

R.E. in H.: I am about to convert to the Roman Catholic Church. I know from your lectures and from the *Midnight Call* that you do not approve of the doctrine of this Church. Because it is my greatest longing however to receive Holy Communion, I see myself forced to take this step! I know myself to be delivered from my sins and have experienced the new birth, but I am so terribly lonely. And the eucharist in the Roman Catholic Church attracts me. There I can receive what I lack.

Answer: If you go this way you will find yourself out of the frying pan and into the fire. What is your longing? Not something, but Someone. You are longing for **real** fellowship with the Living God, through the Lord Jesus Christ. Neither the Evangelical Church, much less the Roman Catholic Church can mediate this to you. The fact that the eucharist in the Roman Catholic Church so attracts you suggests that you allow yourself to be influenced by visible things. There is much visible in the Roman Catholic Church; not only pictures but also relics, hairs of saints, splinters of the Cross, teeth of martyrs, etc. Of course such visible things have great attraction for the natural man, but you will be bitterly disappointed because Jesus is not in all this. Only Jesus, the Son of God, only He alone, can still your deepest longings. And what is more: He is not far from you. But you do not see Him, you cannot feel His presence and you do not know where to find Him. The Lord reveals Himself through the **Word**. He is near to those who call upon Him, who call upon Him in truth (Psalm 145:18). He is standing at the door of your heart and knocking and asking you to let Him in (Revelation 3:20). Moved with compassion, He stretches forth His hand to you (Mark 1:41). What is your trouble??? You don't believe this! You want a visible hold, in this case the Roman Catholic eucharist. In this you grieve the Lord, "for" says Scripture, " . . . he that cometh to God must believe that he is . . . " Faith is the opposite of feeling and touching. "Faith is the assurance of things hoped for, the proving of things not seen" (Hebrews 11:1). Now let me say earnestly; the Lord Jesus Christ is very close as you read these lines, and Scripture says: "Seek ye the Lord while he may be found, call ye upon him while he is near." And the Lord's Supper? "This do" said Jesus **"In remembrance of me."** This is the deep meaning of the Lord's Supper. Not that Jesus is crucified and sacrificed again (Hebrews 6:6); this is a false teaching of great consequence which, I repeat, has an enormous attraction for the natural man; but in this meal of remembrance we actually have fellowship with His death, His sufferings and His precious, shed blood.

I beg of you, go down on your knees and lay hold of Jesus in faith and call upon Him with all your heart, because again Scripture says: "Whosoever shall call on the name of the Lord shall be saved."

Nebuchadnezzar's Palace

N.N. in X.: I have found some most interesting articles in your publication, particularly where Roman Catholicism is concerned. I can only say that the Roman Catholic Church here in "X" is an abomination to me. The priests just about talk away one's faith. When I listen to them talking about the Bible. I have the feeling that they themselves do not even believe in God. The Bible seems to be pure Jewish mythology for them. One Roman Catholic priest even maintained that the Bible cannot be believed because it contradicts itself and is unintelligible. The only thing we can believe is the doctrine of the Roman Catholic Church. As you in your paper have often mentioned, there is obviously something wrong with this doctrine, with its prayers to saints, the ritual of Mass, Mariolatry, prayers for the dead, etc. The tragedy is that the Roman Catholic Church in "X" is almost a State Church and identifies itself with the strongest political party (the People's Party). You can imagine what a powerful influence this Church has here, from which nobody can easily escape. I am a student of Pedagogics and have great difficulty in avoiding Religious instruction (Religious Pedagogics). I cannot leave the Church because this would make it difficult for me to find employment. I would have to reckon with a position as teacher in a school for mentally backward or delinquent children. I am not built for this kind of work and have neither the nerves nor the disposition for it. — I can only hope that God Himself through His Word (the Bible) will strengthen my faith and show me the right way to get out of this "modern Babylon."

Answer: Your trouble has concerned me a great deal. Your position is like that of Daniel in Nebuchadnezzar's palace. Please read in this connection Daniel, chapter 1. What you should do, is the same as Daniel did. "But Daniel purposed in his heart that he would not defile himself with the portion of the kings meat, and of the wine which he drank" (Daniel 1:8). The secret of success my dear young friend, is in the determination: I will not collaborate: I want to belong to the Lord. To put it in New Testament language, my heart is consecrated to Jesus. Only Jesus leads to the living God, and not Mary, not the saints, not the Church and not baptism, but Jesus and Jesus alone. I would like to ask you a direct question now: Do you have the assurance in your heart that you are a child of God? That is, have you received this same Jesus into your heart who shed His precious blood for you (John 1:12)? If this is so, you will have the witness of the Holy Spirit in your heart that you are a child of God (Romans 8:16). That is the primary thing.

Now to your dilemma. Finish your studies, but at the same time, take much time for Bible reading and prayer. God speaks to your heart through the Bible, and you speak to Him in prayer. In this way you will be strengthened in faith and you will grow in the Lord who, according to Ephesians 2:10, has paved the way to the end already. He wants to make something for the praise of His glory out of your life. — You may be assured that if you trust Him, you will not only come through this temporary "modern Babylon" but also be saved for eternity.

Nervous Illness

Z.M. in Z.: Something bothers me which I would like to get off my mind. It is concerning your allusions to children of God who are suffering with a nervous illness. Because you are suspicious of these suffering ones "something must be wrong" you say, you are causing believers much distress...

Answer: I am very sorry if I have offended anyone who suffers from a nervous illness with my statement. I did not intend this in any way. The opposite is true. For I know how many illnesses stem from the vegetative nerve system. The question, however, is in which connection I said "something must be wrong." This statement is to warn those whose nervousness is caused by nothing less than disobedience towards the Lord and wanting to hide with the alibi: "I am a complete nervous wreck." With this I say nothing about truly suffering brethren who probably, as Paul, suffer in their flesh, to replace that which is still missing in the Church of Jesus Christ.

The Devil is a Liar

P.M. in W.: The devil is always around me, day and night: he leaves me no peace. I cannot pray anymore and even less go down on my knees. The enemy has shown me that I am lost and shall never again find peace.

Answer: You are making a fatal mistake. If you did not make this mistake the enemy would have to let go of you immediately and radically. Your mistake is that you believe the devil; such bare lies like "I am lost and shall never again find peace" could never come from our blessed Saviour." On the contrary he says, "Him that cometh to me I will in no wise cast out" (John 6:37). I also see from your letter that you know it is the enemy because you write "the enemy has shown me ... " Now consider and realize that Jesus Christ **has conquered** this enemy who torments you, through His precious blood, His death on the cross and His resurrection! The Bible says, "the Son of God was manifested, that he might destroy the works of the devil." "Yes," you say, "but what help is that to me? What do I have to do? Listen! Go down on your knees now and if you have no counselor available then say out loud, "In the name of Jesus Christ who shed His blood for me, I renounce the power of Satan over me." You will immediately feel pressure within you, because the enemy is now getting afraid. Then you must do the following: Begin to thank God unceasingly for the blood of Jesus. Read aloud the passages which particularly apply, namely Ephesians 1:7 or 1 Peter 1:18-19.

Drug Abuse

R.S. in W.: I am at present in a hospital as a result of abuse of alcohol and drugs. I have tried everything in order to be free from this addiction but all my prayers have been to no avail. One becomes discouraged as time goes on, but this is just what one should not do because it is playing into the devil's hands. Satan is just waiting for this. But what shall I do to be free?

Answer: I am sure you have read the words of the Lord Jesus in John 8:36, "If the Son therefore shall make you free, ye shall be free indeed." It is obvious that all attempts to free oneself are in vain because in this way the addiction and desire for alcohol and drugs remain deep down in your heart. You can only be made free through Him who says of Himself that He is the truth. This will happen the moment you become quite truthful in your bondage. That is, when you confess to the Lord on the one hand your desperate failure but on the other hand cry from your heart, "Lord, I **want** to be free at all costs," Don't say, "I should" or "I would like to be . . . " but **"I want to be."** It does not matter how weak or unstable you are, the nobility of man is his free, sovereign will. The Lord does not expect any exertion of strength on your part. Your strength is not enough. What you cannot do, however, He can. He did it long ago on Calvary's cross. The only thing which He requires of you is an upright, truthful attitude of heart. Now please don't say, "I am so corrupt and dishonest." Have you a genuine desire to be free? Begin to read the Bible prayerfully and the Lord will reveal Himself to you and put His finger on your sins. Be honest then and say, "Yes, Lord, it's true, I know it is." At the same moment, the true cry will arise in your heart which is so decisive, "Lord Jesus, make me truly, really free." Then you will be able to thank Him for the accomplished redemption through the blood of the Lamb and that this redemption is effecting you personally. The fact that you will suddenly not have to drink alcohol or swallow drugs any more will not be the result of your efforts but of your faith. You have believed in the truth that Jesus makes you free. Please do this immediately. Get down on your knees in your desperate weakness, pour your heart out before Him until thanks for the accomplished redemption breaks through in you.

Suicide!!!

S.M. in X.: I am suffering terribly under depression, which is probably caused by my repenting too late. The enemy whispers that for me it is too late. Please pray for me that I may become a joyful child of God. At this time I am about to despair. We have already had two cases of suicide in our family and Satan wants to drive me to commit this sin also.

Answer: Deeply moved I have acknowledged your suffering in the soul, for depressions cause suffering and pain in the soul. However these depressions are not caused, as you write, by repenting too late but they originate (and I am telling you this with great assurance) from the father of lies, that is the devil himself. You would like to be a joyful Child of God? I am asking you, can God lie? "No!" you will answer. Is then His Word totally reliable? "Yes," you will agree. Don't you know how often He gives promises such as Isaiah 1:18, "Come now, and let us reason together, saith the Lord: though your sins be as scarlet, they shall be as white as snow; though they be red like crimson, they shall be as wool." Although I clearly see in view of the two suicides that in your family of three or four generations a dark line is running through on which you are bound too. But these are defeated too, for the Word of God says in Colossians 2:13-14, "and hath he quickened together with him, having forgiven you all trespasses; Blotting out the handwriting of ordinances that was against us, which was contrary to us, and took it out of the way, nailing it to his cross." This Scripture clearly shows that your handwriting of ordinances, sin and guilt have been nailed on the cross too. With it the dark line of desperation which is present in your family and on which you were bound until now. The Lord Jesus said "until now the kingdom to heaven suffereth violence, and the violent take it by force" (Matthew 11:12).

I have prayed earnestly to the Lord that He grant you courage and faith in that you tear apart this line of bondage in the precious name of Jesus and call out loud, "I renounce in the name of Jesus all inherited enemy bondages over my life." You will then experience, after you have thanked the Lord for His precious blood, that the dark bondage in your life will disappear. For as truly as the Lord liveth so true is His faithfulness and so true and unmovable are His promises. He does all this according to the desire of those who fear God.

Incidently I have noticed many letters from different people whom you do not know within your city who have the same problems of demonic depressions. So it seems that in "X" there is a special concentration of these powers of depression. But they are defeated in the name of Jesus!

"Thou Art My Hiding Place"

H.I. in K.: For ten years I was addicted to drugs, alcohol and tablets. Three years ago Jesus came into my life and since then I feel absolutely healthy, happy and free of all vices. Frequently there comes over me a stupid, unfounded fear. It grieves me to death and I pray continuously when my children are in bed at night because I am afraid that they will suffocate in their sleep or otherwise die. Further, when I awake in the morning I am already afraid that I shall not manage the household or fail in other respects, etc. . . . . So I just spend much time praying to the Lord and it always becomes better again afterwards. I know perfectly well that I do not need to be afraid and yet I am still not free from it.

Answer: You have much reason to thank the Lord for your wonderful salvation through the blood of Jesus Christ. Will He nevertheless allow you to sink in a sea of fears??? Never! You must learn Psalm 32:7 by heart where it says, "Thou art my hiding place; thou shalt preserve me from trouble; thou shalt compass me about with songs of deliverance." As soon as the unfounded and truly silly fears come over you then say out loud that the Lord is your hiding place, and your shield.

Apart from this you must realize the **reason** for such inexplicable fears: the firm basis, that is the necessary faith-reserve, is lacking in your heart. Everybody is susceptible to these unmotivated fears which no one can explain — fear of life, fear of death, fear of the night and fear of the day. It is the sickness of our times. You are how you can become free of it. Firstly, as I have already told you, take God's Word seriously and especially Psalm 32:7. Then from the depths of your heart thank God for the power of the blood of Jesus Christ. Thank Him that you are freed and saved from all demonic influences of fear. Have the courage, when the fears come upon you like waves from which you can no longer escape, positively to cry out loud, "Thank you Lord Jesus that you saved me from all fear through your blood." Then there will be that peace of God inside you which passeth all understanding, and it will keep your heart and mind through Jesus Christ.

Spiritual Misery

N.O. in H.: I am in great spiritual misery. I do pray, I read my Bible, and I do attend Church but, it seems as if nothing penetrates me. Sometimes I even have a feeling that I am possessed by demons. Repeatedly, I am being tortured with the thought, Can God be a God of love if He kills people? Please do help me.

Answer: First, I must ask you a question. Have you accepted Jesus Christ on the grounds of John 1:12 as your personal Saviour? If you can answer this question with "yes" then what are you? You are a child of God! Then Jesus Christ lives in you on the grounds of Ephesians 3:17 and Colossians 1:27. And He is the victor over all the powers of darkness. Including those which frustrate your thoughts, read carefully Ephesians 1:20-21 and Hebrews 2:8.

From your letter I believe you are not possessed by demons, therefore, do not give too much honor to the power of darkness. For Jesus has defeated all the dark powers as it is written in Colossians 2:15.

I know too well, what awful results our thoughts can produce in certain areas. For that reason Paul says in 2 Corinthians 10:5, "Casting down imaginations and every high thing that exalted itself against the knowledge of God and bring into captivity every thought to the obedience of Christ." And who is closer at hand to help than He who lives in your heart? How then can you permit yourself to be influenced and impressed from all the evil in the world which is attacking you? Plant your feet securely on the grounds of victory of Calvary. In that you thankfully accept with Paul 2 Corinthians 15:57, "Thanks be to God which giveth us the victory through our Lord Jesus Christ." When you do that and keep yourself constantly to that guideline, you will experience that all the negative dark thoughts will have to retreat, because your thoughts are centered in God who has thoughts about you, about peace, and not about suffering. "The Lord has been mindful of us, He will bless us" (Psalm 115:12).

TEMPTATIONS & STUMBLING BLOCKS

Tried or Tempted?

D.E. in W.: What is the difference in being tried and tempted?

Answer: The meaning of these words in the Bible are often interchangeable. But there is a certain difference to be seen. While trials are testings of God (He tried Abraham Genesis 22:1), the aim of God's testing is Ps. 66:10. David asks the Lord to try and test him in Psalms 26:2 "Examine me, O Lord, prove me; try my reins and my heart." In opposition there is a temptation from Satan to sin: "And when the tempter came to him and said:" (Matthew 4:3). In this manner God would never tempt a person. (see James 1:13). There is also a temptation from our side in relation to God. This is a terrible sin! The Scriptures say: "Ye shall not tempt the Lord your God." (Deuteronomy 6:16 and Matthew 4:7).

Temptations come from three sides: A) from Satan: he fights against the victory of Jesus in us and brings us into defeat. B) from the world: the visible noticeable, and feelable world around us says no to the promises of God because it always stands in contradiction to them. C) from our flesh and blood, which always wants to go the opposite way of the Spirit, (Galatians 5:17). God permits this kind of temptation in our life so that we might prove ourselves (James 1:12).

1. before the visible and invisible world to manifest the victory of Jesus when Satan wants to try us. 2. that we believe the invisible God more than the visible world in spite of contradiction. 3. that we in this last manner of temptation of the flesh prove that we love the Lord more than our flesh. Summarizing:

TRIALS clarify the position of things in us like Faith, Patience, Love, etc.

TEMPTATIONS loosen us from the negative, like rulership of the flesh, lust of the world, power of Satan. Or to say it in other words: God tries us in the temptation to see if that which is in us is of Him. (Deuteronomy 13:4, 8:2). And He permits us to be temp;-ted that the cleansed life in us, stands and resists all other influences (James 1:12).

Origin of Unbelief

M.H. in B.: Where does unbelief and doubt in God's Word originate?

Answer: The original source of unbelief is wellknown. Satan was first to put a question mark behind God's statement when he asked Eve, "Yea, hath God said...?" (Genesis 3:1). That is when the poison of unbelief entered for the first time into sinless man. And because the enemy is permitted to deceive the believers until the return of the Lord, we must decisively stand against these whisperings of Satan, the putting of a question mark behind the Word, with the Word, "resist the devil and he will flee from you. Draw nigh to God and he will draw nigh to you" (James 4:7-8).
We can only honor our Lord with consistent faith. For the Scripture says, "But without faith it is impossible to please him: for he that cometh to God must believe that he is, and that he is a rewarder of them that diligently seek him" (Hebrews 11:6).

Harlot's Dress in Church

L.E. in B.: I have heard of a Church which prayed for revival for a long time but nothing happened until God could show them the reason: It was because their girls and women went around looking like harlots. Now, I wonder where in the Bible it says what harlots wear and look like. Even with the help of the concordance I could find nothing. Could you help me in this matter please, because in our Church young brothers are wearing long hair and the sisters wear trousers with their hair falling all over their faces.
Sometimes I wonder why I worry about such things as some of the parents of these young people also say. Would you please be so good and explain to me what a harlot's clothing looks like?

Answer: Harlots' dress seduces and promotes harlotry. It is the opposite from what the apostle says in Titus 2:4 about young women learning to be sober. Women and girls in the midst of the Church of Jesus Christ today walk around thoughtlessly in immodest clothing and do not want to know that the Scriptures condemn them sharply. Proverbs 11:22 says for instance, "As a jewel of gold in a swine's snout, so is a fair woman which is without discretion." It is grotesque, even brutal how Church members even defend such unchaste clothing, and this because values have become inverted under the influence of the Antichristian spirit. Today people honor what is shameful, undisciplined and provoking (" . . . whose end is destruction . . . " Philippians 3:19). This is how our generation is degenerating under satanic influence. At one of our conferences recently, I was shocked as I started conversing with a young man who had come to Christ after a terrible battle and great burdens of sin. His main problem was drinking and immorality. After his conversion he became a member of a Church and saw the sisters there dressed in a shameless manner. Through the sight of this shameful display of the flesh he fell anew into the same temptations. He could not resist. Then he said to himself "Out of this Christian camouflaged impurity!" — And there he stood before us, helpless, at our conference.

Men who want to have long hair should read carefully 1 Corinthians 11, that is if at all they want to take the Word of God seriously. And for women who want to run around in men's clothing, they should remember what the Bible says in Deuteronomy 22:5, "The women shall not wear that which pertaineth unto a man, neither shall a man put on a woman's garment: for all that do so are abomination unto the Lord thy God." However, don't be surprised too much to see that Christians of today don't take notice of the Word of God, after all we are living in the last times with its apostasy. Not for nothing did the Lord Jesus say. "...when the Son of man cometh, shall he find faith on the earth?" (Luke 18:8).

Zodiac Charms

E.R. in O.: Is it a sin to wear signs of the zodiac as jewelry? I know that horoscopes are connected with superstition and that they can bring people under a bond. I do not believe in horoscopes, however. I have already thrown my three charms Gemini, Aries and Cancer into the dustbin once, but then I fished them out again because I would like to know your answer first.

Answer: You say you do not believe in horoscopes, and yet you do, or you would not have fished out your three charms again. But I would like to ask you a more important question: Are you a child of God? Do you have Jesus in your heart? If so, then how can you wear these three signs as jewelry, as these signs lead many to read their horoscopes? Are you serving the Lord Jesus by wearing them? Of course not! There is only one answer, therefore: away with them! Renounce in the name of Jesus all the powers of superstition which bind you and, "If the Son shall make you free, ye shall be free indeed."

Plagued by Voices

U.M. in W.: For many weeks already...even for months, I am being plagued by voices. Several years ago (this was before my wedding) I worked for almost three years in a hospital, training to become a nurse. Shortly before my graduation I had to break off this training period because it became an emotional strain. I believed that I had fallen in love with one of my teachers and told him so in a letter. It all ended up in a nerve-clinic. Now since almost a whole year, I can hear the voice of this teacher again. He mingles into my marriage. All day long I am plagued by this voice. How can I get rid of it? My husband does not believe me anymore and is suspicious. I can't stand it anymore day after day. How shall my life go on? Please help me!

Answer: The voice that you hear is not the one of that teacher but that of a spirit of imitation. The matter is very harmless in itself, for Jesus Christ at the cross of Calvary has conquered all of hell: principalities, powers, demons etc. Of those, the spirit of imitation is one of the weakest.

I give you a two-fold advice:

1. When you hear the voice again, thank the Lord Jesus for His precious blood, through which you have been redeemed from all these dark powers.,

2. With this kind of thanksgiving, you ignore this voice. It will become meaningless to you; just as meaningless as this spirit really is. But even more important: when you give thanks for the blood of Jesus, you prove that it is much more important for you, what Jesus has done for you and therefore more important and stronger than all the powers from below. True thankfulness is therefore the highest expression of faith. That's why you should begin right now to practice it. The victory belongs to him who can believe!

Card Playing

N.O. in S.: In your January 1970 issue I read your answer on playing-cards and I would like to know the source of your information.

Answer: First of all here is the answer I gave to the question, "Isn't card playing in itself harmless if it does not become a passion?"

"Whoever is familar with the origin of playing-cards, can well understand why such devilish things as fortune-telling are carried on with playing-cards.

The first playing-cards were designed for the personal use of King

Charles of France in the year 1392, at which time he was suffering from a mental illness. The designer of these cards was a degenerate, wicked man who mocked God and His commandments. For his evil creation he chose biblical personalities. The King represented the devil; the Queen, Mary, the mother of Jesus. In this blasphemous way he made our Saviour a son of Satan and Mary. The hearts represent the blood of the Lord and the Jack or Knave (I hardly dare write it) our Lord Himself. The clubs and other symbols symbolize the persecution and destruction of the saints. He expressed His contempt for the ten commandments in choosing this number for the number of cards to a suit. In the light of the devilish origin of playing-cards then, the devilish results are understandable. No wonder fortune-telling by means of playing-cards is so successful, for these are devilish symbols."

Many of our readers have asked for the source of our information. However there are too many to inumerate here in this magazine and besides, most of the international encyclopedias in different languages are contradicting themselves in regard to the origin of playing-cards. We can be assured however, that playing-cards were used already in the 14th century in Europe. Some say they were invented in Egypt. In any case, today, more than 90% of the population of the civilized countries of the world are suffering under the bondage of playing-cards which are used as entertainment games such as Skat, Bridge, Canasta, Rumme, Ecarte, Baccarat, Doppelkpf, Schafskopf, Poker, Sixty six...etc.

We warn every child of God emphatically — have nothing to do with playing cards! That is, those which we mentioned at the beginning of this answer. We are not opposing playing cards which are used for other games without the blasphemous characters and demonical signs. History of black magic is closely united with the development of playing-cards. There is absolutely no question that playing cards with its blaphemous signs are of Satanic origin. The new Brockhaus German encyclopedia describes it as follows:

"To receive information through playing-cards in regard to the future is being used in different ways. The practice is always of a superstitious nature. Success which has been ascribed to fortune tellers, gypsies, etc., are to be based on the fact that psychic powers have been employed."

It is therefore obvious and clear that in this time of the approach of the Antichrist the powers of the occult appear suddenly in many different forms and at the same time especially with playing-cards which harbor a great power of attraction not only to people of this world but also the members of the Church of Jesus Christ. Whoever becomes bound to playing-cards, the enemy immediately has a stronghold on him. Therefore get rid of playing cards now and renounce them in the name of Jesus.

Enduring Sexual Temptations

X.Y. in Z.: I have a problem which not only troubles me but many other young people who are believers, particularly us men. I am just over thirty years of age and have suffered since my sixteenth year from an excessive sexual urge. I was never told about such things and suddenly this strong compulsion broke out in me with full force. I discovered the practice of masturbation which made me a real prisoner to it. I thought that my problem would be solved when I got married, but that is not the case. How often we men are enticed and even outrightly provoked by the clothing of women, which makes the trouble even worse. Please help me, for I want to be freed of it.

Answer: The urge to reproduce has been given to every person. Misuse of it is sin. To put it biblically, "Know ye not that your body is the temple of the Holy Ghost which is in you, which ye have of God and ye are not your own? For ye are bought with a price . . ." (1 Corinthians 6:19-20a). The tensions which arise in every normal person never find their solution in masturbation. The latter merely burdens the conscience of the one concerned, not to mention its other effects. "But what shall I do?" so many people ask desperately. The answer is so plain and simple that many people cannot understand it. First of all let us see clearly that the urge to reproduce is a creative ability which God put within man. The "safety valve" for the apparently unrelievable tensions is fellowship with the Lord by means of a deep sincere surrender of the heart to Him in prayer and through the reading of His Word. In this way the God-given ability (I mean the ability to reproduce) is rechanneled into creative activity for the Lord. Many men and women are not called to be married. Does God not know this? Of course He does and that is why the Scriptures encourage us to "Pour out your heart before Him" (Psalm 62:8). Through intensive fellowship with the Lord, miracles of grace take place especially concerning these particular problems and temptations.

"But," some of you ask, "what happens at the moment of temptation when every part of me wants to sin and when I simply cannot bear it any longer?" The answer is, you cannot do anything about the birds that fly over your head, but you are responsible if one of these birds builds a nest on your head! It is exactly the same with these unclean impulses. Perhaps they come over you suddenly but Christ in you is the hope of glory; He is stronger than all fleshly allurements. As far as married people are concerned, Paul says in 1 Corinthians 7:5, "Defraud ye not one the other, except it be with consent for a time, that ye may give yourselves to fasting and prayer; and come together again, that

Satan tempt you not for your incontinency." The trials of which
we spoke before come to married as well as to unmarried
people. Some may resignedly say, "Why fight it?" I would like to
remind you of the Word in James 1:12, "Blessed is the man (and
therewith the woman also) that endureth temptation: for when
he is tried, he shall receive the crown of life."

Karate?

E.F. in H.: What do you think about our youths taking part in
Karate courses? I find that our time is much too serious to be
wasted with such questionable spare-time hobbies. It would
only take away time for Bible reading and prayer. I am afraid
also that this kind of sport can develop into a very unhealthy
self-assurance and obviously will hinder the child-like trust in
our Lord Jesus. Then another question: What do you think of
chiropractors?

Answer: Karate is a Japanese technique of self-defense without weapons, by striking the attacker's body with hands, elbows,
knees or feet. This is a combat method from the "land of the
rising sun" is blowing stronger to the West today and this is
the reason, I believe, that our youth are so eager to learn more
about it. That is also the reason for the strong desire and great
popularity of Buddhism and other Asiatic religions. This fact,
however, lies on the line of fulfillment of the prophetic Word.
For according to Revelation 16, the kings from the rising sun
will be united with all the kings of the earth against Israel (Revelation 16:12-16). (Please read also the article on China, page
16). Already for these reasons I would reject decisively these
types of sports.

What a chiropractor does is very enlightening. He twists,
pushes, or bounces the bone and muscle structure back into
joint. Sometimes it is very painful, but it is very effective. Often,
however, questionable methods are used which unfortunately
are of occult origin. In such cases, the chiropractor touches
the troubled area but does not physically work with it. With
this, one has already stepped over his set border. Then he is
either an ordinary crook, or a magician. In the first case, the
people are not being helped physically, and in the latter case
they have received noticeable relief. But with this, the enemy
has an open door to the soul. If there is even a little doubt present, we should reject it. For whatever is not done in faith is
sin. Here also it is good to use the motto, "In case of doubt say
no!"

Bound Only To Jesus

M.H. in R.: In your book, "The Rapture," you write that a person can even be bound to a piece of chocolate. If I like to eat a piece of chocolate once in a while, am I bound to it?

Answer: Please be careful that you don't slide from grace into the law and become caught unwilling in the net of the enemy who would like to trap you with doctrines of regulations. It is much better to keep yourself to the clear statements of the Scripture:
1. Unto the pure all things are pure (Titus 1:15).
2. For it is sanctified by the Word of God and prayer (1 Timothy
3. Nothing to be refused, it it is to be received with thanksgiving (1 Timothy 4:4).
   The things I wanted to say in the booklet can be expressed best with the words of Paul in Galatians 5:13, "For, brethren, ye have been called unto liberty; only use not liberty, for an occasion to the flesh." In other words: do not let yourself be bound to anything except Jesus Christ! To be bound to other things is impossible if you keep in mind the three rules mentioned above. Then you will remain under the protection of Jesus Christ and you can have everything, but nothing can have you!

Beat Music and the Gospel

B.R. in O.: I know a group of young people who sing very appealing words to Beat Music and other loud music. In between, the Word of God is preached, testimonies are given and prayers are said. This Beat Music attracts very many teenagers. But the reason for my writing is the following: Beat Music — Jesus Christ. Does the answer which Moses gave Pharoah also apply here, "That is no use?"

Answer: Beat Music came into fashion with the Beatles, in England. It would be superfluous to elaborate on its devilish source. The Beatles have had millions of teenagers in their sway which has resulted in many frightful orgies. The use of Beat Music in the furtherance of the Gospel seems to us to be an unsanctified mixture of holy with unholy. We disagree with the maxim, "the end justifies the means." And even though certain record publishers, i.e. missionary societies, are increasingly using this style, this awful development is on a level with the words of Isaiah 1:5. But the Lord has no pleasure in those that draw back, compare Hebrews 10:38.

Television

X.Y. in Z.: We have inherited a television set. In the beginning I was against it and feared the dangers. Then I relented, not wanting to become a tyrant in the house as my wife and children, three of whom are grown-up already, were looking forward to it. I could not always keep to my decision to stay away from the T.V. screen, but even though I seldom watched it, I always had a guilty conscience afterwards and was aware that I had made a mistake. The results were soon apparent. There was friction between my wife and me and we began to have trouble with our school children. It was worse during the holidays when our daughter and son-in-law also came to watch. Evening after evening they watched the television programs, together with my wife and children. Usually I went to bed but I could not sleep and was annoyed with the group of viewers and myself for having given in . . . When one watches television on Saturday evening until the early hours of the morning it is difficult to get up on Sunday morning and so they miss the church service. I could give you many such examples. My wife once asked me as we were discussing the subject whether I would prefer our son to go to the cinema . . . In this way, at least he is at home. It is obvious that the television set must be removed so that peace can return to our home, but how to do this I do not know. Please can you advise me?"

Answer: Satan has indeed caught you in his net, but let me say right at the start: Jesus is Victor!
We know that firstly, television becomes an addiction, then it violates public opinion and is therefore character destroying and it disrupts families. Young children are in particular danger. Recently a teacher asked one of his pupils, "Have you been receiving additional tuition? Your work has become so much better lately!" The pupil answered, "No — but our television has been broken for a few weeks." There are innumerable families in the same situation as yours today, families in which children who are hardly of school age go and turn on the television of their own accord without asking permission of their parents and watch any program they like. In just as many families children are permitted to view for only half an hour or an hour each day regardless of what is being shown. People are of the stupid opinion that children do not take it seriously and soon forget things, but the soul of a child can be irreparably damaged by what enters and if even television directors have their doubts, such as Dr. C. Munster of the Bavarian Broadcasting Company who stated in a German newspaper, "It is pedagogic nonsense

to sit a child under eight or ten years of age in front of the T.V. screen," how terrible must it be in reality! Dr. A. Weber of the University Clinic in Zurich ascertained that television does not meet a child at its level of development. The so-called childrens' programs do not alter this. Are there television diseases? There are many reasons to believe that headache, backache, eyestrain and even circulation disturbances and epileptic fits can be caused by television. Most of the information contains references to signs of nervousness in all age groups. The symptoms are as follows: tendency to irritation, inability to concentrate, easily distracted, inconsistency in carrying out of work, difficulty in going to sleep and sleeping through the night. According to a report by the Children's Clinic in Dortmund, Germany, television can lead to overexcitement accompanied by fits of temper and screaming. By far the most frequent complaint, however, is disturbed sleep; inner tension can result in nightmares, apart from the harmful rays. In a test made in the U.S.A. it was found that 20% of the 5,000 tested color television sets produced rays which exceeded the safety limit. Health insurance premiums in America will soon cost 5-15% more for owners of television sets. It is no wonder that these harmful results which we have only touched upon briefly here are being brought to light. The television set is actually nothing other than a sort of family altar in front of which the whole family sits, from the oldest to the youngest. Does it not remind one of Deuteronomy 27:15 and Ezekiel 8:12?

All this, my dear brother, you are now experiencing in all its bitterness. What should you do now? Your house has become a television house; every morning it is weirdly dead, and out of one room only shimmers a bluish light. There your family sits, old and young, and stare fascinatedly at the flickering screen. What can you do about it? You can no longer speak with your wife properly, you cannot sit down and read and sing together. In many households the work is often neglected and meals not properly cooked; family devotions are pushed aside by the newsreel. This is what the devil's altar does. What can you do??? It even happens that Bible studies have to be canceled because the "Christian" brothers are more interested in a football game which is being televised than in the Words of life. Whoever loves and is captivated by these pictures loses his hunger for the Word of God and therewith the power which the Word imparts. Say "no" therefore to the television and serve no longer the image because all those who serve graven images will be confounded and those that boast themselves of idols (Ps. 97:7). Here we come back to the question, however, as to what **you** can do in **your** situation where the whole family is already captivated in the devil's snare? Do that which Elijah did when the land was full of idol altars: he built up again the altar of the Lord which had been broken down. That was the first thing he did. It was only afterwards that he dealt with the priests of Baal. In your situation you cannot simply take the television and smash it. You must do the following: after supper you must build up the altar in your family again. Open your Bible in a friendly manner and say, "From now on let us read the Bible together each day" (I presume you have stopped doing this), and then say a short word on that which the Lord has given you through the Word you have read. Then continue and say, "Now let us pray together." Whoever wants to watch television afterwards may do so. If you are persistent in this and build up again the family altar at all costs then Satan will retreat and gradually the power which he at present exercises over your wife and children will be broken, for there is no more blessed and victorious atmosphere in a family than there where the altar is faithfully built up. Even if at first it is very hard going this does not matter. Humble yourself quietly before the face of God over your foolishness in letting the television into your home. If you seriously do set up the altar of the Lord again in your home you will one day experience that the television will somehow disappear from your house and the family will no longer gather around the dim, blue light but around the radiant light of the Gospel which we have through the living Word of God. If your elder son still chooses to go to the cinema, then let him go. He will soon see the difference and have an increasing longing to be around the family altar with his family rather than in the emptiness and solitude which meets him there. May the Lord bless you and give you much grace to do it!

Pinball

W.T. in Z. What would you say the Bible says about children of God playing in the bowling alleys or in restaurants? We have some Christian friends who would like us to play with them. Up till now I have been absolutely against it. I believe what Romans 12:2 says, "Be not conformed to this world, but . . . " Am I being too strict in applying this word to this particular question, or do I understand it incorrectly. I have been told that if we are that particular we may not even eat in a restaurant. What do you say to this?

Answer: Are you allowed to play in a bowling alley or not? The question is wrongly formulated. 1 Corinthians 6:12 says, "All things are lawful unto me, but all things are not expedient" (Amplified Bible). Is such bowling expedient or profitable to the Kingdom of God. Are you being a living witness of Jesus Christ when you are killing precious time in this way? What end does this means have? I fear that your Christian friends do not know the Lord Jesus very well, who said, "I am come that they might have life and have it more abundantly." When I am away from home and go to a hotel or a restaurant for a meal this is quite reasonable because my body needs nourishment. If I, as a child of God, were to go in order to be like the world, however, the question would arise, "Is Jesus with me? Can I do it in the name of Jesus?" This, my dear brethren, is the only proper compass for our lives, as it is written in Colossians 3:17, "And whatsoever ye do in word or deed, do all in the name of the Lord Jesus, giving thanks to God and the Father by him."

This reminds me of the experience of a farmer who had to make a trip to the city each month. He had a wife who had a child-like faith. One day he took her with him. After lunch when he had finished his business he said, "Come on, let's go to the cinema." "What is that?" his wife asked. "You will see; it is something very nice" was the answer. He bought two tickets and he and his wife entered the cinema. As they sat there and his wife continued to ask him what it was, the lights suddenly went out. So the man said to his wife, "Be quiet! It's beginning now!" "What?" she said, "What is beginning?" "The film, of course!" said the farmer. Then his wife said, "Don't we begin with prayer?" "No, they don't do that here," he replied. "In that case I don't belong here," she said and stood up and left.

We are living in the last stage of the end times. There are still millions who are perishing and we still have not fulfilled our commission to fill the world with the Gospel and there is still no revival. Is not the question of a child of God, whether it may go bowling or not, disgraceful? Instead of asking, "How near can I keep to the world and still follow Jesus?" We should much rather ask, "How far can I get away from the world so that I can serve the Lord even better?" May the Lord give you grace to give Him the answer.

Evolution

W.W. in M.: In our Church we had a series of Bible studies on the Creation. The preacher was of the opinion that apart from Paradise there was another world outside. To my question the preacher confirmed that there were descendents of Adam and Eve and also descendents of primitive people and even further back descendents of a primitive cell (i.e. evolution theory). This statement caused considerable confusion among the listeners. What do you think about it?

Answer: It is obvious that there was a world outside of Paradise

because man was sent out of Paradise by God Himself in order
to work the ground (Genesis 3:17, 22-24). Paradise was only intended to be the starting point for man to fill the earth but all
hogwash about primitive man and cells is pure nonsense and
comes from philosophy without faith. It is shameful that so many
people — not only Church people, but also preachers of the
Gospel — repeat this philosophy and continually thresh the
same straw instead of holding on to the living word of God
which says, "God created man in his own image" (Genesis
1:27). In this way they close their minds to the knowledge of the
glory of God, they lose their originality and become robots of
disbelief. As there is nothing as unspiritual, one-sided and
boring, as tasteless philosophy — similar to a line of factory
assembly belts — they can only offer stones instead of bread.
The whole thing is called "Modern Theology" but a better name
would be "Modern Satanology!"

Yoga and Autogenic Training

A.A. in Z.: It is so hard now for us believers, that's what I am
writing to you about. Doctors, these days, give more and more orders that bring people into bondage of Satan. I think especially of
Yoga and autogenic training which are frequently prescribed and
which spread so quickly through gossip that it is frightening.

Answer: Autogenic training is one of many shades of self-
redemption. It represents the attempt to gain peace through inner
concentration. With this however, the finished work of Jesus Christ
is being rejected. Jesus, the Son of God, has — as the Scriptures
say — made peace through His blood, which He shed at the cross
of Calvary. But because the natural man wants to by-pass the
cross he takes refuge in this autogenic training.
Yoga originates from India. Yoga is an attempt to rule the body
through the spirit and there have, in fact, many successes already
been achieved. **But,** the root of this practice is occult. And Yoga
too, is finally nothing but a way from below to above. God has made
a way from above, to us below through the Lord Jesus Christ.
Therefore, both, autogenic training and Yoga, for the child of God
are to be refused and rejected as occultism.
If you have a difficult time, concerning this, among your co-workers,
then why not do as Daniel did who found himself in similar circumstances and he loved the Lord with all his heart. We read of him
in Daniel 1:8 the following: "But Daniel purposed **IN HIS HEART**
that he would **NOT DEFILE** himself . . ." The firm decision to the
"NO" for everything that is against God has to be made in the heart.
Then you will be able, in all these malicious temptations, to claim
the victory of Jesus.

Adoration of Mary

W.M. in B.: With great interest and much inner gain have I read your book *"20th Century Handwriting on the Wall"* (German language edition ed.) Only one thing did not make me happy; the thing which you wrote about Mary. Thanks to a special experience I found the way to the Catholic Church about 15 years ago. The fact that Mary is the mother of God, chosen by the Almighty, should be sufficient reason to hinder anyone from writing such as you did: "But before the hour had come for Him (Jesus), SOMEONE WANTS TO BRING IT ABOUT WITH FORCE. For we know, how Mary had pushed herself into the foreground ... But when she wants to present herself as mediator ... etc." Concerning the adoration of Mary, I have become a Paul from a Saul, if I may express myself in this manner. Today, I cannot love Mary enough and cannot thank her enough for the great grace she has prayed down on me. She is the mediator, she is the mighty intercessor before the throne of God.

Answer: I do not want to go into a discussion, but for the sake of Jesus I will point out the following to you:
—The foundation of your Mary-worship is as you write, a personal experience. To the question: "How shall a young man cleanse his ways"—which is also true for men and women—the answer is in Psalms 119:9 "by taking heed thereto according to thy word," our feelings and experiences are not important, but God's unfailing Word!
—Please read carefully once the New Testament and pay attention to the fact of how little is mentioned of Mary. Is it not remarkable that in the Epistles, written by the Apostles which are inspired by the Holy Spirit, and present the teachings for the believers, she is not even once mentioned?
—Your statement, that Mary is the mediator and mighty intercessor at the throne of God has no biblical foundation at all. Please read what God's Word says in 2 Timothy 2:5 so very clearly and unambiguously.
For the sake of your soul, I beg you: Come back to the ground of the WORD OF God!

The "Emotional Spirit"

X.Y. in a land ruled by Islam. We have a prayer meeting every week. This week we had visitors among us. The brother who was leading the prayer meeting spoke a few introductory words and then suggested that we should just thank and praise the Lord for all He has done for us. We all bowed in prayer. Immediately one of the visitors began to say continuously, "Preis dem Herrn!" (Praise the Lord), while another said "Glory, Glory!" and a third kept repeating the same in yet another language. A Pentecostal sister, from here, continuously said, "Hallelujah!" and threw herself down on the floor in front of the brethren asking them to pray over her, whereupon someone uttered some sort of a prayer. I myself began to praise the Lord in my heart. But as the noise and disorder increased I could only pray, "Lord have mercy on this situation." As it became even louder it seemed to me to be devilish. (Please excuse this expression!) Such a terrible sort of fear and uneasiness came over me that I could not bear to be among them any longer and with all haste returned home to go and pray in my own room. Once there, I just wept and wept. According to my knowledge this "praise" was not produced by the Spirit of God. Is it possible that it was human, or even demonic? Would it be possible among people who testify to being saved through the blood of Jesus? This is my big question. On other occasions I have been in similar situations, but then the question was about baptism in the Spirit and healing of the sick. In each instance the Spirit of God testified to me that these things were not His work. Could I have mistaken the Spirit's leading perhaps?

Answer: I have taken note of your shocking letter. Where prayer is accompanied by much noise, shouting and groaning it is no longer God's Spirit but another spirit. The Lord reveals Himself in a solemn stillness and that is where the Holy Spirit is at work. You ask if it is at all possible that such things can happen among people who testify to being saved through the blood of Jesus Christ. Yes, it is possible! Devilish lies are always revealed in deceptive ways and are always embedded in a piece of biblical truth. That is why such people, who say they believe in the blood of Jesus, are not crucified with Christ. They do indeed have cleansing from sin through the precious blood, but they still deny the cross in their own lives. They would like their natures to be cleansed, but God never cleanses our natures; He cleanses us from our sins, through the blood of Jesus Christ, His Son. Our nature, the "I," must be crucified with Christ (Galatians 2:19-20, 6:14 and compare carefully Romans 6). This gushing, emotional spirit appears in places where the "I," the flesh, is made religious instead of being judged and condemned. The holy and precious blood of the Lord is often spoken of, yet it is often forgotten that cleansing from sin implies the abandonment of the corrupt life into His death. For this reason there are so very many "Hallelujah-Christians" who shout and moan, and yearn for signs and miracles, when they themselves have not experienced the one actual miracle which God intends, i.e. the actual renewal of the heart; because of this they are enemies of the cross. The proud "I" insists on the gifts of the Spirit as a prerequisite, at the expense of the fruit of the Spirit which is received through grace. Therefore the Lord says in Matthew 7:21-23 that He will have to reject such people. Those who truly bear the gifts of the Spirit are humble people, because they have the fruit of the Spirit and received their gifts from God. Those who truly bear the gifts of the Spirit use them to glorify Jesus. For this reason I would like to urge the leader of that prayer meeting to renounce this emotional spirit from below in the name of Jesus, and remember that Hebrews 10:19 emphasizes that we have entrance into the holiest by the blood of Jesus. Verse 20 says in addition, "By a new and living way, which he hath consecrated for us, through the veil, that is to say, his flesh." Only those who go this living way, go the way of the whole truth and are therewith protected from this infatuating, emotional spirit from below. May the Lord grant you the necessary grace to do this, dear brethren. Wishing you the Lord's blessing.

Christmas Trees, Easter Eggs, etc.

N.S. in H.: I am a bit disturbed that we as believers are making so much fuss about holydays such as Easter; sunrise service, Easter egg hunts, etc. Without thinking about it I used to like it but during the last few years I have something against it. When I wish to talk about it to someone, nobody seems to understand.

Answer: Maybe you think this to be sinful, but I have just no time and energy for things such as Christmas trees, Easter eggs, etc. Many have already taken it as a task to write books, booklets and tracts about this subject. I find that this is sufficient.

Let me tell you a secret: I do not have much sympathy for Santa Claus, Easter Bunnies, etc. For me everyday is Good Friday, Easter, Pentecost and Christmas. Let me express this with the words of Paul, "Thanks be to God for his unspeakable gifts." This same Paul also said "to the clean everything is clean" and he further said "ask nothing for the conscious sake." You see, for this reason I can rejoice when my children are glad and happy about chocolate Easter eggs and I also rejoice with them about the burning candles on the Christmas tree. And when someone comes and hands me, with a very serious and pious face, a tract or booklet titled such as the "Heathen Origin of the Christmas Tree" or "Egg Hunting is Heathenism," then I simply answer 'ask not for conscious sake.' I thank God for His unspeakable gifts for the Lord Jesus who died on Good Friday, rose Easter Sunday, and gave us His Spirit on Pentecost. All the sidelines are unimportant to me. Nevertheless he who rejoices in them, let him rejoice in the Lord. If you do not agree please forgive my position. To the actual and terrible sins of the end-times: Apostasy, worldliness among members, a paralyzing prayerlessness in the Church of Jesus, and other vital and urgent matters, these "Easter" and "Christmas" "specialists" have often little to say. Here we measure with two measuring sticks, such as is done in the Middle East and in Africa. The United Nations for instance, does not move a little finger about the massacre of thousands of people in Uganda by their mentally retarded leader. It also does not move and protest against the killing of thousands and thousands of Curds in Iraq and Persia. But this very same United Nations is upset and gets into an uproar when it comes to the point that Israel dares to request secure borders.

Visions

K.A. in H.: At my conversion I had a vision. My room in which I was lying (I did not sleep) suddenly seemed to disappear. It became real bright and shining around me and a very great mass of people surrounded me on all sides. All of them were dressed in long white robes and had palm branches in their hands and looked at me with shining eyes. Then I saw two angels putting one of those long robes on one person. I only could see the person from behind (I believe I was this person). In this same way I also had other visions. During three nights I had visions which filled me with wonderful joy.

Answer: A very decisive statement in your letter forces me to warn you. You write that you had a vision during your conversion which caused you to be filled with wonderful joy. You did not have this wonderful joy because the Lord Jesus in His eternal grace and goodness had drawn you from sin and guilt and made you a child of God, but, your joy is based on the fact that you have seen and experienced something unusual. This is a very dangerous displacement, for the things we see or feel do not count. What counts is the Lord alone and what he says in His Word! If you're not very, very careful in this point, the enemy will have an open door to your soul. The Scripture clearly tells us that Satan himself can be transformed into an angel of light, and therewith, does as much damage as possible.

From my heart I give you this urgent advice: Renounce inwardly all these visions and hold yourself to the Scripture alone! In this case, a translated warning from Jeremiah 23:28 is valid. "The prophet that hath a dream, let him tell a dream; and he that hath my word, let him speak my word faithfully." In His Word everything is being told to us, what we should know, what we are permitted to know, and we have much reason to rejoice in this fact!

SCRIPTURE EXPLANATIONS

Pearls before Swine

M.Z. in O.: How should we understand the warning given in Matthew 7:6 "Give not that which is holy unto the dogs, neither cast ye your pearls before swine, lest they trample them under their feet, and turn again and rend you?"

Answer: To cast our pearls before the swine, means to give the Gospel to such people, who have heard it and rejected it and are now consciously making fun of it. If you tell someone like this about the love of God in Jesus Christ, he will take this statement and use if for slandering. In this way the name of the Lord is being blasphemed, and the person in question draws additional sin and further judgment upon himself. Therefore, one should not try to help such persons through preaching of the Word but through his daily walk should be a readable letter to Christ to them and otherwise be silent.

Predestination and Man's Free Will

A.G. in T.: How would you explain the contradiction between predestination and man's free will?

Answer: Predestination is a wonderful fact. It is based on God's fore-knowledge (Romans 8:29p. That means that God knew you and me before the foundation of the world (Ephesians 1:4). On the grounds of God's pre-knowledge He chose, or elected us because He knew how you and I would choose concerning His Son. Therefore no one can say "I cannot be saved because I have not been elected." That is why the Scriptures say, "WHOSOEVER will, let him take." And Jesus said, "Come unto me ALL ye that labour and are heavy laden!"
But we should not claim to be able to explain election completely because otherwise we could explain God. We believe though what Spurgeon once said: "As a poor sinner I came to the narrow door on which it said, I am the way, the truth and the life: no man cometh unto the Father but by me. I went through this door and looking back saw written over the inside of the door, "Chosen in Him before the foundation of the world."

Least in the Kingdom Greater than John

B.W. in M.: In our prayer group, we came across Matthew 11:11 where it says, "Verily I say unto you, Among them that are born of women there hath not risen a greater than John the Baptist: not-withstanding he that is least in the kingdom of heaven is greater than he." In answer to my question, why John should be the least in heaven when he had such an important office on earth, our pastor answered that he had not been baptized with the Holy Spirit. I am not satisfied with this explanation.

Answer: In heaven, in glory, relationships are quite different. There the Bride will be presented to the Bridegroom, Jesus. The Bride is the closest of all to the Bridegroom. John the Baptist belongs in another category. He was a prophet on the border of the Old and New Testaments, and the Lord says of him in verse 14, "And if ye will receive it, this is Elias, which was for to come." Let no one detract anything from the unique greatness of John the Baptist.

Maybe the following comparison will help you to understand this better: here in the Midnight Call Mission, I occupy the leading position, but if I visit another mission the least worker there is more important than I, because I have no task in their midst. Certainly John's position has nothing to do with the baptism in the Spirit.

Is John the Baptist Elijah?

B.F. in B.: I would like to know the truth about John and Elijah. According to Matthew 11:12-14 and Luke 1:17 etc., John the Baptist must be Elijah. He would have been born twice as a child. But in John 1:21 John the Baptist answers to the question of the priests and Levites if he was Elijah, I am not! How are the words of Jesus and the preceding Bible verses to be understood?

Answer: The Bible does not support the false teaching of reincarnation, according to which the prophet Elijah was reincarnated in the person of John the Baptist. No, this is never true! The Lord wanted to say with the words "And (if ye will receive it), this is Elias, which was for to come" (Matthew 11:14). He simply stated that John the Baptist, in his task as the herald proclaiming the coming of the King was a clear prophetic stature. For in this same way Elijah and Moses will be the last heralds of the coming King in great power and glory, when He comes to establish His kingdom (Revelation 11: Malachi 4:4-5).

An example: The Lord Jesus said of the bread and wine, "this is my body...this is my blood" (1 Corinthians 11:24-25). With this, He wanted to say, when you eat this bread and drink this wine then you have fellowship with me. In this spirit when He said John is Elijah, then He wanted to tell us that John fulfilled that which Elijah will yet do.

The Cursed Fig Tree

P.L. in F.: I would like to know your opinion on Mark 11:13-21 which speaks of the fig tree which Jesus cursed even though verse 13 says, "...for the time of figs was not yet."

Answer: The unique thing about the fig tree is that its early fruits appear on the new shoots of the previous year, from which the leaves grow, the first fruits being ripe in June. The later fruits which grow on the new shoots ripen in about August. But some of these late fruits do not ripen and therefore often survive the winter and only ripen in Spring when the tree comes to life again. These trees with the unripe fruit during the winter usually keep their leaves. So we see that the fig tree has three kinds of fruit: early fruit, late fruit and winter fruit. It is said that the event in Mark 11:13-21 happened in early April. Therefore it was not yet time for figs, as verse 13 says, — as far as early fruit was concerned. But Jesus nevertheless expected the tree to have some unripe winter fruit on it because it had so much foilage. When He found no fruit He cursed the fig tree.

The fig tree is a picture of Israel which is beginning to awaken to new life in our days. We are looking forward to the time when the vine, the olive tree and the fig tree, all three of which represent Israel in particular prophetic ways, will be full of glorious fruit!

Paradise

M.M. in H.: Generally speaking Adam and Eve were sent out of Paradise. However, in Genesis 2, we read only of the garden called "Eden" watered by four rivers of which the Euphrates is well known. The expression "Paradise" never occurs in the account of the creation. How has it then come into this story? In 2 Corinthians 12:4 it says, " . . . he was caught up into paradise," obviously the same Paradise is meant and expressed here which Jesus promised to the dying thief on the cross. But in Revelation 2:7 we read of the tree of life which is in the paradise of God. Where is that? Is it on earth? Or do trees also grow in heaven?

Answer: Everything that God created on this earth is a shadow of heavenly things. Just as there is an earthly Jerusalem there is also a heavenly one. It is the same with Paradise. The earthly

Paradise was a reality because it says so in the Bible. The Garden of Eden and Paradise are one and the same thing. The heavenly Jerusalem is just as much of a reality, for the Lord Jesus said to the thief, "Today shalt thou be with me in paradise" (Luke 23:43).

It is not a good thing always to try and find out the why's and wherefore's with your human understanding. The Holy Spirit reveals to born-again children of God the glorious reality of the Paradise which God created and which will be re-established in the last times, because God's Word and works remain forever. For instance, some of the glorious signs of the Garden of Eden, (Paradise) are beginning to be visible again in Israel. This is simply because God Himself planted this garden (Genesis 2:8), and what He does remains eternally. You can read in Ezekiel 36:35 about the restoration of Israel and what the pilgrims or tourists will say about the land, "This land which was desolate is become like the garden of Eden . . . "

However, God did not intend that the earthly Paradise should be the ultimate goal for man, for in this garden there was the tree of life. One day man would have been allowed to eat of this so far unknown tree and would have lived forever, that is, he would have been transfigured (cf. Genesis 3:22). Not even the heavenly Paradise is the ultimate glory. The ultimate and highest glory will be when the bride, the Church of Jesus Christ, will be given to the Lamb.

Soul Sleep?

K. in M.: A short while ago I heard a lecture about the mortality of the soul. The preacher said, among other things, "when a person dies, his soul dies with him." Surely that cannot be true, because in many places in the Bible it says otherwise, for instance in Matthew 10:28 "And fear not them which kill the body, but are not able to kill the soul: but rather fear him which is able to destroy both soul and body in hell." Please give me an absolutely clear and definite answer.

They also defined Bultmann as a good and wise man from whom we could learn much but who, according to their attestation was generally misunderstood.

Answer: Now listen to me for one moment — let those who believe in the sleep of the soul sleep on! This meaningless and comfortless gospel is nowhere to be found in the Bible. I can well imagine, that the person who refuses to obey God would like to slide into the state of unconscious non-existence; but death does not mean "dead" but a change of existence. What do such people make of Philippians 1:23 I wonder. Paul says there, "For I am in a strait betwixt two, having a desire to depart, and to be with Christ; which is far better." He does not say anything about sleeping or that his soul would die. But I really find such discussion a waste of paper. Our hope is anchored in God's Word which says, "For we know, that if our earthly house of this tabernacle were dissolved, we have a building of God, an house not made with hands, eternal in the heavens." (II Corinthians 5:1). As for Bultmann — let them go on defending him and his doctrine! Just yesterday from somewhere in Germany I received the news that a certain church fellowship had been disbanded because the young pastor had lent his ear to this wretched Bible criticism. It appears as though Churches and Free Churches today are obsessed with suicidal desires, but despite this the Lord is still building His Church. As Martin Luther writes in one of his hymns, "God's truth abideth still!" We believe unchangingly and unreservedly, that the whole Bible is the infallible Word of God, despite "Bultmann & Co."

David's Sin

D.D. in C.: Because of the counting of the people, thousands had to pay with their lives, for the sin that David had committed. How could a righteous God permit it?

Answer: You are speaking of 2 Samuel 24. Please read carefully, before you come to the wrong conclusions; "And again the anger of the Lord was kindled against Israel, and he moved David against them to say, Go, number Israel and Judah." We see, that, (1). The wrath of God over Israel was not stilled yet. God's rightousness is perfect. It has to be completely satisfied. (Thank God for Calvary) (2). For the deed of David the whole nation has to suffer. This proves the terrible severity of sin in general: One man's sin becomes national sin. One can only prayerfully deal with this question, keeping in mind that WE, THROUGH THE CANCEROUS WORK OF SIN IN US, HAVE NO MORE OBJECTIVE FEELING FOR RIGHTEOUSNESS. Only God is perfect in His righteousness and holiness.

David as king is representing the people before God on the one hand and on the other hand, as a servant of the Lord represents God for the people. They have asked for him as king. He represents them before the Lord. His dealings are the dealings of the nation, and his sins are the sins of his nation. In the reconciliation it is the other way around; the sin of all becomes the sin of one: "Behold this is the lamb of God, which takes away the sin of the world." Just as the whole nation had to pay for the sin of David, now all people can be saved through the payment of the heavenly David. That is Godly justice.

Elder's Qualifications

L.S. in Y.: May a man who has unconverted children be a church elder? Here, some say yes and some say no. Yet it is often the case that the children of such servants of the Lord, although "believers" as children, afterwards go their own way when they get older."

Answer: 1 Timothy 3:4 and Titus 1:6 and 7 make it quite clear: Elders of a church have authority to be elders, only when their children are also believers. The fact that there are elders who have unbelieving children only results in their having no authority in their office. It may well be that such bishops, preachers, and elders can give good service, but the power of their testimony is nullified because of their family relationship. Now we should examine the reason for the miserable family relationships even in the homes of some good and busy servants of the Lord. The answer is that they work more as priests in public than as priests in their own homes. I myself, have 12 children and feel it an urgent necessity to pray with and for my children so that the Lord can fulfill His promise concerning my children. "Believe in the Lord Jesus and you will be saved, you and your household." The genuineness of our authority in public is proved by our priestly authority within the family.

Now, if someone is reading these lines who is a church elder and has unconverted children, he should not become discouraged nor weary of his office, but should rather take to heart the motto, "Most important things first." This means — the most important is the salvation of your own house, and not public Christian activities. Then repent and pray incessantly and then two things will happen: Your children will be converted and you will be newly empowered for your office.

Paul or Matthias — Apostle?

As a result of Mrs. Wasserzug's article **"The Bible is True"** we have received many letters asking how it is possible that Paul took Judas' place as an apostle, when Matthias was chosen through prayer, in Acts chapter one.

Answer: We are sure that Judas' place as an apostle of the Lord was taken by Paul. Why are we sure of this? Matthias was chosen by lot whereas Paul was called directly by the Lord Himself, even as the other eleven apostles. This is why Paul himself claims that he is no less than any of the other eleven, (2 Corinthians 11:5). Let us not forget that it was Peter, the man of initiative, who insisted on a replacement for Judas before Pentecost. The Lord, however, corrected this by His calling Paul in Acts 9.

The unmistakable sign of an apostle is not only that he has seen the Lord (cf. 1 Corinthians 15:5-8), but that the Lord Himself has called him, and not another apostle, not even Peter. The acceptance of Peter's competence to appoint an apostle, through prayer, is rather similar to the Roman Catholic teaching concerning the Pope as God's representative here on earth.

Jesus & the Blind Man

C.F. in H.: In one of your publications you have spoken of Jesus' meeting with the man born blind. In John 9:6 it says, "He (Jesus) spat on the ground, and made clay of the spittle, and he anointed the eyes of the blind man with the clay." You connect clay with his blindness and write, "Only Jesus can help you when, like that blind man, you let yourself be convicted of your uncleanness." In John 9:3 however, Jesus says, "Neither hath this man sinned nor his parents, but that the works of God should be made manifest in him." Therefore the blind man had not sinned. So in this case the clay which Jesus made with His spittle cannot be likened to sin!?

Answer: This apparent contradiction which you discovered is the very confirmation! The blind man was not blind because he had sinned but because he was a sinner. Through Jesus' actions he was to be convicted of the fact that by nature, i.e. from birth, he was a corrupt sinner. That is what man finds so difficult to accept but the Holy Spirit wants to convict us of it. This blind man accepted the fact and therefore Jesus could heal him so wonderfully. The question ultimately is not: what does a person have to do to perish, because no one will be lost or perish because of what he has done, but — from birth — he is lost because of what he is, namely, a corrupt sinner. All sins, wicked deeds, thoughts etc. are merely the result of our innate sin. Some people are morally strong and they manage to make their sinful nature look like a decent life on the outside. But the Scriptures say, "There is none righteous; no not one." That is why Jesus claims in John 3:3, "Ye must be born again." The terrible trouble in our Christianized countries is that the person who has grown up within Christianity without meeting Christ personally puts on a Christian show behind which he hides his un-born-again heart. In this way one goes to church, is baptized, married and buried by the church and goes to a Christless eternity because one has never taken seriously the grave words of the Bible. "Man looketh on the outward appearance, but the Lord looketh on the heart."

Cain's Wife

F.G. in Z.: An acquaintance of mine said he cannot understand where Cain got his wife from. It says that Adam and Eve were alone in the world with their two sons and then it suddenly says, " . . . and Cain knew his wife."

Answer: This is a very old and hackneyed question which is always being asked by unbelievers to question the reliability of biblical reports, particularly that of the descent of mankind from one couple. There are those who doubt for the sake of doubting and these cannot be helped, but there are also doubters who want to know the truth. We shall answer these now. The solution is simple enough: Cain's wife was his sister or his niece who went with him. It does not say in the Bible that Cain found his wife in the land of Nod. Mankind at that time in its original strength, which was characterized by very long life and marked propagative powers, can in no way be compared with mankind today. According to Genesis 5:3, the murder of Abel probably took place shortly before Adam's 130th year of life, because according to chapter 4:25 Eve looked upon the next-born son, as a replacement for the first-born, Abel. At any rate, apart from the two who are named, Abel and Seth, many brothers and sisters followed Cain, the first-born, for it says in Genesis 5:4, "And the days of Adam after he had begotten Seth were eight hundred years: and he begat sons and daughters." We do not need to be shocked that Cain took his sister to be his wife. God's command to mankind was, "Fill the earth." It was much later that the marriage relationship was not solely for this purpose and God commanded that unrelated people should marry; but in the beginning, a marriage within the closet family circle was the only possible and practicable thing. Abraham also married his sister Sarah (Gen. 20:12) and Isaac was expressly led to his relations in order to preserve the holy line. Leah and Rachel were also closely related to Jacob.

Predestined to be Lost?

H.L. in L. When I read Romans 9, particularly from verse 11 onwards, I am very sad. My question is, Are there people who cannot be converted because they are not predestined to be saved?

Answer: You have no reason to be sad about Romans 9:11. The two facts which we are unable to grasp with our understanding remain: on the one hand, God chose us before the foundation of the world, before you or I existed, before we could do good or evil, but on the other hand the Bible says quite clearly in

Revelation 22:11, "Whosoever will, let him take the water of life freely." For this reason, every person who hears the Gospel preached in the authority of the Holy Spirit is capable of saying "Yes" or "No" to Jesus. I know very well that this will not satisfy your understanding which cannot fathom or understand the election of God, but this is not necessary. It does not depend on what you or I understand, but on what the Word says. We know that God determined His election on the grounds of His foreknowledge. That means that God knew before the foundation of the world how you and I and every other person would react to the offer of grace in Jesus Christ. Consequently, it is never the case that a person can not be converted because God has not chosen him. Then the Lord COULD CONTRADICT Himself in 1 Timothy 2:4, "Who will have ALL men to be saved, and to come unto the knowledge of the truth." Does this explain the mystery of the election? Never! Our human intellect is incapable of grasping this. The blessed man of God, Charles Spurgeon, explained this in the following manner: as a poor sinner I came in answer to Jesus' call, "Come unto me all ye that labor, and are heavy laden, and I will give you rest." I stood before the straight gate and read above it, "Him that cometh to me I will in no wise cast out." In faith I pushed my way through the gate, looked back and saw written on the back of the gate, "CHOSEN BEFORE THE FOUNDATION OF THE WORLD."

Feeding the 5,000

H.K. in W. During a Bible Study on John 6:1-15, the feeding of the 5,000, the minister who was leading it explained that a spiritual feeding was meant here and not a literal physical feeding, analogous to the spiritual bread which is spoken of in the second half of the chapter. The minister said, among other things, we should have the courage to explain; we do not have to believe that 12 baskets full were left over. (verse 13) What do you think of this?

Answer: This exposition is intellectual, not spiritual. Your minister, who I do not know personally, is evidently still a natural man and that is why he is obliged to come to such foolish conclusions about John 6:1-15. For Paul says in 1 Corinthians 2:14, "The natural man receiveth not the things of the Spirit of God: for they are foolishness unto him: neither can he know them, because they are spiritually discerned." But if a person does not have the Holy Spirit, he cannot discern spiritually, but at the most psychologically and intellectually. A child of God however, who has experienced and tasted that the Lord is good and gracious, and then has to listen to this sort of rubbish, is deeply shocked and goes away empty. It is sad that there are such "ministers" but it is even sadder that such people are let loose upon the Church of Jesus Christ as preachers and pastors to scatter and corrupt the flock. With all due respect, I would like to say to this minister who, according to your letter, says we should have the courage to explain; we do not have to believe that 12 baskets full were left over, "Please have the courage to give up the ministry because you have no right to it and are absolutely incapable of carrying it out, because you are not prepared to fulfill the primary condition for being a preacher of the Gospel: that is unconditional faith in the Word of God, inspired by the Holy Spirit, and in its original text, infallible. We and many of your listeners have come to this decision; and through the grace of God, and through His living Word, we have become new people. The reason we cannot get any closer to one another in our contradicting views, is that you are cleaving to the wisdom of man. You have just swallowed that which Professors have taught you. Have you ever read what God has done with the so-called results of scientific research? "For it is written, I will destroy the wisdom of the wise, and will bring to nothing the understanding of the prudent. Where is the wise? Where is the scribe? Where is the disputer of this world? Hath not God made foolish the wisdom of this world? By the foolishness in the wisdom of God, the world by wisdom knew not God, it pleased God by preaching to save them that believe" (1 Corinthians 1:19-21) That is why we won't remain guileless in spirit and as it is written in Colossians 2:8, see to it that no one spoil you through philosophy and vain deceit, after the tradition of men."

"Whosoeateth My Flesh..."

G.K. in R.: In the Gospel of John, Chapter 6 Jesus says that He is the bread of life, and "Whoso eateth my flesh, and drinketh my blood, hath eternal life; and I will raise him up at the last day" (Verse 54).

The bread of life is Jesus Himself and His blood He has given as a sacrifice for our sins. These we should take to us like food and drink for our bodies. Four times the Lord says that who does this, him will He raise up on the last day.

How can this be understood in connection with the rapture? When is the last day? When is the rapture to take place? I picture the last day as the end of the world and the last judgment is before the great white throne, where people of the second resurrection receive judgment. At this point the rapture and the first resurrection should have long taken place?!

Answer: When the Lord JESUS SAYS, "Whoso eateth my flesh, and drinketh my blood," then it has a very deep meaning. He does not mean this in terms of matter, for in John 6:63 He says, "It is the Spirit that quickeneth; the flesh profiteth nothing: the words that I speak unto you, they are spirit, and they are life." For that reason God sent His Son into the sinful flesh, "for what the law could not do, in that it was weak through the flesh, God sending his own Son in the likeness of sinful flesh, and for sin, condemned sin in the flesh" (Romans 8:3). So when Jesus says "Whoso eateth my flesh,..." then this means that I accept judgment over my sinful flesh — "I am crucified with Christ" — and — "whoso drinketh my blood..." — His blood is His poured out life — this is the payment for my sins. His judged flesh puts my sin, my temperament out of power. His precious blood cleanses me from all my sins and my transgressions. When now the Lord further states, "...and I will raise him up at the last day" then we must remember that the Lord mentions many times different, far removed happenings in one breath. So for instance through the Old Testament prophets, who have seen and told of the first and second coming of Jesus as one. The same we can see with the prophetic Word about Gog and Magog; both are, by the way, expressions for nations living in rebellion. With Gog and Magog, first of all, the Soviet Union is meant (Ezekiel 38 and 39). Concerning the history of salvation, this is not of importance, especially since the Lord is not returning at the downfall of Russia and her satellites. He will return at the beginning of the anti-Christian kingdom with the Antichrist leading. The beast and the false prophet will be thrown into the pool of fire then. In this sense, the rebellious nations under the leadership of the Antichrist have prophetic and historical significance. Then — after the Millennium — the expression Gog and Magog return (compare Revelation 20:8) when Satan i.e. the dragon will be thrown into the fiery pool and is united with the beast and the false prophet in eternal damnation.

So we can see, that it is a principle of God to interrupt the history of salvation again and again. This can also be clearly seen in Israel. Israel of today, is the same as Israel 2000 years ago, it was dispersed into all the world. But Israel as a nation in the history of salvation is the same, in spite of the different periods of thousands of years. The first and second coming of the Lord Jesus and the second step of His second coming in great power and glory is in the eyes of God ONE. In the same sense is the "day of the Lord" to be understood. It consists of a period of judgments. Or let us consider "the last days" (compare Acts 2:17a), which began 2 thousand years ago on the day of Pentecost, yet still waiting for the final fulfillment. Let us compare Hebrews 1:2a, "Hath in these last days spoken unto us by his Son . . . " This period of last days will be completed with the return of the Lord Jesus.

This is also true for "the last day." In my opinion this day consists of the judgment of the children of God at the first resurrection (2 Corinthians 5:10, 1 Corinthians 3:11) the different final judgment of humanity, the judgment of the nation (Matthew 25), and finally the judgment of the "dead, small and great," before the great white throne judgment Revelation 20:12).

Sins — Forgiven & Unforgiven

R.E. in L.: May I also ask a question? According to 1 John 1:7-10 every sin can be forgiven to man. Then how is 1 John 3:15 to be understood, where it says, that no murderer has eternal life abiding in him?

Answer: The one, who reads the Bible superficially only, will always find contrarities, but there are no contrarities in the Bible. We can be cleansed from **all** sins by the blood of Jesus. But when a murderer remains a murderer by hardening his heart, there is no cleansing from sin and therefore has also no eternal life. Simple, isn't it? One only needs to approach the Word of God with a prayerful heart, then much that is dark becomes light and clear.

Book of Life/Book of the Lamb

M.M. in B.: Please explain the meaning of the "Book of Life" and the "Book of the Lamb."

Answer: The Book of Life is the book in which all the names of all people are written in. "For it is God's will that all men will come to the knowledge of truth" (1 Timothy 2:4). They, however, whose names will not be found in the book of life are those whose names have been eliminated.

Moses is a man who had such an exceptionally priestly attitude that he even said to God "Blot me out of thy book." And Paul too said, "For I could wish that myself were accursed from Christ for my brethren; my kinsmen according to the flesh." (Romans 9:2). For that simple reason, we who believe on the Lord Jesus, let us rejoice that our name is written in the Book of Life, as He Himself has told us (Luke 20:2).

Dear Reader, whoever you are, the answer to the question: if your name is written in the Book of Life, is vitally important and is urgently necessary. It is actually frightening how many people consciously ignore the most terrible and shocking message the Bible predicts for those whose names are not found in the Book of Life (Revelation 20:15). How very important it is therefore to render one's life totally to Jesus, so that your name will not be blotted out of the Book of Life.

Transubstantiation — Immortality of Soul

G.P. in S.: I would like to ask you your opinion on the following subjects: 1. transubstantiation and 2. the immortality of the soul.

Answer: Regarding transubstantiation, this is a term used in the Roman Catholic Church which means "the conversion of the eucharistic elements into the body and blood of Christ." This idea is based on a grave mistake, however. If transubstantiation were a fact, this would actually mean that upon every occasion of the celebration of Holy Communion, Jesus Christ would be crucified afresh (Hebrews 6:6). From the Scriptures, however, we know that He entered in **once** into the holy place, by His own blood, having obtained eternal redemption for us (Hebrews 9:12). The Roman Catholic Church, as also some Protestant churches including the Lutheran Church, base their doctrine transubstantiation on the statement of our Lord in Matthew 26:26 where, referring to the bread, He says, "Take, eat; this is my body." Then, with reference to the wine, He says, "Drink ye all of it; for this is my blood" (v. 27-28a). To assume that this means that the bread is transformed into the body of Jesus and the wine into His blood, is to be completely in error. The Lord also said, "**I am** the Good Shepherd — **I am** the Door — **I am** the Vine, etc." By means of these examples He wants to show us what He is in His innermost being. If the Lord's Supper is not a process of transubstantiation then, what is it? According to 1 Corinthians 11:25, it is celebrated in remembrance of the Lord's death until He comes again.

To come to your second question, the soul is indeed immortal. The opponents of this completely biblical doctrine maintain that the words "immortal soul" do not occur in the Bible. This is not necessary, however, because the important thing is that the immortality of the soul is **taught** by the Bible. Just one statement of our Lord may suffice, "Fear not them which kill the body, but are not able to kill the soul" (Matthews 10:28). The Lord is saying how clearly and unmistakably that if the body is killed the soul cannot be destroyed. When we offer this biblical argument, however, there are those who say, "Indeed, the soul is not destroyed, but it sleeps; it is in a state of unconsciousness until the day of the resurrection." This, however, is also untrue, for Paul says, "We know that if our earthly house of this tabernacle were dissolved, we have a building of God, a house not made with hands, eternal in the heavens" (2 Corinthians 5:1). The Lord Jesus also says nothing about sleep to the dying thief on the cross, but says to him, " . . . Today shalt thou be with me in paradise." Such clear statements of the Scriptures contradict the doctrines of the sleep of the soul as also the death of the soul.

"He That Is Not Against Us Is For Us"

S.E. in T.: How can someone do great deeds in the name of Jesus and yet not be known of Him? (Matthew 7:22). Please compare also Mark 9:38-30, where John said to the Lord, "Master, we saw one casting devils in thy name, and he followeth not us: and we forbad him, because he followeth not us." But Jesus answered, "Forbid him not: for there is no man which shall do a miracle in my name, that can lightly speak evil of me. For he that is not against us is on our part."

Answer: The deeds done in His name were signs of the beginning of God's kingdom on earth. For that reason the Lord Jesus clearly said, "no man which shall do a miracle in my name, can lightly speak of me."

In His statement, in Matthew 7, the Lord adds another dimension of miracles. He goes one step beyond the signs of the kingdom of heaven. Those signs, which were based on the Law, were done through the Church and were done to fulfill the Old Testament. The Lord emphasizes this continuously to His disciples, in that He teaches them **more** and **deeply**. Compare John 16:12, "I have yet many things to say unto you." He is speaking of the things which will happen after Pentecost and will be a necessity, namely the fruit of the Spirit. Compare Galatians 5:22. On such occasions the Lord Jesus often gave the disciples a preview of the things to come. For instance in John 7:38, "He that believeth on me, as the scripture hath said, out of his belly shall flow rivers of living water." This was a preview of the things to come, which is proven also by the next verse, "But this spake he of the Spirit, which they that believe on him should receive: for the Holy Ghost was not yet given; because that Jesus was not yet glorified." Another example is John 14:12 where He, with a prophetical view describes the uncounted multitude who throughout the coming centuries will believe in Him and collectively will do greater works than He was able to do through His disciples. "Verily, verily, I say unto you, He that believeth on me, the works that I do shall he do also; and greater works than these shall he do; because I go unto my Father" (John 14:12).

Summarizing, I would like to emphasize with great earnestness that Matthew 7:22 is valid especially for our time, for the time of the Church, for the endtime, because now the time of the fruit has come (Matthew 21:34).

Upon This Rock

I.W. in N.: What is the meaning of Jesus' statement in Matthew 16:18, "Thou art Peter and upon this rock I will build my church"? The Catholic Church bases its election of the Pope on this verse.

Answer: Just preceding this verse Peter answers to the question of the Lord Jesus, who He is, "Thou art the Christ, Son of the living God" (Matthew 16:16). Then the Lord says in verse 18, "Upon this rock I will build my church." In no way does this mean that the Lord will build His church upon the person of Peter, but very obviously on his confession, **"You are Christ."** For He is the precious selected cornerstone, the foundation of the prophets and the apostles, Jesus Christ Himself (See Ephesians 2:20-22).

On the grounds of this false interpretation of Jesus' statement the entire Pope-hierarch of the Roman Catholic Church was established, and as always one mistake is followed by another. For instance, the infallibility of the Pope, the Pope's claim to be the representative of Christ, etc. Then the calling upon, or prayer to deceased saints is another of the many strong deceptions which this church is practicing for almost 2,000 years and will continue to play its role in the end times of the anti-Christian period (Compare 11 Thessalonians 2).

Casting Out Demons

R.S. in Rumania asks what the position is today regarding the laying on of hands and the casting out of demons. Her husband is much troubled in this respect.

Answer: The Scriptures say that we should not be hasty in the laying on of hands (1 Timothy 5:22). Moreover the laying on of hands is only for the sick in body, and this in faith that the Lord at the moment of the laying on of hands meets and blesses the sick person. On the other hand, it is a great mistake to lay hands upon demon-possessed people. The Lord Jesus never did this, but with authority He commanded demons to go out of the possessed person, and He only laid His hands upon the sick. If your husband has acted wrongly in this respect, and for this reason is so troubled, he should on his knees renounce in the name of Jesus every stain on his spirit from this evil power resulting from unbiblical laying on of hands. At the same time he should give thanks for the precious blood of Jesus which sanctifies and purifies him.

Jesus — Holy Trinity — Witnessing

F.A. in N.: I have many biblical questions to ask you. They are: (1) in John 1:1-3, we read that Jesus Christ is God, but in verse 14 (and some other verses in the Bible) we read that Jesus Christ is "the only begotten Son of God." How can God be the Son of God? (2) What is your opinion on the Holy Trinity, that is, God the Father, God the Son, God the Holy Spirit? I understand that They are not three Gods but three in One. Please explain. (3) Was Jesus Christ created? (4) Are Christians commanded to preach from house to house? According to the Jehovah's Witnesses, it is compulsory to preach from house to house. Is this true?

These are very important questions which everybody will like to know. I am very anxious to know more about Jesus Christ our Lord.

Answer: Thank you for your letter. To answer your questions — (1) In 1 Timothy 3:16 we are given a very clear answer although completely unsatisfactory for our human understanding, "And without controversy great is the mystery of godliness: God was manifest in the flesh, justified in the Spirit, seen of angels, preached unto the Gentiles, believed on in the world, received up into glory." Also 2 Corinthians 5:19, "God was in Christ, reconciling the world unto himself . . . ", or John 14:9, "He that hath seen me hath seen the Father." Simply because it is humanly speaking inexplicable people do not want to believe this mystery. We, however, accept and believe the statements in the Scriptures, and are "Looking for that blessed hope, and the glorious appearing of the great God and our Saviour Jesus Christ" (Titus 2:13).

(2) The same applies to the trinity of God — God the Father, God the Son and God the Holy Spirit — but one God. If I could explain this I would be able to explain God and whoever could explain God would Himself be God. The church father, Augustine, thought about this matter for a long, long time until it became a real problem to him: how can I understand the trinity of God? One day he was walking along the beach and saw a small boy going back and forth to the water's edge filling his bucket with water from the ocean and then emptying it into a hole which he had dug in the sand. He asked the boy, "What are you trying to do, my boy?" He answered, "I'm trying to empty the ocean!" Augustine suddenly realized that he was trying to do exactly the same. He said to himself, "I am trying to fathom out the unfathomable ocean of God's Being." And then he just praised God!

(3) No! This is the teaching of the Jehovah's Witnesses but it is not biblical. From eternity Jesus was the Son of God who was actively present at the creation of the world, as the eternal Word, compare John 1:1-4 and 14. The trinity of God created the world in that the Holy Spirit moved over the earth that was WITHOUT FORM AND VOID (Genesis 1:2), in that God the Father decided to make a new creation and finally in that God the Son, the Word, said, "Let there be light: and there was light" (Genesis 1:3-4). Concerning this act of creation you should also carefully compare Colossians 1:15-16. This is why Jesus, when He was here on the earth, said of Himself, "Verily, verily, I say unto you, Before Abraham was, I am" (John 8:58).

(4) No! The gifts and tasks of the individual members of the body of Christ are absolutely varied. Colportage work is one type, one method of evangelization, but there are many other methods. There is no scriptural proof that we should go from house to house.

I hope that I have answered your questions satisfactorily and wish you the Lord's blessing.

Sons of God (Genesis 6)

X.Y. in Z.: I still don't understand who the sons of God were in Genesis 6.

Answer: You must read Genesis 6:2 very carefully. It says, "The sons of God saw the daughters of men . . . " If the sons of God had been human beings it would not say "the daughter OF MEN." The difference in these two expressions tells us that these sons of God in Genesis 6 were FALLEN ANGELS. They are exactly the same beings as those mentioned in Job 1:6. These were also not human beings but angels.

"Snare"

L.T. in M. I have always wondered what a "snare" is, because Jesus uses the word in Luke 21:35.

Answer: A snare is a concealed, purposefully placed rope on the ground or else a sudden and cunningly thrown noose, used to catch animals. The Lord used this picture in the text you quoted, "For as a snare shall it (i.e. the day of the Lord) come on all them that dwell on the face of the whole earth"; that means — as unexpectedly and inescapably as animals are caught in a snare, in the same way, carnally minded people who have lost their love for the truth will be overtaken in their confidence, and surprised by the appearing of Jesus Christ when He comes to judge them.

Sin Unto Death

E.S. in O.: In 1 John 5:16 we read, "If any man see his brother sin a sin which is not unto death, he shall ask, and he shall give him life for them that sin not unto death. There is a sin unto death: I do not say that he shall pray for it." By his last sentence the question arises; by the *sin unto death,* does he mean the sin against the Holy Spirit, for all other sins can be forgiven?

Answer: Here it definitely does not speak about the sin against the Holy Spirit. But there is a sin unto death for children of God. It occurs when death takes them away, that is, *the unfruitful branches.* They lose their life. Such can be caused by the sin of fornication. If the believer in question, in spite of warning will not cease to commit this sin, or by unceasing and continuous slander of brethren or servants of God, then such sins can become *sins unto death.* In such cases only the Lord knows the moment when this sin has become a *sin unto death.* In certain cases the Apostle Paul did not pray anymore for such people, but in Apostolic authority gave over their bodies to Satan in order that their souls be saved (1 Corinthians 5:5; 1 Timothy 1:20). An example: I have experienced often that on the sick-bed of a brother or sister I had great confidence and joy to pray for the healing of that person. In other cases I was kept back powerfully from doing that. The latter however could have been caused by two different reasons: One, the Lord was ready to take His child home, for he had fulfilled his task on earth. Two, the sin unto death was present and the continued life of such a person on earth would have been a blasphemy to the name of the Lord. In this connection I ask you to read and observe the two above mentioned statements of the Apostle Paul carefully.

"Sin Wilfully"

A.H. in B.: In Hebrews 10:26-27 we read, "If we sin wilfully after that we have received the knowledge of the truth, there remaineth no more sacrifice for sins, But a certain fearful looking for of judgment and fiery indignation." How am I to understand "sin wilfully" in this connection? If we have been overtaken by a sin, we more or less sense immediately that it is wrong, even before we do it, and in that way we "sin wilfully."

Answer: Please note carefully that it says "after that we have received the knowledge of the truth." Most people who sin are aware that they sin but have not the *knowledge of the truth.* That means:

1. They have not recognized that Jesus is life to overflowing. They believe more in the lust of the sin than the all embracing satisfaction we have in Him.

2. They have not recognized the truth. Namely, that Jesus Christ liberates totally, for He said "the truth shall make you free" (John 8:32). If however, someone has the *knowledge* and has tasted how good and friendly the Lord is, and in spite of it holds willfully unto sin, then there is no   more sacrifice for his sin. One cannot be converted twice. One cannot be saved twice! That is furthermore confirmed in Hebrews 6:6. That believer will then fall into the judgment of God. Often it is the case that such believers are being taken away before their time was up, so that the name of the Lord will not be blasphemed, but their soul shall be saved (1 Timothy 1:20).

The Lord Jesus also points to this fact in John 15:2. When Hebrews 10:31 warningly says "It is a fearful thing to fall into the hands of the living God," then it lies on the same level with 1 Corinthians 3:15. The believer who sins wilfully loses enormously. Although he himself will be saved (1 Corinthians 3:15), nevertheless, everything he has done in his life will be burned up in the fiery judgment of God. He loses his reward, his inheritance, his crown. He will not be glorified with Him (Romans 8:17). The Scripture throughout, speaks about this *second part of salvation,* (not a second blessing) which the believer can lose, can waste. Salvation, that is eternal life he cannot lose, for that has been given unconditionally and absolutely free on the grounds of the works of Jesus Christ on the cross of Calvary. But the *second part of salvation* is to be inherited. It is that which Hebrew 1:14 speaks of, "For them who **shall** be heirs of salvation." The believer is called to inherit, but through his willful sin he can lose this inheritance.

Someone may now think: "Well, as long as I have eternal life I am satisfied." How dare you think like that! Don't you know that through your worldly attitude and living in the flesh you not only lose the glory of the Lord, but you actually miss God's original goal for you? (Ephesians 1:4). Therefore, beware that you lose nothing which the Lord in His suffering on the bloody cross has accomplished for you! Hold that fast which thou hast, that no man take thy crown!

Hebrews 10:26-31; Romans 11:22

S.P. in D.: How am I supposed to understand Hebrews 10:26-31, especially verse 29 and also Romans 11:22?

Answer: Hebrews 10:26-31 lies on the same level with 1 Corinthians 3:11-17. This text deals with the unbelieving people of Israel, or to be more precise, about disobedient members of the people of God, who were to be punished because they had broken the law. Nevertheless they were still members of the nation of Israel. On this same line lies the **God-child** relationship of the New Covenant. A born-again person is in Jesus and in the Father's hand and no one can pluck him out of the Father's hand. (John 10). But according to 2 Corinthians 5:10 we must stand before the judgment seat of Christ and will be revealed through fire. There is no such thing as a second conversion, but there is, or can be such a moment when a disobedient believer can lose his inheritance, his crown. He will suffer an unspeakable great loss, but he himself shall be saved yet so as by fire (1 Corinthians 3:15).

Romans 11:22 again lies on the same level with John 15:6. We have in the Bible two types of Salvation; on the one hand the Salvation which we can receive without deserving it, through the works of Jesus Christ through faith. On the other hand Salvation is the receiving of wages, the crown, the glory we will inherit through faithfulness (Romans 3:17, Hebrews 1:14). This second kind of Salvation can be lost by a child of God. Hebrews 6:4-8 also speaks about this. That is the reason why the Scripture admonishes us in so many ways to hold on and to remain in Jesus.

Parable of the 10 Virgins

D.R. in P.: In one of your *Midnight Call* magazines you wrote about Matthew 25:9 and according to your statement, those to whom the five foolish virgins should go, were "peddlers," or "false teachers." I believe also that the five wise virgins received their oil from these peddlers, otherwise they could not have told them to go and buy the oil from them. And oil in the Scripture always means the Holy Spirit, which also was needed for the wise virgins to keep their lamps lit. If these peddlers had the oil they could in no way be false teachers.

Answer: In analyzing, or interpreting parables, one must never be catagorical, that is, to say that there is no other way to interpret the parable. Especially through this parable, the Lord is speaking deeply to us and at the same time it has a manifold meaning. In this passage it is clearly revealed that these peddlers were the wrong people, and place for the foolish virgins to go to because they should have been there where the bridegroom was (Matt. 25:10-12). Peddlers (the King James Version has no name for it and calls it 'to them that sell'), are those who deal with material goods in order to make a profit, in this case by selling the oil. And here, I hear the warning of Peter, "Not for filthy lucre," (1 Peter 5:2). This peddler spirit, outside the Church of Jesus, does not sell the true oil, but an imitation.

Furthermore, we have in this a message which the Lord wants to tell us: a tremendous warning on a world-wide basis, not to get the oil from below as opposed to the oil from above, which is the Holy Spirit. Because, the OPEC nations, (today's peddlers), are able to shut off the oil at any moment, which subsequently means the total collapse of the Western industry. The heavenly oil, the oil from above, it is totally different, of which the Lord Jesus later said, "How much more shall your heavenly Father give the Holy Spirit to them that ask Him," (Luke 11:13). Please note, "give," not "sell"! What a treasure, at the beginning of the Church of Jesus He FIRST gave the Holy Spirit. With His son, He, the Father, gave us all things and FIRST His Spirit! He who has an ear to hear, let him hear!

Heroes of the Old Covenant

H.S. in W.: How do you understand Hebrews 11:39-40? And why should they be not made perfect without us?

Answer: The heroes of faith of the Old Covenant have seen, as we see in verse 13, "the promise...afar off" and received satisfying comfort by it. Why was it so? Obviously, the New Covenant had to be established yet! Jesus had to come to carry away the sins of the world! We, the believers of the New Covenant had to be saved yet! This mighty all embracing truth in God's plan of salvation is thus expressed in verse 40, "without us should not be made perfect." God's plan of salvation will "be made perfect" or as another translation says, "completed" not only when the last one will be added to the church, but in general, to the uncounted multitude of the saved.

In this connection it is important to notice that there are many types of eternal salvations, for instance, those who have been made perfect of the believers of the Old Covenant do not belong to the Bride of Jesus, but they do belong to the multitude of the saved. The classification of glory is something else again. It will be processed to the unlimited variety of the glory of God. On this line, 1 Cor. 15:23-24 describes this succession and especially in verse 41. Altogether however the believers of the Old and New Covenant are sinners saved by grace and washed clean by the blood of the Lamb. This is how we see Hebrews 11:- 39-40 according to our understanding.

Wine In "The Cup"

W.P. in G.: I have read your German language publication *Nachrichten Aus Israel* of August, 1978, where you wrote, "He (Jesus) took the cup of wine and said, 'Drink ye all of it, for this is my blood of the New Testament which is shed for many for the remission of sins,'" I am familar with this verse, but find in no place in the Bible that wine was in the cup.

Answer: What was the cup that Jesus used at the initiation of the Lord's Supper? It was the cup of the Passover (Matt. 26:17-21)! Until this very day believing Jews bless the cup of wine and drink it at the beginning of the sabbath. We already see a prophetic illustration in Genesis 14:18 when Melchizedek, the king of Salem, (Jerusalem), brought forth bread and wine to Abraham.

You still may protest and say, but the word wine was not used in the institution of the Lord's Supper. But that is not necessary, for the word "the" cup points clearly to the Passover cup in which wine was used. Moreover, the Lord Jesus adds, after He has given the cup to His disciples and asked them to drink, "This is my blood of the New Testament which is shed for many for the remission of sins, but I say unto you that I will not drink henceforth of the fruit of the vine until the day when I drink it anew with you in my father's kingdom," (Matt. 26:29). Because it is written in Leviticus 17:11, "The life of the flesh is in the blood and I have given it to you upon the altar to make an atonement for your sins, for it is the blood that makes atonement for the soul," and because the Lord has shed His life on the altar of the cross it is absolutely clear that wine is the perfect illustration for its unlimited duration, thus giving us a picture of the everlasting validity of the precious blood of the Lamb.

Baptized In The Name Of?

G.H. in K.: It says in Matthew 28:19, "...baptizing them in the name of the Father, and of the Son, and of the Holy Ghost." But then I read in Acts 8:16 "...only they were baptized in the name of the Lord Jesus." And in Acts 10:48, "And he commanded them to be baptized in the name of the Lord." What is right?

Answer: In the very nature, or substance, there is no difference in being baptized in "the name of the Father, the Son, or the Holy Spirit," or in "the name of the Lord Jesus Christ." It is of no difference, because when baptizing, we are confronted with the Trinity of God. That means, whoever is baptized in the name of Jesus is also baptized in the name of the Father and the Holy Spirit. For that reason the Scripture mentions these two forms (Matthew 28:19-20, Acts 8:16, Acts 10:48).

Arabs

P.S. in F.: Who are the descendents of Ishmael today? Can one pinpoint the descendents of Keturah today? Is the description, *Arabs,* a collective description for all non-Israelite Semites?

Answer: The Arabs are not pure Semites anymore because Ishmael had Egyptian blood from his mother, Hagar. The Ishmaelites are without doubt Egyptian Arabs. The Moabites and Ammonites live in today's Jordan whose capital city is Amman. (Compare Genesis 19:37-18). They are descendents of Lot and are more Semitic than the Ishmaelites, although they are children of incest. The Edomites (Edom lies south of the Dead Sea) are the Bedouins who still live there and are descendents of Esau. These also are not pure Semites because Esau had taken wives from the daughters of Canaan (Genesis 36:2). The Syrians have more Semitic blood in them inspite of the fact that they are the most bitter enemies of Israel. They descended from Abraham's brother Nahor (Genesis 22:20-21). From Keturah, Abraham's second wife, the Midianites descended. They can be traced in the Scripture rather extensively, especially in the book of Judges 6:2. They did unite with the Amalekites against Israel. Amalek again was a specially selected son of Eliphaz, the son of Esau (Compare Genesis 36:12). We assume that the other sons of Abraham from Keturah have spread across the nations and have become assimilated.

The description, *Arab,* is therefore a collective name for all nomadic races. They all have a promise of blessing of God through Abraham (Please compare Genesis 17:20 and Genesis 37:39-40, etc.), but His covenant of promise, the Lord established with Isaac and Jacob (Genesis 17:21).

MORE QUESTIONS

"Why Didn't God Create Only Good People?"

M.P. in E.: A young girl in my neighborhood asked me a question which I cannot answer clearly enough. "Why didn't God only create good people? Surely He is almighty, and nothing is impossible for Him." I tried to give her an explanation, but I would be grateful if you would tell me more.

Answer: God did only create good people, without spot or wrinkle. The answer to this young girl's rather rebellious question is the lofty statement: God made man in His own image! God furnished man with sovereignty and a free will. A will is only free; however, when it can be exercised. Now I hear the reply, "Why did God allow the exercise of the will?" The answer is because He is love! God created in man a being that had the ability to love, and which was to love Him. But love always on a free-will basis. This is the nobility of man. Is it not heartbreaking to read in Genesis 6:5, that when God saw that the wickedness of man was great in the earth, it repented Him that He had made man on the earth? This not only because His love for man was scorned and rejected, but also because He saw the immeasurable sorrow which would inevitably follow. But God's love was stronger than His regret, because God so loved the world that He gave His only begotten Son. Of course we can never understand God, because then we would be God. This, however, was exactly what Satan lied to man about when he seduced him, "Ye shall be as gods" (Genesis 3:5). With this, the circle is closed. Ultimately all rebellious questions are the result of a refusal to humble oneself beneath His almighty hand. You, who ask such questions, are not submitting yourself to Him, but defying Him. You want to make Him responsible. You, who would understand Him with your sin-darkened understanding, I know a better way for you, for thus saith the Lord in Isaiah 57:15, "For thus saith the high and lofty One that inhabiteth eternity, whose name is Holy; I dwell in the high and holy place, with him also that is of a contrite and humble spirit, to revive the spirit of the humble , and to revive the heart of the contrite ones." The place where you can humble yourself, He has shown you: Calvary — Jesus. Here He does not only reveal Himself to you through your understanding, but in your heart. And in wonder and adoration, you will never again ask "why," but "what for."

Heart Transplants

E.H. in S.: Since hearing of heart transplants, I cannot help wondering whether, — supposing that our thoughts come from the heart — the thoughts and character of the 23 year old Denise Ann Darvall were transferred to the operated Washkansky. Is it possible that thousands of years ago man thought that the heart was the center of the thought life, because the function of the brain was not yet discovered? In a newspaper extract from the Hanover Press (December 22, 1969) it said, "Obviously it (the heart) is more than merely a muscle; but it has never been proved that the heart is the seat of the soul." Even if such assertions are made by faithless scientists, it still makes me think.

Answer: Have we not noticed how with every new scientific achievement, man becomes more and more insolent towards God, just as here in this newspaper cutting, . . . "But it has never been proved, that the heart is the seat of the soul." Science and faithlessness march along hand in hand. You ask what we say about heart transplants? "Man's heart is evil from his youth" whether it is transplanted or not. But will heart transplants be successful? Even if from a medical point of view it appears so fascinating and to open up such great new vistas, we still know that God has set man his limits. When he reaches this limit, God calls an irrevocable "stop." In any case it is striking that the first man to receive a replacement-heart, Louis Washkansky, lived 18 days after the operation, which is 3x6. A dog into which they put another heart lived for 18 months, which is also 3x6. How long Doctor B. in Cape Town will live, we cannot tell. At the time of the second heart transplantation, the now renowned surgeon, Mr. Barnard, said that for operations of this kind, in twenty years' time they would probably be using pigs' hearts. When this happens, human beings will be walking around with pigs' hearts. Truly a satanic mockery! Just as space travel is a poor caricature and a satanic imitation of the mighty journey into space which the children of God will make at the Rapture, which will soon take place, so is this exchanging of hearts a distorted imitation of the wonderful and glorious promise in God's Word which the Lord gives in Ezekiel 36:26, "A new heart I will give you, and a new spirit I will put within you, and I will take away the stony heart out of your flesh and I will give you an heart of flesh." Let us beseech the Lord from the bottom of our hearts, that many thousands will come forward for such a spiritual heart transplantation in these last times. With God all things are possible.

Blood Transfusions

G.M. in C.: I work in a laboratory and had to examine the blood of two patients, who were both Jehovah's Witnesses. Now both told me that they, for biblical reasons, refuse to receive blood. Blood transfusions are not permitted according to the Bible, they say (Acts 15:20). The patients remained on their viewpoint and had to be released. Our doctors do not want to take a chance, because both faced a big operation.

Answer: The Bible talks about the EATING of animal blood. It is not permitted to eat this, as for instance in blood sausage. For the reason, mentioned in Leviticus 17:11, "For the life of the flesh is in the blood." I'm sure God does not want to identify the human life with that of animals. The blood transfusions of human blood is however a wonderful blessing of God. I am personally very thankful for that. My youngest son, when he was one month old had to be operated on and his life was saved by blood-transfusions. But above all we thank the Lord for the "heavenly blood-transfusion." Romans 6:23 says: "The wages of sin is death," but Jesus Christ the Son of God, has poured out His life in His blood. Blessed are those, that have part of this holy, sinless blood, through faith, they have eternal life. (John 6:53, 56, Ephesians 1:7, Revelation 12:11 etc.) Praise God for the giving of blood of people to their fellow-man, but eternal thanks and praise to the Lord for the blood of the Son of God, which gives eternal life. In regard to the false teaching of Jehovah's Witnesses it seems to be wasting time writing about it.

Judas Iscariot

M.K. in G. I would like to ask you for an explanation concerning Judas Iscariot for my cousin. Was he really elected by God to go this way?

Answer: The statement in 1 Timothy 2:4 stands firm, "Who **will** have **all** men to be saved, and to come unto the knowledge of the truth." But God knows in advance — even before the foundation of the world — how we, you and I, will react to Jesus, for nothing is concealed from Him. This is why it says in Romans 8:29, "For whom he did foreknow, he also did predestinate." God acts according to His foreknowledge. This does not mean that Judas was predestined for eternal damnation, but it means that God recognized Judas as one who would never continue to follow Jesus. Although God knows from eternity how a person will react in the confrontation with His Son, He still has the Gospel preached. The free will of man is no theory but something very real. For this reason the Scriptures say, "And whosoever will, let him take . . . " (Rev. 22:17). And Jesus calls, "Come unto me all ye . . . " (Matt. 11:28). God, therefore, does not have an election in this sense. When God, on the one hand, as Ephesians 4 says, predestinates people for eternal life, he never, on the other hand predestinates a person for eternal damnation, but He knows in advance when a person does not want to be saved. Thus the call of grace applies to all. "**Today** if ye will hear his voice, harden not your hearts" (Heb. 3:15).

O. T. Food Laws & Beards

O.B. in G.: May I ask you to answer in your Correspondence Column the question, whether the New Testament Church has to keep the commandments regarding food in Leviticus 2, and thus abstain from eating the flesh of unclean animals. A second question: is it the Lord's will that a man who confesses Christ should grow a full beard?

Answer: When we begin to observe the laws concerning food as given in Leviticus 2 we are returning to the pathway of the law. The Scriptures, however, clearly declare that by the work of the law no one can be justified. For centuries there has been much disagreement about this question. On the occasion of the apostolic council in Acts 15 it was first discussed whether or not the Gentiles who had come to believe on the Lord Jesus also needed to keep the Jewish law. Peter answers in verses 10 and 11, "Now therefore why tempt ye God, to put a yoke upon the neck of the disciples, which neither our fathers nor we were able to bear? But we believe that through the grace of the Lord Jesus Christ we shall be saved, even as they." Herein lies the answer to your second question also, whether it is the Lord's will that a believer grows a beard. If a brother feels led to grow a beard, let him do so. This sort of thing has to be a matter of personal guidance. But he must not require his other brethren to do the same, however, because the Lord Himself does not require it. Otherwise we would have to begin keeping the **whole** of the law and depart from grace. But we are told in the Bible to keep the "royal law," "If ye fulfill the royal law according to the scripture, Thou shalt love thy neighbour as thyself, ye do well" (James 2:8). James adds, with reference to the keeping of the Old Testament law, "For whosoever shall keep the **whole** law, and yet offend in **one** point, he is guilty of **all**" (v. 10).

What you need to do is to consider anew the two ways: the

way of the law and the way of grace, in order to be righteous before God and to stand immaculate before His holy face. The first
way makes sin immensely sinful but it does not make anyone
righteous for it is written that no man is made righteous through
the works of the law (Galatians 2:16). The other way leads from
glory to glory in that we receive grace upon grace out of His
fulness. Take time to consider these two ways before you act.

Adam's Skin Color

A.H. in I.: Did Adam and Eve have red, brown, black or yellow
skin?

Answer: God created man in His own image. As I have never
seen this image I am not able to tell you what the first people
looked like! But what **you** look like in God's eyes is the decisive
factor concerning your eternal destination. It is not the color of
your skin which counts, but your spiritual color. Man has lost
that wonderful image of God through sin, and through this indwelling sin his face has become distorted and scarred. Then
God sent His only begotten Son who said, "He that hath seen
me hath seen the Father" (John 14:9). Imagine the overwelming
fact, which millions of people have now experienced — the individual is now able through the conviction of sin by the Holy
Spirit to receive Jesus into his heart as his personal Savior by
faith. At the same moment begins that miracle of retrans-
formation into the original image, into the image of God. And
even more than this, the saved person begins to radiate the
glory of God, that is, the Lamb (Revelation 21). This is what the
Bible calls sanctification. Thirdly, Jesus has not only given His
precious life-blood so that we can be saved from the power of
sin and from its guilt, but in His resurrection we have the trium-
phant guarantee of our transformation. This is what the Bible
says in Romans 4:25. Was raised again for our justification.
Read Romans 8:30 very carefully sometime, ". . .and whom he
justified them he also glorified." Are you already experiencing
this saving process of transformation? It begins, I repeat, with
the new birth (2 Corinthians 3:18, Romans 8:29, and Galatians
4:19). And then on that day when we stand before Him, the
question of our skin coloring will be irrelevant because ". . .we
shall be like him; for we shall see him as he is" (1 John 3:2b).

Call a Doctor? Yes or No?

H.S. in D.: I had a growth and the doctor said I would have to
have an operation. I had faith, however, and did not want to do
this, but the growth became as large as a ball. Years later I am
still in doubt whether I should have taken the doctor's advice.

The pain has come back again. I am not sure what I should do: simply trust the Lord as my doctor, or receive medical attention.

Answer: The Scriptures say, "Whatsoever is not of faith is sin" (Romans 14:23). The Lord leads us in different ways. Sometimes He gives us freedom to trust Him directly in times of sickness without calling a doctor, and other times we have to go to a doctor. After reading your letter I advise you to go to a doctor as quickly as possible and ask the Lord to lead the doctor in his diagnosis and treatment. The alternative is not: Shall I consult the doctor or let the Lord be my doctor? That is misleading. The Lord often helps wonderfully **through** doctors.

Women Laying on Hands

D.X. in T.: I am in the Lord's full time service and was asked by a sick lady to practice James 5 on her (laying on of the hands etc.). I was very much against it because I felt incapable of it as a woman; but the patient never relented till I consented. The lady concerned is much better now and I was strengthened in faith, but afterwards came a defeat.

Answer: You have intervened in an office which is not intended for you. James says expressly, "Is any sick among you, let him call for the **elders** of the church; and let them pray over him, anointing him with oil in the name of the Lord" (James 5:14). The elders do not necessarily need to be presbyters for they are often themselves godless, but it means, call for the **fathers in Christ** who have had experience in counseling others. In doing this you have crossed over a boundary which was not allowed for you. I would advise you to humble yourself before the Lord and ask Him to clean you through His precious blood. God has given sisters ample room in other spheres to serve Him in many different ways!

Oath's Permissible?

E.H. in E. I often hear your radio programs, which are always very helpful to me in my faith-life. May I come to you with a question concerning the Christian faith? Is the oath — that is, to swear by God — permissible according to the Bible? Those who are against it base their views on Jesus' statement in Matthew 5:33. Those who are for it quote such texts as 2 Corinthians 1:23 and Hebrews 6:16 as the grounds for their opinion. What is right in your opinion?

Answer: As far as I understand, the Lord Jesus wants to say to us in Matthew 5:33-37 that swearing flippantly, as it was often

done in Old Testament times, comes from evil and for this reason
He says, "Let your communication be Yea, yea; Nay, nay: for
whatsoever is more than these cometh of evil." This does not include the oath which is taken before authorities or in a court of
law, but merely the abuse of it.

Best Years on Sickbed

I.T. in W.: Now for 5 years I've spent my best years of youth
chiefly on the sickbed. Three times I sought healing according
to James 5:14. Deep spiritual blessing resulted yet without
physical success. I have been bothered by believers again and
again with Isaiah 53:4-5 as follows: "Why not take in faith, what
has been prepared for you, healing, and health," or "Jesus
healed them all..." This and much more reaches my bed. I
only have one wish, to go the way my Saviour finds best for me.
Please give me very openly your opinion, even if you might
have to hurt me.

Answer: It is right and necessary, that we apply the promises
which God has given to us in His Word! You did this.
Repeatedly, hands were laid on you. The physical healing didn't
take place. What does this mean? The Lord wants to make you
on your bed a blessing for many others, in spite of your bodily
weakness. I believe firmly that the Lord even today touches the
sick and heals them, when it is to His own glory. But I know from
experience that our God will not permit us to force Him into a
pattern. There are those which say on hand of the Word: if you
believe, you are healed; if you are not healed you did not
believe. And there are others that say on hand of God: today the
Lord does not heal anymore. He only did so in earlier times.
Neither of these are right, because the Lord teaches everyone
of His children in a different way. He directs them, in that way in
which they should believe. A well known missionary spoke in a
touching way about the need in India: "God searches for
workers in His vineyards. Who will give his life to serve the
Lord?" A young girl stood up. "I will serve the Lord," she said.
At the day of her departure to India she was suddenly paralyzed.
Nothing helped! Now for more than 35 years, she is on the sickbed, but she is a bright light and a great blessing for her
surrounding. Therefore, dear sister, remain faithfully in the
Lord's hand. The fact that you are willing to go anyway, gives
Him opportunity to do with you that which He desires to do.

Head Coverings While Praying

H.H. in B. A brother in the Lord wrote that a woman should
always wear a head covering, especially when praying. He said
that a woman without a head covering is like a harlot with whom

any one may do as he wants. I find this outright brutality! There are instances when it is absolutely impossible to have a head covering when praying. I have experienced this myself, for instance at work, and the Lord has wonderfully helped, despite no hat. What do you say to all this?

Answer: We have already written in the *Midnight Call* many times about women wearing a head covering but I will nevertheless go into it once again.

Paul is speaking about the order in the church; according to our knowledge of the Scriptures, 1 Corinthians 11:15 is the key to understanding this question, where Paul says, "But if a woman have long hair, it is a glory to her: for her hair is given her for a covering." (margin, vail) Whoever thinks otherwise should not quarrel with the sisters or with the brethren but should rather take to heart what it says in 1 Corinthians 11:16, "But if any man seems to be contentious we have no such custom, neither the churches of God."

I will tell you why I am writing once again about this question despite the many previous discussions. All unbiblical doctrines fall into blasphemy. The Universalists, for example, dare to say, "Surely God cannot be so terrible that He would let people perish in hell." With this statement they are blaspheming the Lord. The Jehovah's Witnesses blaspheme the trinity of God. In the above case a brother is blaspheming by trying to enforce his praying without her head covered is equal to a harlot. With this the whole teaching of wearing a head covering is exposed as a deviation from the truth of the Scriptures.

Most of the confusion in the Church of Jesus Christ is caused by such false movements, which want to have the monopoly on salvation. I once heard an "apostle" of the "new Apostles" sect say, "Jesus said 'In my Father's house are many mansions.'" When asked what happens to those who do not belong to the New Apostles, he explained, "many mansions" means a beautiful house and they would belong in there. There would also be barns and stalls where the rest would belong.

I could quote many such things. Let us hold fast to the Head — Jesus Christ!

Try to avoid the "specialists" in the kingdom of God: those who harp on secondary things and do not cling to Jesus Christ alone, the crucified, risen and returning Lord!

Religious Insanity

S.A. in T. Why are there so many people in insane asylums, who fell for religious insanity?

Answer: There are different categories: 1. People who were always demonically bound. As long as they didn't come in touch with the Word of God, these spirits were still. But now they hear the Word, see themselves in its light and are reluctant to be obedient to the Lord. The Holy Spirit works in them but now the indwelling demons become active too. Because these people do not say a whole "yes" to the Lord, their spirit will be taken over by these spirits which means they are surrounded by darkness.

2. There are also children of God to be found in these institutions, who for years resisted the Holy Spirit in a certain area of their life. In other words: they do not want to open themselves to the truth completely and fall prey, to the powers of lies around them. (2 Thessalonians 2:10-11).

3. There are also those which are spiritually bound through abominable sin of their parents and forefathers. Demons have room there, where there is unknown sin, especially sin of abomination, until the third and fourth generation according to the Bible. These people desire to be freed. In this respect, the prayer, which our Lord showed us, should be prayed with more earnesty: "The field is White for harvest, ask therefore the Lord of the harvest, that He send workers into His harvest." Spiritually mature workers know what it means, to free these poor bound souls in the name of the Lord Jesus from these inherited powers (Matthew 18:18).

Does God Send Illness?

W.D. in H.: There are many people who are of the opinion that God never sends illness and cannot hurt anyone, because God is Love and He can only be good and do good to people. I turned to the Scriptures with this question, but came to a totally different conclusion. As I have met with some resistance however, since seeing this, I would like to ask your advice.

Answer: I agree with you: even the powers of darkness have to submit themselves to the will of God. However, the Lord does not command Satan, because Satan was disobedient to God's commands and became God's enemy, whom God conquered, judged and deprived of power, through the Lamb on Calvary's cross. For this reason, God does not command Satan anymore, but allows him to attack us, as in the case of Job. He often allows a messenger of Satan to buffet us in order that we do not exalt ourselves (2 Corinthians 12:7), and so that He can show us more grace (2 Corinthians 12:9). Our obedience of faith, however, is of utmost importance. This is what Paul means in Romans 6:16 "Know ye not, that to whom ye yield yourselves servants to obey, his servants ye are to whom ye obey; whether

of sin unto death, or ot obedience unto righteousness?"
Whoever heeds God's Word, in his weakness, with a willing
heart, and accepts Calvary for himself is obedient. Such a person, Satan has no right to attack, and if he does attack him, then
it is only with God's permission. Whoever is not willing to heed
the Word, however, withdraws himself from God's protection,
which He gives us through His angels which are sent out as
ministering spirits to serve those who are the heirs of salvation
(Hebrews 1:14).

It follows then, that we cannot possibly pray with every sick or
afflicted person alike. Often I have great inner freedom to pray
for a child of God who is afflicted in body, soul and spirit, in the
assurance that the Lord will mightily intervene. Often I do not
have this confidence because repentance is lacking in the afflicted person. To such, applies the Word. "He that committeth sin
is of the devil; for the devil sinneth from the beginning" (1 John
3:8a). To those who follow Jesus though, applies the Word of
the apostle in 1 John 5:18, " . . . that wicked one toucheth him
not." In other words, even if Satan buffets us, he is not able to
touch us, because we are in Jesus' hand and our Father's hand,
from which no one can pluck us.

O. T. Law Today

P.R. in S.: Which of the commandments are crucified (with Jesus) and which of them are still valid in the New Testament?
Most of the religious fellowships say: "We are free of the law;
only the commandment of love still exists." Is this true, or how
should we understand this? We would like to know what the
law demands of us and whether the 10 commandments are still
valid in the New Testament including the commandment of the
Sabbath-day. Does the Sabbath-law have the same validity today
as it did then? Please explain on hand of Bible-verses!

Answer: Let me first of all say this: the law is the written, holy
will of God — and God's will is never canceled, neither are His
demands. But this law is (according to Galatians 3:24) our
schoolmaster to bring us unto Christ, especially since the natural
man cannot keep the law, since he is weakened through the flesh
(Romans 8:3). But then Jesus Christ came and proclaimed: "Think
not that I am come to destroy . . . BUT TO FULFILL." (Matt. 5:17).
He fulfilled it completely and not only that. He also took upon Himself the curse which befalls us — has to befall us because we have
broken the law over and again. Therefore, we read in Galatians
3:13, "Christ has redeemed us from the curse of the law, being
made a curse for us: for it is written, "Cursed is every one that
hangeth on a tree." So, Jesus Christ IN US (Ephesians 3:17) is

the fulfilment of the law. IN HIM, God sees us spotless and completely righteous (Romans 8:1, 30-34; Ephesians 1:6). Under which law are we then, today, if we have Christ Jesus living in our hearts? Answer: "For the law of the Spirit of life in Christ Jesus hath made me free from the law of sin and death." (Romans 8:2) We are subject to the law of the SPIRIT. The Lord Jesus told us, that the Holy Spirit leads us into ALL truth and tells us, how we should follow Jesus. The compass for our life to follow in Colossians 3:17 "And whatsoever ye do in word or deed, do all in the name of the Lord Jesus, giving thanks to God and the Father by him." Because of this Word, we know exactly what we should or should not do. For example: You cannot smoke cigarettes in the name of Jesus, or be glued to the TV set with thanksgiving.

About the Sabbath-question: The sabbath is strictly for the Jews. It was and is a sign between God and His people as we can read it in Exodus 31:13, "Speak thou also unto the children of Israel, saying, verily, my sabbaths ye shall keep; for it is a SIGN between me and you throughout your generations, that ye may know that I am the Lord that doth sanctify you." Under this law, the Jews live TOWARDS this day of rest, but we live ONWARD from this peace which has been gained for us. This also was God's original plan. For man was created on the sixth day, but on the seventh day God rested, so that man's first day on earth was a day of rest. His life started with a day of rest. Now we start every new week with a day of rest: The Sunday, because this was the day of the resurrection of our Lord Jesus. As we read in the New Testament, the disciples came together on the FIRST day, also they broke the bread in the homes here and there on that day. As you can see, this has nothing to do with the installment of the Sunday as the day of rest by the Emperor Constantine. Summarizing: There are two ways to God: On one of these no-one can succeed; that is the way of the law (Galatians 3:11). The other, the only way which really leads to God is Jesus Himself (John 14:6). Only he, who walks this way, comes to the Father.

Baptism For The Dead?

H.P. in W.: Please can you give me a brief explanation of 1 Corinthians 15:29. On this one Word of the Scriptures the Mormons based their whole body of thought of the temple baptism, baptism on behalf of the dead. Such theology can no longer be called biblical, can it?

Answer: There are many interpretations of 1 Corinthians 15:29. But let me say one thing first: it is not always necessary that we can understand everything. According to my understanding of the Scriptures, when Paul said, "Why are they then baptized for the dead?" he meant that the act of baptism is the individual's acceptance of the death of Jesus; this act takes place in front of the gathered Church, which means that the Church, the body of Christ, is a witness to it. According to the Bible there is also a cloud of invisible witnesses around us (Hebrews 12:1). Here too the Bible explains the Bible. If the dead are not alive, if they are not raised, then there is no point in being baptized, also from the point of view of the cloud of witnesses.

Science and Theology

R.E. in B.: By chance your radio message on John 16:22-23 fell into my hands...You preached about something you haven't understood yourself. This proves that when you want to interpret a text of the Bible and preach on it, you must use Theology. In the paragraph; "Jesus is the answer to science" you mention "I will destroy the wisdom of the wise, and will bring to nothing the understanding of the prudent . . ." — This verse does not refer to science, but to people who just want to know everything better and do not want to heed the Word of God which is preached. These are the wise of this world. Those are meant who to themselves seem smarter than the Word of God, who without Christ think they are just as good or better off. Science, however, has to try to discover truth, especially theological science. It is vital in our world today, that preachers receive the right tools to proclaim the gospel rightly. — That the church has been made powerless by Theology, you surely cannot believe yourself!

Answer: Dear Pastor, what kind of Theology are you trying to advertise, the Bultmann's? I hope you know that a majority of German speaking Theology is entangled in the devilish question-mark "Yea, hath God said?" (Gen. 3:11). We are deeply thankful to God for Theologians, who today still believe, that the Bible **is** the Word of God and not just **contains** it. I am surprised over the certainty in your tone with which you mention "theology," which really is no Theology at all but only tries to tear up the Bible. You have to ask yourself too, why there is such a shortage of pastors in Germany? Don't you know the young believers had their faith destroyed completely by so-called Theological studies? Don't you know that it was partly the fault of the Theological science of which you are talking about, that the **Third Reich** (Nazi Germany) came into being? Where was the clear Theological testimony that explained the position of the Jews?

Surely we have no reason to be proud of such a Theology! What is very much needed now is to fall on our knees before the Almighty God in humility under His strong hand. It is still true: there are two different kinds of wisdom, according to I. Corin-

thians 1:19, 21, 27 **The Wisdom of Men,** that if not bound to God,
is empty and dry and produces dead things and **the wisdom of
God.** This wisdom of God you and I need. We will receive it in
the measure in which we subdue our sin darkened mind under
the obedience to Christ. It is given us in the person of Jesus
Christ (1 Corinthians 1:30). In other words: A person starts to be
truly fruitful and wise, not by studying a lot of "modern
Theology" - on the contrary, when he becomes often more foolish
than before and stumbles like a blind man — but when he heeds
what the Scripture says in Proverbs 1:7, "The **fear** of the Lord is
the **beginning** of knowledge." There could be a very educated
Theologian with many theological accomplishments, who is in
the eyes of the Lord a foolish babbler as long as he doesn't
begin to fear the Holy Word of God (Isaiah 66:2) and obey it. You
must not forget that God goes exactly the opposite way than we
do. He gives His wisdom to the simple, as it is mentioned in
Psalm 119:130, "The entrance of thy words giveth light; it giveth
understanding unto the simple." We could say it in still another
way: The intellectual — in your case theological — knowledge
of the Word of God is the same as the "eating of the tree of
knowledge of good and evil," it does not renew a person. It
doesn't free him of the power of sin. It doesn't give the preacher
authority in his preaching, but might only permit him to look down
upon the simple. The heart-knowledge of the Word — that is
Godly Theology — changes a person, lights in him a fire and
gives the messenger of God power in his preaching.

That's why I would like to tell you in closing: I have great
respect for your occupation, for you have great responsibility.
But when you get stuck on your intellectual knowledge, then
your preaching will remain effectless in your own life and in the
lives of your listeners. I plead with you for the sake of your soul,
for the sake of Jesus and the people who hear you: Come from
your intellectual to a spiritual knowledge. Stop at the cross of
Calvary. That is the real study of Theology!

FALSE TEACHINGS

Victims of False Doctrine

B.Y. in Q.: Why are there believers who know the Bible and later fall for false teachings?

Answer: Better let us ask: Who becomes a victim of false doctrine? 1. Believers, who according to 2 Thess. 2:10-11 never accepted the love for the truth. That's why God sends them strong delusions, so that they should believe a lie. An earnest warning for us! When we as children of God will not come into the light before God, we cannot hear the voice of Jesus (John 18:27b) and open ourselves to the spirits of lies.

2. Unbelievers who search for peace but never find it because of the failure of believers around them. These are trapped easily by false teachings. That's why we as Christians have the important task to be readable letters of the Lord, to be read by everyone, so that we clearly point the way to Jesus. I have experienced many times when traveling that some signposts are unclear and they could be read different ways and are therefore misleading. Is your life a clear signpost to Jesus or is it foggy and unreadable because of some secret sin in your life? This is often the reason why so many searching people cannot find the way and fall prey to false doctrines.

Ecumenical Movement

H.J. in U.: You see the Ecumenical movement as a sign of the end-times and of a negative nature, while many true Christians look at it as such of a positive nature. Isn't it true that you view the Ecumenical movement too one sided and too negative, even with an Antichristian aim? How can searching people still find the truth?

Answer: You confuse the ORGANIC unity of all children of God in Jesus Christ (we are the members of His body) with the ORGANIZATIONAL unity of the Ecumenical movement. The church of Jesus Christ is not an ORGANIZATION but an ORGANISM. When this invisible organism of this body of Christ also takes visible organizational forms, then it should never appear in the form where believers and unbelievers are organized together, as the Ecumenical Movement does. — There is a separation that is wanted by God, a radical separation. It is made with all who say "no" to the consequence of the cross (1 Corinthians 1:18). "I am crucifed to the world." Thank God, there are still spiritual leaders in our time, who recognize this danger of the end-time and are strongly opposed to the Ecumenical Movement. Those who believe on the whole Bible as the Word of God and allow no compromise.

World Council of Churches Supports Terror!!!

K.S. in B.: In the March issue you published an article under the title "World Council of Churches Supports Terror," which has caused some unpleasant thoughts in me. I myself have been very critical of the World Council of Churches for a long time, but I cannot simply view a closer relationship with all the churches as negative. During my youth, we were strongly divided between Roman Catholic, Christ Catholic and Protestant who rather fought than loved each other. If these same people today are drawn to a communal service, a change must have taken place in their hearts.

Your statement that the World Council of Churches has become a political instrument of the atheist Soviet Republic is very sad. Whoever goes that far to compare the World Council of Churches with the Soviets leaves obviously no room for discussion.

For years I have experienced that Christ calls His members from all denominations, even from the Roman Catholic Church. Respect and honor towards such brethren and also towards unbelievers is the precondition for a Christian fellowship and to become one in Christ.

Answer: You have obviously not recognized the purpose and goal of the Ecumenical Movement or the World Council of Churches, otherwise you would not have written me such a letter. Do you for instance know that the WCC's leading people, during the Congress of the WCC in Utrecht, Holland have made the following statement: "The Christ-presence is to be found in all religions; Buddhism, Hinduism, Islam, etc.?" In other words Jesus is not anymore the only "way, the truth and the life." Have you not recognized that the Ecumenical Movement in its substance is anti-Christian? And to this you ask us to be silent? Then I would fall under the judgment of the prophet Isaiah who describes the preachers of that time, "They are all dumb dogs." (Isaiah 56:10).

The Ecumenical Movement is the greatest danger of the end-time. She is preparing the way for the Antichrist. Her works will climax in the terrible World-Unity-Church on whose top will stand he who is **instead** of Christ: the Antichrist, the beast (Revelation 13:13-15).

I know too well that the truth hurts, but does it not also make you free? Do I have to be silent out of respect for other people, even if I clearly recognize that the Churches within the World Council of Churches are approaching a terrible destiny? Never!! Even if thousands of people would write letters like you. The opposite is true. It would be a strong confirmation that I must continue to warn of this Satanic World-Unity-Church!

Your statement however at the end of your letter is true. I too have many brothers and sisters within the Roman Catholic Church and other false teachings. They are members of the body of Jesus, they believe in the blood of reconciliation of the Saviour and put their trust in Him alone. We must differentiate this matter between persons: there are good representatives of a bad cause, such as the Ecumenical Movement and the Roman Church, but there are also bad, very bad, representatives of a good cause: the Church of the Reformation.

The New Evangelicalism

P.S. in S.: With horror, I read the paragraph in the April issue with the heading "The New Evangelicalism." I believe your presentation of the New Evangelicals in this article is out of line and does not do justice to the faith and life of the New Evangelical Christians in any way. Since you write the concluding remarks to the presentations of Rev. Oatley Villis, I identify both opinions as one and the same. Assertions are being made which are not proven by examples. So, for instance, it is said that the New Evangelicalism is far more subtle than Modernism. Such a statement in my opinion is anti-Christian and is done in the spirit of judging.

The next problem is the intellectualism of the New Evangelicals. Yes, they do try to bridge the gap between God and world, but not outside of the redemption in Christ. With this, the mind, the intellect, is not excluded, but integrated, for faith and mind do not constitute opposition but they compliment each other. He who teaches that faith and intellect contradict each other makes the Christian faith unbelievable. The intellect only has to recognize its limits. The mind is a great gift of God to man and it would be a shame if we would not put this gift to His use. What you are doing here is putting New Evangelicalism into a wrong light.

Answer: The New Evangelicals do not want to take their position fundamentally against the anti-Christian Ecumenical Movement, even if they claim to be against it. Just recently, a "New Evangelical" brother had to leave the church committee be-

because he took a strong position against the Ecumenical Movement.

You are also infected, as I can see from your letter. Your glorification of man, of man's intellect, is against the teachings of the Bible. Scripture teaches exactly the opposite of what you say. You assert the human intellect has to be united with faith. You say that human thinking supplements the faith. Then you have moved away from the center of the cross. Please read I Corinthians 1:19-21:

"For it is written, I will destroy the wisdom of the wise, and will bring to nothing the understanding of the prudent. Where is the wise? Where is the scribe? Where is the disputer of this world? hath not God made foolish the wisdom of this world?"

This is not New Evangelicalism but Evangelical. Let him who has an ear to hear, hear!

Billy Graham Preaches Jesus Christ

X.Y. in Z.: In a magazine published by Mr. Albert Springer we read with horror that Billy Graham is numbered among the Christian deceivers of the end times!

Answer: Albert Springer's description of Billy Graham is a severe departure from the truth. Billy Graham proclaims, as he always has, the one and only message which we have been given, namely, Jesus Christ and Him crucified. One may question the way he goes about it and the methods he uses, but these are only of secondary importance. Each one of us either stands or falls before the Lord. What Mr. Springer has done is too much hair-raising. He wrote, among other things, "We asked Billy Graham, 'How would you define your calling?' " When Billy Graham answered this question, the full text of which in our opinion was purposefully not quoted, Mr. Springer falls upon this servant of God in a "holier than thou" manner, on page 15, "A true servant of the Lord does not speak about his calling; he is unable to do so because he feels unworthy of it and incapable of fulfilling it." I would like to ask Mr. Springer: why do you ask Billy Graham about his calling, if you do not want an answer to it? However, even worse than this seems to us to be the wicked suggestion on page 16 of his May issue that Billy Graham works with strange powers, that is, those of the other world, and not with the power which comes from God. We are not in a position to be able to answer all questions concerning Billy Graham but I repeat: during the Dortmund Crusade millions of people were presented with the clear message of Jesus Christ who was crucified for us and afterwards rose again. We are convinced that Billy Graham has the task of reaching the people of these end times with the message of Jesus Christ, so that no one can say later that they did not know. Instead of being pleased you take it upon yourself to speak disparagingly of this servant of the Lord, and even without any further proof or details you summarize the matter with one curt phrase: "Our readers can take our word for it." As I think about this it reminds me of the words of the Lord Jesus which He said when speaking of the wicked servant in Matthew 24:28-29, " . . . that evil servant shall say in his heart, My Lord delayeth his coming; and shall begin to smite his fellow servants."

Strangely enough in this same issue of his magazine he attempts to weaken the glorious hope of the rapture through an obvious misinterpretation of the Scriptures which we shall quote here. On page 10 he writes about Elijah's rapture. "Elisha asked that he might receive a double portion of Elijah's spirit. That was unheard of audacity! Had not Elijah brought fire down from heaven; had he not closed the heavens that it did not rain for three and a half years . . . " Then he continues. "To this request of Elisha, Elijah says, "Thou hast asked a hard thing: nevertheless, if thou see me when I am taken from thee, it shall be so unto thee; but if not, it shall not be so" (2 Kings 2:10)." And now for Mr. Springer's explanation. "What is the meaning of these words of Elijah? If Elisha was filled enough with the Holy Spirit he would see Elijah's rapture — and understand. For this a double measure of Elijah's spirit was necessary!" Dear Mr. Springer, do you not see that you are perverting biblical truths? The double measure of the Spirit was promised to Elisha **if he were to see Elijah going up to heaven,** and not vice versa as you say. Your deceptive comments about Billy Graham are similarly incorrect. With this, your credibility is severely shaken. As a preacher of the Gospel you cannot afford to strike other faithful servants of God. This of necessity results in delusion in your own interpretations, as already seems to be the case.

Universalist Teacher

H.B. in B.: For some time I have been going to a house Bible study group which is led by a man who is a Universalist. He does not emphasize this teaching and the study of the Bible is definitely centered on Jesus and Jesus alone. Would you think twice about attending such a group?

Answer: Yes, I certainly would think twice about it and not so much because of the brother who loves and confesses the Lord Jesus Christ, but more because he is spreading a "strong delusion" (see 2 Thessalonians 2:11), which as we see with our own eyes has done the Church of Jesus Christ endless damage.

Paul warns us expressly concerning this in Colossians 2:18, "Let no man beguile you of your reward in a voluntary humility and worshipping of angels, intruding into those things which he hath not seen, vainly puffed up by his fleshly mind." With the teaching of aeons which makes eternity a limited time, many simple children of God are either consciously or unconsciously led astray. In Revelation 14:11 it says about eternal damnation, "And the smoke of their torment ascendeth up for ever and ever." The Universalists say that this means that judgment of the lost lasts for several aeons, that is, not for ever. If that were so, then the existence of the eternal Son of God would also be limited, Who says in Revelation 1:18, " . . . I am he that liveth, and was dead; and, behold, I am alive for evermore . . . " God the Father, too, would not be infinite. In Revelation 20:10 and 1:18 the same Greek expression is used as in Revelation 4:9, "...who liveth for ever and ever..." Compare Revelation 4:10 and 15:7.

What is the reason that today so many children of God are falling prey to this false doctrine? It is because it is humanly logical and convenient for the flesh. But in no way does it correspond to the whole doctrine of the Holy Scriptures.

Pope Paul "Separated Brethren"

P. in T.: What should be our attitude of Pope Paul's statement that we are "separated brethren"?

Answer: This is just the point: we are the separated brethren who by means of the Ecumenical Movement are supposed to return to the lap of the only life-giving faith, the Roman Catholic Church. Many people let themselves be dazzled by friendly and nice words but they forget that Rome has not changed her false doctrine one little bit. At the last Council every individual priest had to take an oath of faith as follows:

"I acknowledge that during the Mass a truly expiatory sacrifice takes place; effective for the dead and those alive, and in the holy sacrament of the Eucharist the body and blood of our Lord Jesus Christ with His soul and whole Godhead is in truth present. I believe in Purgatory and that the souls who go there are helped by the prayers of believers.

I believe that the saints who rule with Christ are to be honored and prayed to, that they offer prayers on our behalf to God and that we should honor their relics.

I affirm that we should keep, protect and pay due honor to pictures of Christ, the never-changing Virgin Mother of God and the other saints.

I also declare that Christ gave to the Church the power to remit sin and that great blessing comes to every Christian nation which makes use of this.

I acknowledge that holy Roman Catholic Church as being the mother and teacher of all churches. I swear and promise to obey the Roman Pope, the successor of Saint Peter, the prince of the apostles and representative of Christ on earth.

Similarly, I condemn, reject and declare accursed everything contrary to this, including, all false doctrines which The Church has condemned, rejected or cursed. I herewith confess openly The Catholic faith without which no man can be saved. I promise to keep this faith pure and unadulterated until the day of my death."

So much for the "Oath of faith." In view of such a faith, blessed are the brethren who remain separated from it!

Acupuncture

W.X. in Z.: What do you think about Acupuncture of which we hear so much these days.

Answer: Acupuncture is a method of treatment whereby needles are inserted into the body in specific places. It is of Chinese origin and is mentioned in a book written as early as the year 2,800 B.C. Through the insertion of these needles the disturbed equilibrium of the body is supposed to be righted. Acupuncture is scientifically speaking absolutely unfounded. Neither the energy centers, the so-called "life energy Ki" nor the "king channels" in which the energy of life is supposed to circulate have ever been proved. The doctrine of Acupuncture, however, is completely rooted in the religion of ancient China.

On radio I heard the voice of a man who had his tonsils removed painlessly through Acupuncture. It was most obvious that the man was under hypnosis. He answered that he felt well but as if he was in a trance. The Californian Professor Kroeger said, "The only reasonable explanation for Acupuncture is hypnosis, or more explicitly "slow-motion-suggestion-hypnosis." This is also in accordance with the various experiences, for instance:

—

1. Each Acupuncture school inserts needles in different places and according to different rules. This has no effect on the success or failure.

2. Serious illnesses, infections or cancer, for instance, remain uninfluenced. Improvement is cited mainly in the case of diseases which have a nervous origin. It has been proved that wherever witchcraft and sorcery are concerned, people who are taken ill through occultism can also be healed by means of occult practices, whereby they become even more satanically bound.

3. Acupuncture does not work on children, although all important nervous functions are present at the age of five years.
4. The doctor practicing Acupuncture must also believe in it, the more skeptical the doctor or patient is towards the method, the more seldom a successful result is obtained.

These few points should suffice for God's children to see that we are concerned here with a heathen, demonic practice. In the Antichristian time in which we are living occultism is making itself felt in ALL SPHERES of life in order to prepare the way for the revelation of the Antichrist. "Even him, whose coming is after the working of Satan with all power and signs and lying wonders" (2 Thessalonians 2:9).

"God Does Not Exist"

H.S. in H.: I read the following article in a German newspaper (*Pfalzner Merkur*).

Theologian in Mainz: God does not exist. Nuremberg, Dr. Manfred Mezger, Professor of Theology, made a vehement attack on the traditional concept of God in the Evangelical Student Center of the "Holy Spirit." During his lecture, which was entitled "The Language of Faith Today," he compared the concept of "God" and "Holy Spirit" with a "currency which actually has long since ceased to be covered." The radical way of thinking of our day questions the existence of a mighty God in another world. It is the task of present day Theology, therefore, to make God explicable.

Mezger explained that the Christian picture of God in the past can no longer be accepted. "The lake of Constance exists and Himalaya exists, but God does not exist." All conceptions of God, however pious and reverent they may be, must disappear. The holy vocabulary of the Church and the cult of the language of the pulpit must be revised. The biblical statements concerning the resurrection of the dead, the last trump and the rapture in the air are regarded by this theologian in Mainz as expressions of a bygone concept of the world, which can be done away with today. The prophecy of the Revelation of St. John he compared with horoscopes or romantic films in which "everything is promised" and "everything is an illusion." The Christian hope for the future is revealed for the scientist on the other hand, in a quiet composure in being responsible for the present and not worrying about the future.

What do you think of all this?

Answer: Firstly, a church must be in a miserable and shocking state to allow such a man to speak on such matters.

Secondly, it seems almost blasphemous that he delivered his

scornful speech in the Evangelical Student Center of the Holy Spirit.

Thirdly, although this Mr. Mezger has acquired the titles of Doctor and Professor of Theology, the Bible describes him as a fool, "The fool hath said in his heart, There is no God" (Psalm 14:1). "Professor of Theology" may sound very impressive to simple people, but the Word of God tears this imposing facade away and says, "Professing themselves to be wise, they became fools" (Romans 1:22). And yet this speech is not only blasphemous to every believer, but also very revealing, for Dr. Manfred Mezger lays bare his inner emptiness in that he thinks he is being intellectual when he compares the Holy God and the Holy Spirit with a currency which has long since ceased to be covered. We can well understand that this is the case in your life, Dr. Mezger, because the natural man — such as you are — "receiveth not the things of the Spirit of God: for they are foolishness unto him." But there are millions of people, and by the grace of God I am one of them, who through the living God who lives from eternity to eternity, have been born again to a living hope through the resurrection of Jesus Christ from the dead.

As Elijah the prophet stood before the godless king Ahab, he said in 1 Kings 17:1, "As the Lord God of Israel liveth . . . " This God, who lives, has inseparably linked his name with the name of Israel. Whoever cries "God is dead" is an enemy of God and is inevitably an enemy of Israel. The rejection of the Son of God took place firstly through the religious authorities in the person of Caiaphas, the high priest. Afterwards the worldly authorities, in the person of Pilate, had Him executed. The liberal Theology of thirty years ago, which was mild in comparison with that of our day preceded the extermination of Israel which Hitler had in mind. The cry "God is dead" is consequently, "The God of Israel is dead." And the next conclusion is "Israel must also die!" With this spreading "God-is-dead Theology" the first step has been taken to the final worldwide anti-Semitism, according to the prophetic Word where it says that the Lord will gather all the nations against Jerusalem. And, I repeat, when God is dead, Israel will have no more right to exist. It is relevant that Dr. Manfred Mezger, Professor of Theology, came from Mainz to Nuremberg to proclaim his "God-is-dead theology." Nuremberg is the same city in which Hitler passed the two notorious so-called laws of Nuremberg on the 15th September 1935,which led to the terrible persecution of the people of Israel. Just remember, Dr. Mezger, that there where you recently made your speech, another spoke from the height of his pedestal, the ruins of which were still to be seen a few years ago in Nuremberg. Today you are saying, "God is dead." Before you, the one who hated the

Jews cried, "Defeat to the Jews."
May the living God, in His condescending grace, open your eyes
to see whose instrument you were in your lecture, and by which
spirit you were led. Do not be surprised when, in the not too
distant future, the whole world, including Western Germany, is
gripped by a much more terrible wave of anti-Semitism than that
of Hitler's time. The coming strong man who will deceive the
whole world, is described in Revelation 13 and 17, — in the
Revelation which you compare to romantic films and
horoscopes. Your whole appearance, by the way, as well as your
thesis, makes a ridiculous impression, anyone can see that
you have nothing original to offer, and know nothing of God and
His Son, Jesus Christ, but you merely repeat what others in Germany, England and America have said to you. Begin to cry to
this God from the bottom of your heart, because this God will
have mercy on you too, through Jesus Christ. I don't think I am
wrong in the assumption that there is a desperate heart behind
your desperately hollow sounding thesis.

Jehovah Witnesses

D.Z. in H.: I have your tract entitled "Too Late." You are waiting
on a rapture, a departure of the children of God to heaven. I
have understood it in the Bible in this way; all people in general
have the hope to be on earth for eternity, and only a very small
number will go to heaven. In this regard, I'm thinking of the
144,000.

Answer: The Scripture references of your very detailed letter,
are first of all meant for the people of Israel, which in actual
fact have earthly promises from the Lord. For this reason Israel
has an earthly calling. The Church of Jesus, however, has a
heavenly calling and future.

Although you do not mention this in your letter; I nevertheless, have the impression that you have been influenced by the
teachings of the Jehovah Witnesses. I urge you therefore; for
the sake of your soul, reject that teaching! Because especially
the Jehovah Witnesses, lead away from the main thing of all
things — Jesus Christ the Son of God! They lead you away from
the Crucified One, from the necessity of the rebirth of individuals. If you are however; honest and upright, then I am full of
confidence for you, for it is written, "He is a buckler to them
that walk uprightly" (Proverbs 2:7).

SATAN & DEMONS

Why Did God Make Satan?

O.S. in D. Why did God make Satan especially since He knew that men would be misled by him, and away from God into darkness?

Answer: You have come to the wrong address with this question. What do you think I am? Do you think that I, an unworthy human being, have a right to decide what the living God does or doesn't do? If we could understand and reason out God in His doings, then we would be like God. Besides, in your question there lies hidden a rebellion against God, isn't it so? You are probably still an unbroken person and live in sin, and now the living God should be at the end responsible for your sin. You inherited sin, already Adam turned the blame around, against Him who made him when he said, "The woman whom THOU gavest to be with me, she gave me of the tree, and I did eat" (Genesis 3:12). Whosoever asks of God with stubborness never gets an answer. But whoever asks humbly "What for" will look into the depth of God. (1 Corinthians 2:10). By the way I can inform you that this Satan (who was not created by God as Satan, for He created Him as a sinless angel of light) was already overcome by the beloved Son of God, Jesus Christ at the cross of Calvary. In case you do not know this yet: no man has to remain in darkness any longer but whoever accepts the finished work of the Lord Jesus in faith and obedience, may thank the Father "Who hath delivered us from the power of darkness, and hath translated us into the kingdom of his dear Son" (Colossians 1:13).

Laying On Hands

S.R. in Z. In one of your previous letters in the Correspondence Column, you mention something with which I am unable to agree because my experience has been quite different. A sister — I might call her a servant of the Lord — has laid hands on me on various occasions when it was necessary and with "success" according to James 5:14-16. The first time was because of sins of witchcraft, and later, on various occasions, because of sickness. The Lord always honored this holy act. Praise and thanks to Him! Of course, this was always preceded by "house-searching" and the confession of sin. I am not aware of the fact that this sister was subjected to any particular trials and temptations afterwards. It is obvious that the "liar from the beginning" makes himself felt when an attack is made on his kingdom. I just wanted to inform you of this because of the help I have received.

Answer: Your experience is not at all relevant. What **is** relevant is what the Word says. This sister who has "success' in the laying on of hands is on a false, unbiblical path. She will reap what she sows. She should not take the office of another upon herself. Whoever lays hands upon a possessed person usurps a function which not even the Lord Himself performed. She could also learn from the archangel Michael, who as an angel prince did not take it upon himself to rebuke Satan directly. (Please compare Jude verse 9.) He remained within the limits of his office and commission which God had given him, even though he is one of the mightiest and highest angel princes who is mentioned in the Bible. According to Daniel 12:1, he fights for the nation of Israel. — I am not unfamiliar with the peculiar atmosphere which is prevalent where sisters practice the laying on of hands. The Spirit of God is not at work in such places, but another strange spirit instead.

Casting Out Demons

R.A. in H.: The entire article by Dr. Wasserzug in the February issue of the *Midnight Call,* collapses with the words of Jesus in Mark 16:16-20.

Answer: You are speaking of the article, "The Believers Position Toward Satan and Demons." We had expected a strong reaction to it and we did receive many letters, good and bad. To the good letters I count also those who give opposing arguments, but are nevertheless spiritual. Bad letters are those which contain scolding and insults. Here now, the reasons why I was inwardly moved to publish this article:

1) Because the victory of Jesus Christ is an absolute and total victory, our omnipotent God has set His Son at His own right hand in the heavenly places, far above all principalities and power and might and dominion, every name that is named, not only in this world but also in that which is to come (Ephesians 1:20-21).

2) Because we live in the period of the end time, when satanic activities are increasing to the utmost and his work of deception is so cleverly formulated that even many believers fall for it, for Satan himself is transformed into an angel of light (2 Corinthians 14:11).

3) I am totally convinced that the application of the victory of

Jesus is all sufficient to liberate the obsessed, the possessed, the depressed, and the demonically enslaved, for it is written, "In all these things we are more that conquerors through Him that loved us," (Romans 8:37). And that is the summarizing point of this mentioned article.

How do we apply the victory of Jesus? Do we directly address Satan and the demons, or do we claim the victory of Jesus in the presence and in facing God? I have chosen the latter way and that one is not against the Scripture. The opposite is true. The many letters which claim Mark 16:17 do in no way contradict the article, but confirm it, we cast out devils in that we utilize the victory of Jesus in prayer! We do not cast out the devil by taking up a direct confrontation with him or going into a dialogue. In other words, I do not speak with the demons, but with the Lord. That is how I understand the Bible when it says, "In my name shall they cast out devils." That is exactly what I do when I call on the name of Jesus over a possessed person!

We are thankful for a letter such as from R.S., who after reading the article writes the following:

"First of all allow me to express my full agreement to the article! In temptations, I don't pray anymore, such as, 'in the name of the Lord Jesus I command you to depart!' But now I pray differently, 'I thank you Lord Jesus, that you have defeated Satan on Calvary, and that he has no more power over me!' This prayer has already had great success in opposition to the first mentioned prayer."

Should however, someone feel he must go the other way, as many do, through which unspeakably much misery is created, he may do it in his own responsibility before the Lord.

Another question is asked, "what about the many souls who testify gladly that through the command of counselors, they have become free?" Are they really free? Of course! Through what have they become free? Through the claim, in faith, of the victory of Jesus in the face of the enemy! The choosing of words is, of course, another question again. We could compare this with the baptism of infants. We believe that it is unbiblical because we do not find the baptism of infants in the Bible. Does that mean that these children which are baptized are not blessed? Of course they are, if the parents dedicate these children wholeheartedly to the Lord of the baptism. God looks at the heart. The blessing and the power does not lie in the procedure, that is the choosing of words, but in the surrendering of the heart and in faith!

Summarizing, we have again experienced that also in this connection, that whosoever emphasizes the unconditional and perfect victory of Jesus stirs up a hornets nest. The enemy arises mightily, and even through believers...!

ISRAEL

Will All Israel Be Saved?

H.P. in A.: We read in Romans 11:26 that all Israel will be saved. Can we take this verse literally; does it mean that no Israeli will be lost regardless of the attitude of the individual?

Answer: When Paul says in Romans 11:26, "and so all Israel shall be saved," he means the REMNANT which will be in the land of Israel at the return of the Lord Jesus as MESSIAH. For this reason the same Paul says in Romans 9:27, ". . . a remnant shall be saved," and he refers to Isaiah 10:20-22. We must never forget that the whole remnant of Israel will see the Messiah coming in the clouds of heaven and this whole remnant will be converted (Zechariah 12:9-14) so that your phrase "regardless of the attitude of the individual" is pointless. Israel as a nation is today being prepared by the Lord Himself, without the aid of any missionary society, in order to meet Him as a whole, that is the whole remnant.

"Salvation Comes From The Jews"

P.A. in G. Jesus said . . . "I am the way, the truth and the life; no man cometh to the Father but by me." According to this word, all those Jews who have not accepted Jesus are lost, as opposed to those who as a remnant have the privilege of being converted when they see Him at His return. What do you think of this difference?

Answer: The difference lies in the fact that we Gentile Christians do not bear the roots (Israel) but the roots, Israel, bear us (cf. Romans 11:18). We Gentile Christians have the tendency to think the wrong way round, e.g. we think of our salvation and forget that our salvation comes from Israel. "Salvation comes from the Jews." When we consider the question of Israel's salvation correctly starting with the Lord Jesus, we find ourselves already in the center of Israel. The Lord Jesus has not changed His nationality. He is the Son of God and a son of Israel. There is ultimately no difference between Israel and the greatest Israelite, Jesus Christ, but there is a difference between Israel and us Gentiles. It is unfathomable that God will in the end save Israel, but we should find it much more incomprehensible that God has saved us, because we belong by nature to those described as "dogs" in Mark 7:27. In spite of the fact that Gentile Christians today are beginning to recognize the great and glorious calling of Israel there are still many who are bound in their Roman-anti-Semitic way of thinking. They are like Lactance, that scholar of the middle-ages, who said, "Are there really such foolish people who believe that there are men who are made upside down, or trees whose fruit hang upwards, or rain, snow and hail which fall the other way? These people say, in answer, that the world is round!" (from *The False Wisdom 3,* Chapter 24). So it is with Israel, that was God's chosen people before the Church of Jesus Christ, which was the nation of His own possession, but which afterwards through disobedience became "Lo-Ammi" i.e. "not my people" (Hosea 1:9). The soul (namely, the salvation which was to come from Abraham's seed for all the nations of the earth) has departed from the historical body which has now become a corpse. Since then, Israel has for centuries wandered around like a ghost, as a living proof of the truth of prophecy, of its promises as well as its threats, in order to testify to the truth of Christianity, till the end of her days. Hosea 3:4 has been exactly fulfilled for Israel, where it says, "For the children of Israel shall abide many days without a king, and without a prince, and without a sacrifice, and without an image and without an ephod, and without teraphim." Throughout the centuries we have seen this nation to be unique in her ways, scattered over the face of the whole earth — and yet not intermingled, much persecuted, vexed and oppressed — and yet not weakened nor diminished. Without a fatherland, they have maintained their nationality, without any ritual they have preserved their religion and without support their hope. And now we behold — and praise the Lord that we are alive and able to observe what is happening today — Ezekiel 37 is being fulfilled before our very eyes. The dry bones are coming to life again! As truly as this is happening, so will the rest also come to pass. The children of Israel will be converted and they will seek after their king, David, Jesus Christ (Hosea 3:5). At the last moment they will honor the Lord and His grace. Truly ". . .blindness in part is happened to Israel, until the fulness of the Gentiles be come in. And so all Israel shall be saved" (Romans 11:25 and 26a), for the gifts and calling of God are without repentance (verse 29). Even if for thousands of years Israel has become "Lo-Ammi," today the wonderful promise of Hosea 1:10 is nevertheless beginning to be fulfilled, which says, "Yet the number of the children of Israel shall be like the sand of the sea, which cannot be measured nor numbered; and it shall come to pass, that in the place where it was said unto them, "Ye are not my people," there it shall be said unto them," Ye are sons of the living God." The Gentiles in the time which has been granted to them, have been equally as slow as the Jews in their time, in recognizing the things which belong unto their peace. They have taken no notice of the grace of the One who called them. As Israel, years ago, deserted Christ, so have they crucified Him in His Church. The Christianity of today is "Lo-Ammi," "not my people!" in order that the Gentiles may never dare to boast over Israel, but rather that God's revealed mercy receive all the praise and glory.

Anti-Semitism

M.O. in C.: Explain how it is that there is so much anti-Semitism in the latter days? And where does it originate?

Answer: From hell! When the nation of Israel was in the making in Egypt, the first anti-Semite appeared: Pharaoh! After him, throughout the centuries there were always new anti-Semites. This is not a surpise, for God has and will bring His salvation in this world through Israel. In Israel Jesus reconciled the world with God. In Israel He arose, in Israel He ascended into heaven and according to Zechariah 14:4 He will come again and His feet will stand on the Mount of Olives. Starting in Israel He will erect His kingdom of peace. That's why the whole world and hell concentrates on this little nation, which God calls a little worm. But nobody will succeed in destroying Israel. God will fulfill His aim with it. It is sad to see that among believers there are satanic inspired anti-semites who dislike the Jews...They know not what they do. The Lord says: "For he that toucheth you toucheth the apple of his eye" (Zechariah 2:8). History proved that those nations which turned against Israel or persecuted it, were judged by God. Every consecrated child of God has a special great love for Israel.

Israel Cast Away?

K.I. in B.: Many Calvinists and also the Jehovah's Witnesses claim that ISRAEL HAS NO FUTURE ANYMORE, BUT IS CAST AWAY ENTIRELY BY GOD.

Answer: Yes, there are groups of BELIEVERS and teachers of FALSE DOCTRINES, that believe that they are the spiritual Israel. To those should be read slowly and clearly Romans 11: 25, "For I would not brethren, that ye should be ignorant of this mystery, lest ye should be wise in your own conceits; that blindness in part is happened to Israel, until the fullness of the Gentiles be come in." What presumption, to believe the Lord has forsaken His own people! Never! Paul says in Romans 11:1, "I say then, Hath God cast away his people? God forbid." And in verse 2, "God hath not cast away his people which he foreknew." (see also Romans 11, 28-29) All Gentile-Christians, who would like so much to leave the cursings in the Bible to Israel and keep for themselves the blessings, I would like to give you this to think about: It is very humbling but nevertheless very true: The casting away of Israel for a SEASON has become our salvation. God has put aside Israel until the fullness of the Gentiles has come in. In the words of Paul: "Have they stumbled that they should fall? God forbid: but rather through their fall salvation is come unto the Gentiles, for to provoke them to jealousy."

"Jewish Christian"

W.S. in A.: The term "Jewish Christian" does not seem right to me. If a Jew for instance is converted in a Baptist Church and becomes a member of it then he is no longer a Jewish Christian but a Baptist Christian or else a Jewish-born evangelical Christian.

Answer: I am in full agreement with you that the term "Jewish Christian" is unpleasant. However, it does show the dilemma in which many Jewish believers in Jesus find themselves: they are Jews and Christians, that means, they have their Jewry but they also have accepted Christianity in the same way the Gentiles practice it. Such people are unhappy about it as far as I have seen from many such contacts. They are neither the one thing nor the other. The fact that they have been led to the Lord through the testimony of some Gentile or other who did not take into account what a Jew really is in his being means that something may have taken place but it is always questionable. Why is this?

Most Gentile Christians are unable to understand the foundation of the Jewish Testament, the Jewish Bible or "tenach." People evangelize Jews in the same way as they evangelize Gentiles. In this way they become Christians and do not know what to do about their Judaism. Yet their Judaism is the very source of salvation, for "salvation is of the Jews," said Jesus Christ. If I pass on this Jewish salvation — for Jesus Christ is the Son of God and as man Son of a Jewess — to the Jews from my Gentile point of view without reference to the **testimony of the whole of the Scriptures** then they become spiritual bastards. Such a Jew does not know afterwards if he is Jewish or Christian or both. Therefore, we call saved Jews **Messianic-believing Jews** and not Christians, as we call converted Gentiles. The Jew already has the foundation, compare Ephesians 2:20. It would be terrible if a Jew gave up his Judaism — apart from all the wonderful promises — and degenerates into a long-faced and dissatisfied so-called "Christian" as we see millions around us now. I am sorry to say but I have noticed that a comparison between a Jewish person who does not know Jesus and a born-again Gentile turns out in favor of the Jew because the child of God does not know the whole fullness of Christ. So this is not the way for the Jew who finds Jesus. The most healthy Messianic believing Jews are those who come to believe through the testimony of another Jew, or through a direct revelation of the Lord to them, compare Acts chapter 9. We also need to see the difference between the Jew in dispersion and the Jew who has returned to Israel. The first category can be evangelized without any problem. Nevertheless, always in the face of the Old Testament because the Lord Jesus said in John 5: 43-47, "For had ye believed Moses, ye would have believed me: for he wrote of me. But if ye believe not his writings, how shall ye believe my words?" From these clear words of the Lord it is obvious that the Jew in dispersion must first be led back to his Bible. Only then will he be able to believe. The second category, however, which have returned to Israel **has already taken the first step whether consciously or unconsciously:** he has returned to the land of his fathers and therewith is in the center of God's will who so often said through the prophets, "And I will bring them out from the people, and gather them from the countries and will bring them to their own land . . ." (cf Ezekiel 34:13 etc.) Such Jews, i.e. Israelis, are already under the influence of the Holy Spirit. Upon them lies the subsequent promises that the Lord will finally pour out His Holy Spirit over them. That is why we **reject** missionary work among the Jews **in Israel** because no one should presume to interfere with God's work on His people.

Through Israel

G.M. in N.: In a back issue of your magazine you write that God is concentrating His activities today on the central point of this earth again — Jerusalem — which is the reason for the hatred not only of the Arab world but also increasingly of the whole world. My question is: Are not God's activities directed towards the whole world? Certainly Israel has no small part in God's plan, but I find your attitude very one-sided, looking exclusively at Israel. This also applies to the one-sided contents of your magazine.

Answer: Indeed, God's activities are directed towards the WHOLE world, for, "God so loved the WORLD that He gave His only begotten Son, that whosoever believeth on Him should not perish but have everlasting life" (John 3:16). And how does He do it? Through Israel! The nations as such — and this is going to disappoint you with your views — play a very unimportant part in comparison to Israel, because world history is only there as the scaffolding for God's plan of salvation of the world, to be realized through Israel. A practical example is found in Isaiah 40. In many words God speaks about Jerusalem but in verse 15, almost as an aside, the Lord says of the nations, "Behold, the nations are as a drop of a bucket, and are counted as the small dust of the balance: behold, he taketh up the isles as a very little thing." And in order that no nation in their national pride should attempt to put themselves on a par with Israel or even above her, it is said again in verse 17, "All nations before him are as nothing; and they are counted to him less than nothing, and vanity." These are only two of the many examples in the Bible which show that God Himself concentrates His activities on the little land and nation of Israel. Concerning the land it says in Deuteronomy 11:10-12, "For the land, whither thou goest in to possess it, is not as the land of Egypt, from whence ye came out, where thou sowedst thy seed, and wateredst it with thy foot, as a garden of herbs. But the land, whither ye go to possess it, is a land of hills and valleys, and drinketh water of the rain of heaven. A land which the Lord thy God careth for: the eyes of the Lord thy God are always upon it, from the beginning of the year even unto the end of the year." Also the position of the people is specifically emphasized by God Himself when He says in Exodus 19:5, " . . . ye shall be a peculiar treasure unto me ABOVE ALL PEOPLE: for all the earth is mine." And the last words of Moses were, "Happy art thou, O Israel: who is like unto thee?" (Deuteronomy 33:39). Innumerable further statements of the Holy Scriptures confirm the absolute privileged and special position of Israel in this world. Those who recognize this and act accordingly are blessed, but those who rebel against it will find that their spiritual vision becomes darkened.

144,000 Jewish Survivors?

P.B. in B.: I have heard that in a future war against our beloved Israel only 144,000 Jews will survive. This is extremely depressing to me. I ask myself time and again for what have these brave, intelligent and industrious Jews sacrificed so much if later on, for the greatest part, they will be destroyed? It makes me so sad when I think about this. In Israel, there are about 3.5 million people living today. So most of them are doomed to die, if it is correct that 144,000 are to survive. One other thing: if everything is going according to God's fixed plan, which was decided thousands of years ago, why is it important or at all necessary to pray for Israel? God has everything under control, even without our prayers, as He controls the whole course of the history of all the world.

Answer: Concerning the 144,000 you are wrong dear brother. There will not be 144,000 SURVIVORS after the Great Tribulation but 144,000 SEALED ones. That is those sealed by the Spirit of God. They are those Jews which throughout the Great Tribulation and the anti-Christian reign were converted to the Lord. These will then be hidden and spared by the Lord. The other remnant will be converted as a whole at the return of the Lord Jesus in great power and glory (compare Revelation 7:1-8 and Zechariah 12:10-14).

To your second question; why is it important to pray for Israel? Because God has chosen us as His co-workers. Compare to this I Corinthians 3:9. Fundamentally speaking this means: God realizes and speeds up the fulfillment of His plans through the prayers of His children. For this reason, true prayer does not stem from the heart of the believer, but from the heart of the heavenly High Priest, so that it is the Spirit of God which prays through us (Romans 8:26). Very practically, this means that the Lord has placed us in His service, especially in the holy service of prayer, to realize His plans (Compare also Ezekiel 22:30).,

Should Christians Support Israel?

J.W. in M.: With a deep respect for your scholarship and love of God's Word, I am having a difficult time in my own mind determining why the United States Government and the American people should give whole-hearted support, come what may, to the nation of Israel. Originally, President Harry Truman recognized the nation of Israel, over the strong objections of his Secretary of Defense, James Forrestal. Subsequently in 1948, Zionist financial support enabled President Truman to win a dramatic victory over his opponent in the Presidential election, New York Governor Thomas Dewey.

Answer: We as born-again Christians support and stand behind the Word of God UNCONDITIONALLY, come what may, and because the nation of Israel is an intergrated part of the WORD

OF God we also stand and support Israel UNCONDITIONALLY. Israel as it stands today is a part of fulfilled Prophecy of God. You may object now and say; but Israel as a nation is making mistakes domestically and also politically. This is true, but it does not eliminate the POSITION and the high CALLING of Israel. Whoever dares to attack Israel because of their mistakes or weaknesses attacks also the high calling of Israel by God. The Lord Jesus said: "Whoever is not WITH me is against me." The same thing is valid for the people of God. Whoever says, he has nothing against Israel is actually saying he has nothing FOR Israel either. To summarize I would say the following: If God said to Abram "I will bless them that bless thee, and curse him that curseth thee;" (Genesis 12:2) that means practically to us Christians who believe in the whole Bible should without hesitation, and come what may, and without any objection BLESS ISRAEL. This is God's condition to bless us. America's internal political condition is completely meaningless in regard to the motive of "why" America has helped and still is helping Israel. We as Christians are only interested in what God says. And when God says, "I will bless," that means, I will help them that help you. If the help or the recognition of Israel by the United States was financed by the Zionist, it is not decisive either. Because we know that God guides and leads the hearts of those who have authority. May it be Senators, Governors or Presidents. The Bible says, "He guided them as a river." The only thing that is important, is that America helps Israel unconditionally and that is what counts before God. However, I understand that if you, my dear friend have lost the first love to the Lord Jesus Christ, you cannot love Israel. You will sense increasingly an offense against Israel, you will turn against the people of God (this is the reason why all communist, all false religions and imitated Christians are anti-semites). This offense will be in your heart and actually you yourself will not even be able to identify it. That is the sin of anti-semitism in your heart. You should rejoice and be happy for the things America was permitted to do and still is permitted by God to do for Israel. Because America has helped Israel, that is the only reason this country has been blessed inspite of our internal and external troubles and many setbacks. Until this day America is blessed because of the help given to God's people. A parable may help you to understand better: When people are converted to the Lord JESUS Christ they all have different motives. Some people have experienced a so-called Paul conversion, suddenly they are confronted with the Lord, they are born-again and saved for eternity. Other people are burdened so much under their sin that they cry out to the One who can save from sin, the Lord Jesus, these people also are born-again of the Spirit of

THE Spirit of God and saved for eternity. But there are also "rational" conversions. People who use their common sense and think; If I continue the life I live now I will end up to be condemned for eternity. They go down on their knees and receive the Lord Jesus as their personal Savior. These people also are born-again and saved for eternity. Whatever the motive may be, "why" they did do it is not important at all. But that they DID DO IT is decisive.

The Ten Lost Tribes

After preaching a sermon on Israel in Strassburg a friendly brother came and asked my opinion about the "ten lost tribes" to which we the people of the West belong. I first asked him a counter question: If you and many other Germans think you belong to Israel why did you not wear the Jewish star during the Nazi regime and side with the suffering Israel? His answer was rather weak — Because we do not belong to the House of Judah but to the House of Israel.

Answer: I tried to make clear to him that among those who have returned, and still are returning, to Israel there are Israelis of ALL the tribes. Further I pointed out that the condition was the same in Jesus' time when that Gentile woman came to Jesus and He initially rejected her saying, "I am not sent but unto the lost sheep of the house of Israel" (Matthew 15:24). I assured the questioner that the Lord in His perfect time would reveal to which tribe every son and daughter of Israel belongs. But because this question continually recurs and produces all sorts of speculation we would like to publish what the theologian C.I. Scofield writes about it:

"There are not, as some assert, 'ten lost tribes,' known only to God and later to be found by Him, variously conjectured to be the Anglo-Saxon people , the gypsies, or certain peoples of Central Asia or Africa. These misconceptions arise from a misreading of passages such as 2 Kings 17:7-23 (c.f. 2 Chronicles 6:6-11), and especially v. 18. The expresson 'tribe of Judah' (v. 18) is here used idiomatically for the southern kingdom (Judah) in contrast with the northern kingdom (Israel), as vv. 21-23 compared with 1 Kings 11:13, 32, make clear. In these contexts everyone out of all the tribes who remained loyal to the house of David is included, as well as the two tribes of Benjamin and Judah who unitedly and officially stood by the Davidic house. The removal of the bulk of the people composing the northern kingdom does not mean that only two tribes of Israel continued in the land. Verses 7-23 (see v. 20, "cast out"), implying that the portion of the nation taken into captivity by

Assyria is excluded from any promised future return to the land, are in harmony with the principle of Romans 9:4-7, which explains that the total physical descendants of Abraham were not the 'nation' to whom the promises were made. Before the Assyrian captivity, substantial numbers from the ten tribes had identified themselves with the house of David. This began at the time of the rebellion of Jeroboam 1 (1 Kings 12:16-20; 2 Chronicles 11:16-17) and continued when reformations, invasions, and other crises led many to repudiate the northern kingdom and unite with the southern kingdom in a common allegiance to the house of David and the worship of the Lord. Thus in God's view all the tribes were represented in the kingdom of Judah and constituted His continuing Israel. These facts show the correctness of this view: a) the remnant who returned from Babylon is represented as the nation, not simply two tribes; b) our Lord is said to have offered Himself not merely to two tribes (Judah) but to the nation, 'the lost sheep of the house of Israel' (Matthew 10:5-6); and c) other tribes than Judah are mentioned specifically in the New Testament as being represented in the land (Matthew 4:13, 15; Luke 2:36; Philippians 3:5)."

Although Israel is now in an age-long dispersion because of their rejection of their Messiah, nevertheless they still continue as a people, preserved distinct from other peoples, known to God though not knowing Him. A partial restoration of Israel to the land in unbelief has already taken place in accordance with prophecy. The Scriptures clearly state that there will yet be a spiritual restoration, through the salvation of substantial numbers, which will heal the ancient political division (Ezekiel 37:15-28).

"Israel, Temple and Jews"

W.K. in M.: I heard your radio program again this morning. I am always glad to hear it, but there is something which I think is wrong. You have often said that the circumstances of the revelation of the Antichrist refer to Israel first and foremost. I think you are taking the words "Israel, temple, Jews" in the book of Revelation too literally. Paul says in one place, "Ye are the temple of God." He is talking to Christians here. The true temple of God is the Church of Jesus Christ. Thus it is to be understood that the Antichrist will be seated in the Church and have his picture (image) upon the altar (the altar being in the form of a television). I believe the Antichrist is much more likely to come from the so-called Christian nations, like his forerunners: Napoleon, Stalin, Hitler.

Answer: We find the terms "Israel, temple and Jews" not only in the book of the Revelation, but throughout the whole Bible. Many thousands of promises speak of the time in which Israel will return to her land and re-possess Jerusalem. You only need to read the prophets Zechariah, Isaiah, Haggai or Ezekiel. Paul says in 1 Corinthians 6:19 that our bodies are the "Temple of the Holy Ghost" and in another place that we are the "Temple of God." This is the absolute truth but it has a time limit, just as the Church of Jesus Christ is merely an interval in God's dealings with Israel in world history. Christian presumption and arrogance is rooted in the belief that the Lord has rejected Israel once and for all because He has given this interval of grace for the world and the Church of Jesus Christ. This is by no means the case! What does it say in Romans 11:1-2, "I say then, Hath God cast away his people? God forbid. For I also am an Israelite, of the seed of Abraham, of the tribe of Benjamin. God hath not cast away his people which he foreknew." But here comes the Christian pride once again, which says, "Of course God has not rejected the nations; whether Israelis, Dutch, Swiss, Germans, English or Americans, God does not reject any nation. They may all come to God through the Lord Jesus." This is an insidious error, a half-truth, as far as Israel is concerned. God does not put Israel on an equal footing with the nations from which, by grace alone, a great company have become members of the body of Christ. Read once again the text in Romans 11:1-2 very carefully. It says here quite clearly that, "God hath not cast away his people." This obviously refers expressly to Israel. We now, in this interval of grace between the rejection and re-acceptance of Israel are a spiritual temple, or as Paul puts it in Ephesians 2:22, "a habitation of God through the Spirit." Till when? Until God re-accepts His people. Zechariah 1:14-16 is being fulfilled in our day, "Cry thou, saying, Thus saith the Lord of hosts; I am jealous for Jerusalem and for Zion with a great jealousy. And I am very sore displeased with the heathen that are at ease: for I was but a little displeased, and they helped forward the affliction. Therefore thus saith the Lord: I am returned to Jerusalem with mercies: my house shall be built in it, saith the Lord of hosts." As far as the Antichrist is concerned, he will not sit in a church but emerge from out of the church and bring Israel into extreme distress. Modern Christianity without Christ is preparing the way for the Antichrist.

PROPHECY & END TIMES

Rejoice, The Lord Is Near!

S.B. in L.: Recently you said on your broadcast that all the signs of the times have been fulfilled now and that Jesus will return soon. I was really pleased because I am going through great tribulation. However someone has said that the return of the Lord cannot take place for a long time because the Bible still has to be translated into 2,000 languages so that the Gospel can be preached to all nations. What do you say to this?

Answer: You can rejoice, because the Lord Jesus can return at anytime! There is no sign to be fulfilled before the rapture of the Church of Jesus Christ because all the signs of the end times are ultimately meant for the nation of Israel. Read in this connection Matthew 24:16 where it speaks of the land of JUDAH and in verse 20 of the SABBATH. On the other hand however, is the resurrected Israel the great sign for the church that the day of redemption is at hand (Matthew 24:32;33). You have fallen prey to a false teaching and a deceptive belief. Where does it say in the Scriptures that there must be more translations of the Bible before the Lord can return? Perhaps this person was referring to Matthew 24:14 where it says, "And this gospel of the kingdom shall be preached in all the world for a witness unto all nations; and then shall the end come." The end referred to here is the day of judgment which takes place after the millennium. During the millennium the GOSPEL OF THE KINGDOM, the kingdom of peace, will be preached to ALL the nations through Israel, as a testimony. We are now living in the age of grace and have the command, "Go ye into all the world and preach the gospel unto every creature." What gospel? THE GOSPEL OF GRACE! Through the proclamation of this Gospel the Lord is choosing for Himself a people out of the Gentiles, but not all nations (Acts 15:14). Be of good cheer, don't despair or let anyone rob you of your hope through vain philosophies!

Where Is The End-Time Message?

P.H. in E.: Today, we need more than ever the clear and unab-breviated message of salvation and of our soon returning Lord. I always ask myself the question, "where are those who are responsible for the millions of church-attending people? Why is there so little preached about the prophetic Word?" In a discussion in regard to the interpretation of Scripture, I was told "leave it to a minister; he should know for he has studied it!"

Answer: The argument, "leave it to a minister, he should know for he has studied it" is very poor. For intellectual education is not spiritual education. One can learn a lot with his intellect from the Word of God but can remain a spiritual baby. According to Psalm 103:7, one can see and recognize the **acts** of God, but not recognize His **ways.** In order to see His ways, the Holy Spirit must enlighten my spirit and that is exactly what He does if I subdue myself under His Spirit, 'If ye be led of the Spirit," (Galatians 5:17).

You must never overlook one fact, namely that the eternal God does not speak through the intellect to the heart of men, but rather in the opposite direction, He goes from the heart to the intellect! He has destroyed the wisdom of the wise, according to 1 Corinthians 1:19.

We are living in a dispensation where man is always inclined to keep a distance from the truth. That is, he takes as his guide-line scientific knowledge as the ultimate truth, and with this his sin-darkened intellect begins to exalt himself above the eternal truth of the Bible. For that reason, spiritual insight into the mysteries of God, into His ways, is today decreasing.

We are so thankful to the Lord that He revives individual people who in humility of their heart subordinate their intellect to the wisdom of God. Such receive light inwardly, they are friends of God. I am reminded of Abraham, of whom the Lord said: "Shall I hide from Abraham that thing which I do?" (Genesis 18:17). Or think on the statement of our exalted Lord of Revelation 1:1, "The Revelation of Jesus Christ, which God gave unto him, to shew unto his servants things which must shortly come to pass."

Therefore, the more we humble ourselves before the pres-ence of God, the more light He will give us about the things He is doing in our days. For that reason we heed the admonition of Peter, "We have also a more sure word of prophecy; where-unto ye do well that ye take heed, as unto a light that shineth in a dark place, until the day dawn, and the day star arise in your hearts" (2 Peter 1:19).

Russia Attacks Israel!

O.W. in S.: If I understand prophecy right, then the attack on Israel by Russia with their allied countries will happen first, and with this the end of the powerful Soviet-bloc-countries will come. After that, the power of the Antichrist will be revealed openly. Between these two powerful world-shaking events, will there be a time of rest in between? A time of intermission?

Answer: Yes, it is clear that there is an intermission between the falling of the Soviet Union with their satellite countries on the mountains and valleys of Israel, and the appearance of the Antichrist. This intermission however will be disastrous and fateful for Israel because then "peace" will have come their way. This peace, of which the Scripture says "For when they shall say, Peace and safety; then sudden destruction cometh upon them, as travail upon a woman with child; and they shall not escape" (1 Thessalonians 5:3). "Great Israel" will then be established and all potential enemies such as the Soviet Union and with them the Arab people will be eliminated by God in one move. Jerusalem will then become world headquarters, and the Scripture describes it in Revelation 11:8; "which spiritually is called Sodom and Egypt." Yes indeed, that will be a very dangerous time, for then the Antichrist will have appeared on the horizon and will deceive Israel, who will then dwell in safety and security.

Zechariah Speaks Of Today!

J.T. in U.: In Zechariah 2:12-13 is written, "And the Lord shall inherit Judah his portion in the holy land, and shall choose Jerusalem again. Be silent, O all flesh, before the Lord: for he is raised up out of his holy habitation." Does this Scripture refer to our time today and the political happening in the Middle East, or is this in reference to another time such as the Millennium? I strongly feel that the first instance is right. But if this is the case, and the Lord has raised up from His holy habitation since the choosing of Judah and Jerusalem, how very close must His return be today?!

Answer: This prophecy of Zechariah is without doubt speaking about today's situation in the Middle East, for Zechariah is that prophet who speaks about the dispensation which has begun in our century and closes with the return of the Lord in great power and glory. Zechariah prophesied during 520 B.C. during the time of Israel's return from Babylon. And through this he saw prophetically todays wonderful return of Israel.
Very noteworthy is the fact that Zechariah, in 2:13 sees much further than Habakkuk, who prophesied the same thing in chap-

ter 2:20, "but the Lord is in his holy temple: let all the earth keep silence before him." Whereas Zechariah said, "For he is raised up out of his holy habitation." With this we have another proof how very clearly Zechariah saw the return of the Lord (See Zechariah 14:4).

Indeed you are right, the Lord is raised up. His return is very close! On this same line we can continue and quote Acts 15:16, where we are told that the Lord, after He has taken a people from among the gentiles (v. 14), will come again and build the tabernacle of David. James is quoting here Amos 9:11-12. In this case, too, we can rightfully say, when our Lord has begun to rebuild already in 1948 the fallen tabernacle of David, which according to the promise He will complete only after the fulness of the gentiles has come in, how very close the Rapture must be!

Therefore you are right dear brother, the return of Christ is standing at the door! It can happen at any given moment but nobody knows the hour. For that reason we should be ready at all times. But should He nevertheless tarry, then it is for the reason that none should perish, "but that all should come to repentance." (2 Peter 3:9).

Adventists Speak For A Great Part of Christianity

About Adventists. Having once published warnings against the teachings and Bible courses of the Seventh Day Adventists, we received a letter from the Paris office of *"The Voice of Hope"* which contained the following statement:

> "The Church of the Seventh Day Adventists is watching with interest the happenings within the young state of Israel today. But she does not in any way see the present-day settlement of part of today's Jewish people in Palestine as the fulfillment of the old biblical promises to the chosen people. She is of the opinion that in reality political motives surpass the religious ones and therefore acceptance of them as a fulfillment of prophecy cannot be justified. Despite the admiration that the Adventists have for Israel's courage and sagacity, we must not forget that the Jews must seek salvation within the framework of the Church as the apostle Paul teaches in his letter to the Romans, chapter 11."

Answer: The Adventists speak for a great part of Christianity. How can it be otherwise, because throughout the years she has appropriated for herself the thousands of promises without giving a thought to God's people, Israel. It testifies to an inconceivable Christian blindness when people believe that the state of Israel as a political structure cannot possibly have anything to do with the fulfillment of biblical promises. It is only BECAUSE Israel is a political reality — which in itself is one of the greatest miracles of history — that the fulfillment of the promises in the Bible is proved. Israeli politics and the fulfillment of Bible prophecy can no longer be separated.

The second foolish statement here, is that Israel must seek her spiritual salvation within the framework of the Church as Paul teaches in Romans 11. I wonder of which Church?! In this case Israel would be facing a terrible dilemma; in Israel alone there are twenty-four differing churches! Israel is waiting for her Messiah! When Jews are converted in the Diaspora through the preaching of the Gospel they individually become part of the body of Christ. Nevertheless, Israel as a whole will be saved and that will be through her Messiah, but never through the Adventist, or any other Denominational-way. Israel's conversion will be a unique happening in biblical history: they will all, and at the same moment, recognize Him and lament over Him, after which the Church of Jesus Christ will then exercise her heavenly work on earth, while converted Israel will carry out in a wonderful manner her earthly task throughout the whole world.

The Mark Of The Beast

M.P. in S.: What is the meaning of the mark of the beast in Revelation 13? Will it be visible on the hand or on the forehead?

Answer: The mark of the beast, that is, the number of the beast, is the number of a man cf. Revelation 13:18, " . . . and his number is six hundred threescore and six (666)." Without doubt the intellectuals — those who work spiritually — will bear the mark on their foreheads while the manual workers will have it on their right hand (Revelation 13:16). This mark will be a VISIBLE one. But the spiritual meaning seems to me to be more important for it reveals in numbers the highest potentate of wickedness. Paul names these three-times-six antichristian characteristics in 2 Timothy 3:1-5, and then he concludes his list with the comment, " . . . from such turn away" (verse 5). In other words Paul is saying that the end-time people will preach the Antichrist in person through their three-times-six characteristics. He then warns us not to let ourselves be deceived by the appearance of godliness because Christianity of the end times will be anti-Christianity. It will profess to be Christianity in just the same way as the Antichrist will say he is Christ. "From such turn away," Paul warns. It is basically wrong to look for the number 666 everywhere, as for example in Nero, Napoleon, or the Pope, Hitler or most recently in the case of Kissinger and it is also

wrong not to read or see it in those places where it is very obvious. I would ask you to study carefully the three-times-six antichristian characteristics in 2 Timothy 3:1-4. You will then be
amazed and shocked to see how many already obviously bear
the number of the beast.

Resurrection Of The Dead

S.B. in O.: Revelation 20:4-6 talks about those that did not accept the mark of the beast and that they will rule with Christ for
a thousand years. Now, some people believe that the meaning of
verse 5b: "This is the first resurrection" is, that all believers
have to go through the Great Tribulation at the time of the beast
and that all will have to be martyrs to be resurrected, at that
time. These brothers say it is unscriptural to believe that the first
resurrection is not a single moment but a period of time in which
the saved will rise (starting with the rapture of the Church of
Jesus Christ to the resurrection of those that became believers
during the Great Tribulation which died for their faith). They
base this on the fact that Revelation 20 mentions nothing of a
longer period of time or of different phases in the first resurrection. Are there any other Bible verses that would either prove or
disprove their point of view?

Answer: There has been much talk about the resurrection of the
dead, also much has been written and speculated. Let us try to
understand this wonderful hope of ours and put it in a few
words.
The Lord Jesus is the first one of those resurrected (I Corinthians 15:20). He predicted His own resurrection (John 10:18;
Luke 24:1-8). Then, the resurrection of Christ followed a
resurrection of the bodies of many saints (Matthew 27:52, 53),
also the Apostles raised up some dead (Acts 9:36-41; 20:9-10).
Two resurrections are still before us and they include **all.** The
Bible speaks, first of all, of those THAT ARE IN THE GRAVES.
(John 5:28). Those that died, believing in the Lord Jesus Christ
will have part in the "first resurrection," which is a
"RESURRECTION OF LIFE" (John 5:28, 29; I Corinthians 15:22-
23; I Thessalonians 4:14-17 and Revelation 20:4-6). But God's
Word speaks of a "second resurrection," which is a resurrection
"of damnation," that is for judgment (John 5:28-29; Revelation
20:5-6 and 11-13). These two different kinds of resurrection are
separated by a time period of a thousand years (Revelation
20:5). The "first resurrection" to eternal life will follow at the
second coming of Christ (I Corinthians 15:23). The believers of
the church age will meet Him in the air (I Thessalonians
4:16&17). And the martyrs of the time of the Great Tribulation

will be raised at the end of that tribulation, when Jesus returns to the earth to establish His Thousand-Year-Kingdom. These also are part of the first resurrection. Therefore, the first resurrection will take place in different phases. The believers of the Old Testament will also take part in the first resurrection. We suppose that these believers are already included in the first phase of the first resurrection, that is with the church of Jesus Christ at the rapture (I Thessalonians 4:16-17. I Corinthians 15:51-53), which will happen before the Great Tribulation. But there are interpreters which believe it to be more scriptural and according to the Old Testament will take place following a Great Tribulation (compare Isaiah 26:16-21 and Daniel 12:1).

Also, we want to point out that the physical body relates to the resurrection body as the seed in the ground relates to the fruit of wheat in the harvest (1 Corinthians 37-38). The body of the resurrection will be unperishable, glorious, powerful and spiritual (I Corinthians 15:42-44 and 49). The bodies of the living believers will be changed in one instant at the same time. (1 Corinthians 15:35-53, Philippians 3:20-21). This changing of the living and the resurrection of the dead in Christ is called the redemption of the body (Romans 8:23, compare also Ephesians 1:13-14). And finally, after a thousand years the resurrection of damnation will take place (John 5:29). We are not told what the body of the resurrection will be like, but the Bible teaches that they will be judged according to their deeds (Revelation 20:7-15). From all this we can learn that the resurrection of life has different phases the second and last resurrection, however, has only one phase.

The Anti-Christ And The Return Of The Lord

E.A. in N.: According to our opinion, the Antichrist must reveal himself before the coming of the Lord Jesus; but according to your opinion the Lord could come at any moment. We know that especially in this era there is much diversity and obscurity. Please give us once more your views.

Answer: The return of the Lord will happen in two phases: First, the return **for** His own, and second, the return **with** His own. The coming **for** His own is the Rapture, of which the New Testament speaks clearly and unmistakably. After the Rapture, begins the seven year tribulation period when the Antichrist will rule and terrible judgments will break forth upon the earth. Then the Lord will come **with** His own, that is His Bride, in great power and glory, and then through the Spirit of His mouth make an end of the beast (2 Thessalonians 2:8). I hope that you also will take part in the Rapture. For then, the promise of Revelation 12:12, will be fulfilled, "Therefore rejoice, ye heavens and ye that dwell in them. Woe to the inhabiters of the earth and of the sea! for the devil is come down unto you, having great wrath, because he knoweth that he hath but a short time."

The reasons why we are convinced that the Antichrist will be revealed only after the Rapture are the following:

1. The Scripture says in 2 Thessalonians 2:7, "He who now letteth will let till he be taken out of the way." (The German translation says: He who now hinders him will be taken away.) The presence of the Holy Spirit in the congregation of God on the earth is hindering the Antichrist to reveal himself. Therefore the Holy Spirit with the Church must first be raptured from the earth.

2. The Church, which is bought with the blood of Jesus is the Light of the World. Paul says "Ye are all the children of light, and the children of the day: we are not of the night, nor of darkness" (1 Thessalonians 5:5). As long as there is one spark of light on earth it is impossible that the black and dark night of the anti-christian rulership can break through in its full force.

3. The Lord has promised that He will protect them who have kept His Word from the hour of temptation which shall come upon all the world (Revelation 3:10).

4. Already the Prophet Isaiah said "The righteous is taken away from the evil to come" (Isaiah 57:1).

5. Clear prophetic pointers of the time of the Rapture are Enoch and Lot: Enoch was raptured before the flood came, and Lot was taken out of the city of Sodom before judgment broke loose.

For these reasons we are not waiting for the Antichrist but call out: Maranatha, come soon Lord Jesus!

Ten State Empire

H.K. in K.: Will the ten state Empire come into existence before the Third World War or sooner? According to my opinion, I think Russia must first be destroyed and America must not be a super-power anymore. Only then comes the last world ruler that will rule the last world Empire.

Answer: According to my understanding of the Prophetic Word the Third World War and the destruction of the Soviet Union with its satellites on the mountain and fields of Israel will fuse together. Because in the midst of this judgment we read in Ezekiel 39:6, "And I will send a fire on Magog, and among them that dwell carelessly in the isles: and they shall know that I am the Lord." When we observe the pressure the Soviet Union is exerting today to the south, that is Israel, to the West, that is Europe, and to the East, that is China, we immediately recognize clearly that these are signs of the coming and shocking Third World War. The center point of this war, according to my opinion will be the south, that is the Middle East. As we understand the prophetic Word the United States will serve as the uniting link between the re-established Roman Empire, that is the United Europe and the Kings from the Rising of the Sun. These developments are in full swing today and visible.

The Last Days

G.K. in R.: In the Gospel of John, Chapter 6 Jesus says that He is the bread of life, and "Whoso eateth my flesh, and drinketh my blood, hath eternal life; and I will raise him up at the last day" (Verse 54).

The bread of life is Jesus Himself and His blood He has given as a sacrifice for our sins. These we should take to us like food and drink for our bodies. Four times the Lord says that who does this, him will He raise up on the last day.

How can this be understood in connection with the rapture? When is the last day? When is the rapture to take place? I picture the last day as the end of the world and the last judgment is before the great white throne, where people of the second resurrection receive judgment. At this point the rapture and the first resurrection should have long taken place?!

Answer: When the Lord JESUS SAYS, "Whoso eateth my flesh, and drinketh my blood," then it has a very deep meaning. He does not mean this in terms of matter, for in John 6:63 He says, "It is the Spirit that quickeneth; the flesh profiteth nothing: the words that I speak unto you, they are spirit, and they are life." For that reason God sent His Son into the sinful flesh, "for what the law could not do, in that it was weak through the flesh, God sending his own Son in the likeness of sinful flesh, and for sin, condemned sin in the flesh" (Romans 8:3). So when Jesus says "Whoso eateth my flesh,..." then this means that I accept judgment over my sinful flesh — "I am crucified with Christ" — and — whoso drinketh my blood..." — His blood is His poured out life — this is the payment for my sins. His judged flesh puts my sin, my temperment out of power. His precious blood cleanses me from all my sins and my transgressions. When now the Lord further states, "...and I will raise him up at the last day then we must remember that the Lord mentions many times different far removed happenings in one breath. So for instance through the Old Testament prophets who have seen and told of the first and second coming of Jesus as one. The same we can see with the prophetic Word about God and Magog; both are, by the way, expressions for nations living in rebellion. With Gog and Magog, first of all, the Soviet Union is meant (Ezekiel 38 and 39). Concerning the history of salvation, this is not of importance, especially since the Lord is not returning at the downfall of Russia and her satellites. He will return at the beginning of the anti-Christian kingdom with the Antichrist leading. The beast and the false prophet will be thrown into the pool of fire then. In this sense, the rebellious nations under the leadership of the Antichrist have prophetic and historical significance. Then — after the Millennium — the expression Gog and Magog return (compare Revelation 20:8) when Satan i.e. the dragon will be thrown into the fiery pool and is united with the beast and the false prophet in eternal damnation.

So we can see, that it is a principle of God to interrupt the history of salvation again and again. This can also be clearly seen in Israel. Israel of today, 1975, is the same as Israel 2000 years ago, it was dispersed into all the world. But Israel as a nation in the history of salvation is the same, in spite of the different periods of thousands of years. The first and second coming of the Lord Jesus and the second step of His second coming in great power and glory is in the eyes of God ONE. In the same sense is the "day of the Lord" to be understood. It consists of a period of judgments. Or let us consider "the last days" (compare Acts 2:17a), which began 2 thousand years ago on the day of Pentecost, yet still waiting for the final fulfillment. Let us compare Hebrews 1:2a, "Hath in these last days spoken unto us by his Son..." This period of last days will be completed with the return of the Lord Jesus.

This is also true for "the last day." In my opinion this day consists of the judgment of the children of God at the first resurrection (2 Corinthians 5:10, 1 Corinthians 3:11) the different final judgment of humanity, the judgment of the nation (Matthew 25), and finally the judgment of the "dead, small and great," before the great white throne judgment (Revelation 20:12).

Earth Destroyed!?

A.P. in C.: We read in Isaiah 24:19-22 "The earth is utterly broken down, the earth is clean dissolved, the earth is moved exceedingly. The earth shall reel to and fro like a drunkard, and shall be removed like a cottage; and the transgression thereof shall be heavy upon it; and it shall fall, and not rise again. And it shall come to pass in that day, that the Lord shall punish the host of the high ones that are on high, and the kings of the earth upon the earth. And they shall be gathered together, as prisoners are gathered in the pit, and shall be shut up in the prison, and after many days shall they be visited." Does this mean that our earth will be totally destroyed and we will live on another planet?

Answer: Indeed, heaven and earth shall pass away! Inspired by the Holy Spirit, Peter said, "But the day of the Lord will come as a thief in the night; in the which the heavens shall pass away with a great noise, and the elements shall melt with fervent heat, the earth also and the works that are therein shall be burned up" (2 Peters 3:10).

On the grounds of this fact, and also the one you mentioned in Isaiah 24:19, we are being admonished in 2 Peter 3:11, "What manner of persons ought ye to be in all holy conversation and godliness." And in verse 13, Peter expresses his confidence that we can expect a new heaven and a new earth wherein dwelleth righteousness. John also saw the new heaven and the new earth on the isle of Patmos, and he said in Revelation 21:1 very expressively, "for the first heaven and the first earth were passed away." The new heaven and the new earth will be unimaginably beautiful. For it says in Revelation 21:3, "Behold, the tabernacle of God is with men, and he will dwell with them." The great city, the Holy Jerusalem, will come down like a satellite from the heavens and will hover above the new earth. From this city, an all-penetrating clear light will go over the earth. That is the glory of the Lord, for the Lamb is the light thereof (compare verse 10 & 23). The people who will live, as you expressed it on a new planet, will walk in this light. Evidently, there will be an open gate from the new earth to the heavenly satellite, for it says in verse 25, "and the gates of it shall not be shut at all by day: for there shall be no night there." These are only little indications from the glory which is to come, which lies before us. Therefore blessed is he who prepares to meet his God (Amos 4:12).

Who's on Earth During Millennium?

L.L. in N.: If everyone, who takes the mark of the beast will be eternally lost, who will live on the earth during the Millennium? I thought that it would be all those that survive the battle of Armageddon. But won't it be impossible to live without having accepted the mark of the beast?

Answer: All those who accept the sign of the beast surrender to the Antichrist. But it is not written anywhere, that they will all be lost eternally, however they will have to go through the period of judgment (trumpets-vials of wrath). But just as all of Israel will be converted at the return of the Lord Jesus Christ, also masses from all nations will accept Him when they see Him, whom they have pierced. Please don't forget it was a Roman soldier who pierced His side. This helps us not to blame the Jewish people alone for the crucifixion of Jesus. **All of us,** our sins have crucified Him. Besides, we also should keep in mind that not only Israel will see Jesus at His second coming, but **all** generations onearth. At the beginning of the Millennium many of the repentant nations who previously followed the anti-Christian rule and have worn the mark of the beast, will say to one another: "Come, let us go to the mountain of the Lord, to the house of the God of Jacob that He teach us His ways and that we walk in His paths!" It is understood, however, that all the nations will be also judged for all the evil they have done to Israel (compare Micah 4:3 and Matthew 25:31-46). But then the Millennium of Peace will begin and the earth will be covered with the glory of the Lord just as the water covers the sea (Isaiah 11:9).

The Riches of Israel

C.T. in O.: Gog from the Land of Magog will come to the Middle East, especially Israel, to *take a spoil* and *to take a prey* according to Ezekiel 38:12. From an economical viewpoint this country is not rich today and could fit into the category of an under-developed country. Are we to expect an economic giant in this region later or what else would Gog see and count so valuable that he would start a war?

Answer: You are absolutely misinformed when you count Israel as an underdeveloped country, even in spite of the fact that through the heavy burden of war and defense they are poor and deeply in debt. Do you know for instance that the mineral resources in the Dead Sea are far greater than all the mineral riches in the rest of the world? Have you heard about the renowned diamond industry of Israel? Have you been informed in regard to the tremendous technological developments of this country? Besides, the Middle East is the center of energy for the world. For Gog and Magog there are many other things which will lead him to *take a spoil and to take a prey,* not to mention that this country has a unique strategic position: it lieu between three continents: Asia, Africa, and Europe. These are only a few of the powerful drawing magnets, or *hooks* which the Lord God has put into the jaws of Gog (Ezekiel 38:4) to draw him with all His powers to Israel.

The Trumpet Judgments

H.H. in B.: Could you tell me in what Biblical period we are now standing? In other words, in which trumpet judgment?

Answer: As far as I can recognize this part of the Scripture, I believe that the seven trumpets will be blown during the time of anti-Christian reign. And moreso because the seven seals are being opened. You must not overlook the fact that during the short time of the terror reign of the Antichrist, the above mentioned judgments of God will come upon the earth in compact and quick succession. On the other hand, we must keep in mind that it is not impossible that the Church of Jesus Christ may still experience, for instance, the Third World War, with all its horrors before the Rapture. The Church of Jesus Christ however, will be protected from the reign of the Antichrist.

Holy Spirit Raptured

J.N. in F.: According to your answer in the May 1977 issue of *Midnight Call,* you do not believe that the Holy Spirit will remain on earth for eternity. With this you're wanting to say that the Holy Spirit will not remain with the believers. But that is a false teaching. Our Lord Jesus is calling you to recall this statement for it is a lie of the devil and many children of God will be deceived by it. The devil, whose helper you are in this case, will proclaim this false teaching quickly!

Answer: You have a zeal dear brother, but not according to knowledge. You are trying to break into an open door! Who denies the fact that the Holy Spirit will remain with the believer for eternity? In that particular answer we gave, we spoke of the Holy Spirit being raptured with the Church before the Great Tribulation. Why then do you hit such big holes in the air? Why do you use such super strong language which in this case is not valid anyhow?

The description "false teaching" and your claim that I am a "helper of the devil" points very clearly to unsolved inner tensions of your soul. Why not shed all your heart before the Lord? He will free you from all inner conflicts in a wonderful way.

Now to your subject, the Scripture teaches unmistakably clear that with the revelation of the *wicked one* on earth, the Holy Spirit has fulfilled His task on earth and will be taken away with the Church. Think for once on the wonderful fact of Genesis 24, and the wonderful prophetical illustration as Abraham's old servant, a picture of the Holy Ghost, who leads the Bride to the Bridegroom, but then disappears himself! Have you never understood that the Lord Jesus Himself expressively emphasizes in view of His own person, although in the opposite succession, "It is expedient for you that I go away: for if I go not away, the Comforter will not come unto you; but if I depart, I will send him unto you" (John 16:7). When the Lord emphasizes repeatedly that He **must** go in order for the Holy Spirit to come, how is it that you cannot grasp that this must also happen in the opposite succession — that is the Holy Spirit must be removed from the earth, in order for the Lord to come again on earth, or don't you have in your Bible 2 Thessalonians 2:7, "For the mystery of iniquity doth already work; only he who not letteth will let, until he be taken out of the way." How sad that you have not understood this yet. The spirit of the wicked cannot be fully revealed on earth as long as the Holy Spirit is present. It can never be totally dark as long as there is light on earth.

And finally, the Holy Spirit who constantly illuminates the Son on earth (John 16:14), will lead the Bride without spot and wrinkle to the heavenly Bridegroom.

Babylon

E.R. in D.: I have heard someone say that you believe that the "Babylon" described for us in Revelation is Moscow. Is that true?

Answer: Babylon is a collective description of all the nations which according to Psalm 2, imagine a vain thing, and take councel together against the Lord and against His annointed, and then come to the conclusion, "Let us break their bands asunder and cast away their cords from us" (Vs. 3). And to these people, without doubt, the atheistic Soviet Union belongs, but she is not alone. The false church who has committed fornication with the nations is also part of it. In Revelation 18:1 we read of a mighty, powerful angel whose glory lightens the earth and his message is: (Verse 2 and 3) "And he cried mightily with a strong voice saying, Babylon the Great is fallen and has become the habitation of devils, and the home of every foul spirit, and the cage of every unclean and hateful bird. For all nations have drunk of the wine of the wrath of her fornication and the kings of the earth have committed fornication with her." And after the final fall of the world church, or the worldly church, for the first time in the New Testament, (chapter 18)), we hear the "Alleluias" of heaven, because then the glory of Jesus and His bride will become visible to the world.

Babylon, the picture of rebellion against God, is planned to be rebuilt as a city in Iraq today, according to latest report. That is a visible personification of the spirit of the Beast, "who opposeth and exalteth himself above all that is called God (2 Thes. 2:4).

Moscow — "Meshech"; Tobolsk — "Tubal"

M.Z. in P.: From where do you get the interpretation that before Napoleon's assault on Russia, Moscow, and Tobolsk were called "Meshech" and "Tubal"?

Answer: We can only assume that the "Meshech" and "Tubal" mentioned in Ezekiel 38:2-3 and also the "Rosh," are none other than the European and Asiatic "Russia" with its two chief cities, Moscow and Tobolsk. According to the findings of linguistic experts, Meshech and Tubal are the ancestors of the settlers in Northern Russia. Jewish historians are of the opinion that the Mosheni, the people who lived in the Moski Mountains, to the east of the Black Sea, descended from Meshech. Moscow is derived from Moskowi and Moskown from Meshech. As for Tubal, he was the ancestor of the Tubalites. The name Tubal — like the names of many cities in Russia — has taken on the suffix "sk", thus becoming Tobolsk. In the Biblical Encyclopedia which was published by H. Zeller in 1866, these last two names were referred to as originating from the river Tobol in Siberia.

Deliverance in Jerusalem

E.B. in G.: In Joel 2:32 it says, "...for in mount Zion and Jerusalem shall be deliverance." Who will be saved? The Jews? Or has this verse something to do with the rapture?

Answer: Mount Zion is in the first place the city of David. Compare 2 Samuel 5:7 and 1 Kings 8:1. Salvation goes forth from this city into the whole world because it was in Jerusalem that God reconciled the world to Himself in and through Jesus Christ (cf. 2 Kings 19:31 and 2 Corinthians 5:19). Zion, or Jerusalem, has a particular significance concerning Israel's future as a whole, for Joel 3:21 says, "for the Lord dwelleth in Zion." Read also Zechariah 1:14-17. As there is not only an earthly Jerusalem but also a heavenly Jerusalem, so we also have a heavenly and an earthly Zion. In Hebrews 12:22 it says of the Church of Jesus Christ, "But ye are come unto Mount Zion, and unto the city of the living God, the heavenly Jerusalem." And finally the Bible also says that the 144,000 out of Israel will stand with the Lamb on Mount Zion (Revelation 14:1). That will be when He returns to the earth.

Animal Sacrifices in New Temple

L.H. in B.: Will animal sacrifices be re-instituted in the new Temple during the Millennium? To my Christian thinking it would be impossible that after the sacrificial death of Jesus, animals will have to be offered again.

Answer: The subject, if during the Millennium the Old Testament's sacrifice will be reinstituted, because the new Temple will be rebuilt, has moved many. One question immediately arises. What sense and reason would it have since the Lord Jesus Himself through His substitutionary suffering and dying has fulfilled already all of the Old Testament offerings? (Compare Hebrews 9:14 and 29).

Let me say this right now: the Old Testament sacrifice will be re-instituted in the Millennium without a shadow of a doubt because the Scripture says so (compare Ezekiel 45 and 46). This newly re-established offering and sacrifice has a wonderful and glorious meaning; namely, just as the millions of sacrificed animals in the Old Covenant pointed to the substitutionary sacrifice of Him who was to come, in order to fulfill in one sacrifice once and for all an eternally valid Redemption; in this same way the sacrifice during the thousand years of peace will illustrate and testify what Jesus has done. That is biblical prophecy in its total outreach and all embracing. The prophet does not only see ahead (that means the future) but also the happenings which are way back in the past. I am reminded of Isaiah 14:12 where the Prophet describes the fall of the King of Babel. But suddenly he receives a back view; he sees behind this King the shadow of Satan, in this case it was before the foundation of the world (compare Ezekiel 28:16).

New Jerusalem

T.V. in A.: In Revelation 21:24 it says, "And the nations of them which are saved shall walk in the light of it: and the kings of the earth do bring their glory and honour into it." What kind of glory and honor is this speaking about?

Answer: Here it speaks about the time after the 1000 Years Peace, that is the millennium, when the nations will have gone through terrible judgment and through it will be cleansed and renewed. We recognize this from verse 1 where it talks about a new heaven and a new earth. The whole earth will then be penetrated through and through by the glory of the Lord and all the nations on the earth will be included in this. These then will bring in turn their own glory to the New Jerusalem. This will be a wonderful and glorious interchange: in the same way children of God, today, are being translated into the image of Jesus and this image will later be accepted and recognized by the Lord Himself. We however will cast our crowns, which we will have received then, at His feet.

^{IS} PROPHECY BEING FULFILLED?

See clearly God's Plan for Today and Tomorrow
As a serious Christian you need to know how to be prepared for the Second Coming of Christ. The unique prophetic magazine **MIDNIGHT CALL** can help. Timely articles will enlighten the present day fulfillment of Bible Prophecy before your own eyes. Read articles like these . . . Is the Anti-Christ already among us? • Israel and the Bible • World Currency, World Religion and World Dictator coming soon • The terrifying goal of the Ecumenical Movement • Roman Empire on the rise • . . . and many more subjects . . . 16 to 24 inspiring pages every month . . . Spiritually Packed . . . Challenging . . . Informative . . . Uplifting . . . Christ Centered.

This dynamic magazine is read in all States, Canada and in over 100 foreign countries. Available in six languages. English, French, Dutch, German, Portuguese and Spanish.

To order use ORDER COUPON or ask for the MIDNIGHT CALL magazine. Subscription is $3.00.

By The Same Author

ISRAEL'S GOD DOES NOT LIE
by Wim Malgo $3.95
This book is a must for every serious Christian, who is waiting for the Second Coming of Christ. The Author penetrates deeply into the Spiritual background of the latest events in the Middle East, including the "Yom Kippur War". Illuminating these events in the light of Bible Prophecy, many astonishing truths are clearly revealed as never before.

Some of the Chapters contained in this book ● The Yom Kippur War ● Jerusalem's Border ● Will the Antichrist come from the tribe of Dan? ● The Destruction of the Nations ● The First and the Last King of Jerusalem . . . and more.

1 book $3.95   **2 books $5.00**
          4 books $10.00

1000 YEARS PEACE . . . A UTOPIA?
by Wim Malgo $2.95
A refreshing outline on the much debated subject; the millennium. Without discussion and argument the author goes direct to the source; the Bible, to show the clear teaching of the coming 1000 years peace. The millennium is the answer to Jesus' prayer "Thy Kingdom Come." The patriarchs, prophets, kings and priests looked forward to the thousand year reign of peace.
Some of the chapters in this book: Israel's position in the millennium . . . Where will the church be during the millennium? . . . What will happen after the millennium? . . . etc.

1 book $2.95   **2 books $5.00**
          3 books $7.00

SHADOWS OF ARMAGEDDON

by Wim Malgo **$3.95**
What began in 1948 in the Middle East as a
seemingly insignificant local matter has taken on
world-wide proportions today. The Author shows in
unmistakably clear terms that even political conflicts such as Vietnam and Cyprus are definitely
signs of the preparation for the battle of Armageddon.

20th CENTURY HANDWRITING ON THE WALL

by Wim Malgo **$3.95**
Daniel the prophet interpreted the Handwriting on
the Wall for king Belshazzar . . . today, there is
ANOTHER Handwriting on the wall seen and read
by all men. It is the Handwriting which predicts
the coming 3rd World War . . . The Collapse of the
Free World . . . The return of Christ . . . and the
Battle of Armageddon.

PRAYER AND REVIVAL

by Wim Malgo **$3.95**
What can we do to cause a Revival? How does a
Revival begin? Does God want to send a Revival?
There are divine conditions we must first meet in
order to have Revival. Analyzing these conditions
for Revival through the Bible, this book will help
serious Christians to find the pathway to Revival.

Jerusalem Focal Point of the World
by Wim Malgo $2.95

Jerusalem is not just another city, it is the city of God, the future capital of the world. This city is unequaled in the history of mankind and is today back in the spot-light of the world.

The Arabs claim Jerusalem, so does the Catholic Church and the United Nations . . . but God has a different plan!

Wim Malgo clearly shows, on hand of the Scripture, how Jerusalem will reach God's ultimate goal in the near future.

Some of the chapters in this book:
* Jerusalem Focal Point of World Peace
* God's Oath concerning Jerusalem
* Rome versus Jerusalem
* The Significance of the Number 666
* The heavenly Jerusalem . . . etc.

1 book $2.95   **2 books $5.00**
3 books $7.00   **10 books $15.00**

CALLED TO PRAY
by Wim Malgo $2.95

An enlightening and reliable guidance to a victorious prayer-life. Read in this book how Prophets, Apostles, Priests and Kings used PRAYER to overcome the enemy. Tells how your life in Christ can become a powerful testimony. PRAYER is one of the most important subjects in your Bible. 17 INSPIRING CHAPTERS TO FILL YOUR HEART. A REAL TREASURE IN EVERY CHRISTIAN HOME.

1 book $2.95   **2 books $5.00**
3 books $7.00

ORDER FORM

Fill in, Clip, and Mail this Whole Page to:
MIDNIGHT CALL   P.O. Box 864   Columbia, SC 29202

How Many	Title		Total Price
____	Shadows of Armageddon	$3.95	_____
____	20th Century Handwriting on the Wall	$3.95	_____
____	Prayer and Revival	$3.95	_____
____	The Last Days	$2.95	_____
____	Jerusalem Focal Point of the World	$2.95	_____
____	50 Questions about the Second Coming	$2.95	_____
____	Israel's God Does Not Lie	$3.95	_____
____	1000 Years Peace	$2.95	_____
____	Israel Shall Do Valiantly	$2.95	_____
____	Called To Pray	$2.95	_____
____	The Rapture	.95	_____
____	Seven Signs of a Born-Again Person	.95	_____
____	Terrifying Goal of Ecumenical Movement	.95	_____
____	On The Border of Two Worlds	.95	_____
____	Group Dynamics, New Tool of the Antichrist	.95	_____
____	Signs and Wonders	.95	_____
____	Begin with Sadat	$1.95	_____
____	Biblical Counseling	$3.95	_____
____	How to Walk With God	.95	_____

☐ Enclosed $3.00, please send a one-year
subscription to MIDNIGHT CALL magazine. _____

Total Enclosed $ _____

NAME Mr. Mrs. Miss _____
                              Please Print

STREET _____

CITY _____ STATE _____ ZIP _____